THE MYSTERY OF JESUS FROM GENESIS TO REVELATION

YESTERDAY, TODAY, AND TOMORROW

THE MYSTERY OF JESUS FROM

GENESIS to REVELATION

YESTERDAY, TODAY, AND TOMORROW

—— VOLUME ONE ——

THE OLD TESTAMENT

Dr. Thomas R. Horn, Donna Howell, Allie Anderson

DEFENDER
CRANE

The Mystery of Jesus from Genesis to Revelation: Yesterday, Today, and Tomorrow
Volume 1: The Old Testament
By Dr. Thomas R. Horn, Donna Howell, Allie Anderson

All Scripture is taken from the King James Version of the Bible unless otherwise noted.

Cover design by Jeffrey Mardis

ISBN: 978-1-948014-61-8

CONTENTS

INTRODUCTION

By Dr. Thomas Horn

I
t was the year 2012. I was speaking at the Prophecy in the News conference in Branson, Missouri, when I concluded my address by rapidly listing how Jesus is at the core of every book of the Bible. My goal was to share how and why Christians can have great faith in the future because, if the Word has been so consistently accurate regarding the predicted First and Second Advents of Jesus, then we can trust our futures in the hands of the Alpha and Omega, who will continue to bring about the perfect fruition and finality of Christ's mission to earth for humanity. (For those who do not know, the sixty-six books of the Bible were written over thousands of years and contain more than twenty-five hundred prophecies, more than two thousand of which have already been accurately fulfilled.)

At the end of my 2012 narrative, the crowd came to life in response, ultimately giving me a standing ovation for this effort to illustrate *The Mystery of Jesus: From Genesis to Revelation—Yesterday, Today, and Tomorrow.*

Immediately following that oration, and on numerous occasions since, I have been approached by people through letters, emails, and even face to face, wanting me to further elaborate on just how Jesus is the core of all truly inspired Scripture, and what that means for us today and for our future. What I discovered is just how much this mystery is unknown to most churchgoers, and, once people discover these forceful, supernatural revelations, they are extraordinarily stirred by these apparently hidden truths, amazed they've never seen or heard anything about them in their local houses of worship.

This three-volume work is the culmination of years of scholarly effort to peel back the onion layers of this mystery, in order to finally put on display an unprecedented work filled with fresh revelations that most readers will undoubtedly find amazing and inspirational.

Nothing like this collection has been written before. It is a groundbreaking work, as readers will discover lost and forgotten revelations involving the enduring mission of the God-Man commonly known as Jesus (Yeshua).

I went into this project knowing such an immense objective would be beyond my singular ability, so I invited Donna Howell (a celebrated scholar whose degree is in theological/biblical studies) and Allie Anderson (a theologian with a degree in psychology) to join me in this comprehensive effort. We were blessed by God along the way, and this research has produced what I have told my coauthors will unquestionably be perceived as a magnum opus.

In many instances, we have stood on the shoulders of experts who paved the way before us, and our sincere prayer now is that your faith will be strengthened as you read and treasure this unprecedented work—which uniquely puts on full display just how "the testimony of Jesus is the spirit of prophecy" (Revelation 19:10b).

VOLUME ONE

THE OLD TESTAMENT

S tart in Matthew," the preacher said, "and proceed through Mark, Luke, and John, and then go back to Matthew and read them all again. Just read the four Gospels over and over, and don't deviate from them until you have that material so inside of you that you feel you can quote all four books. This is the redemption narrative. The rest of the books in the Bible can wait, but this section of Scripture tells you who Jesus is, what He came to do, and what that means for your salvation."

This was the advice given from the pulpit of a Pentecostal evangelist on the West Coast who pastored a church of approximately two hundred people. Another teacher, a messianic rabbi who is active on YouTube, had something completely different to say. His advice, generally, was: "Don't even bother with the New Testament until you've mastered what the Old Testament said about the coming Messiah. Who Jesus was and is, and what He came to accomplish on the cross, starts in Genesis and moves through the history of Israel. Jesus was a Jew! You can't know the Messiah by starting in Matthew until you know who He was to the Jews."

Neither of these speakers was responding to what the other had said—they weren't even aware of each other as far as anyone can tell—yet their guidance on getting to know Jesus through the Word of God staunchly opposed to the other. I might suggest in the most respectful manner possible that although each of these approaches to the Word would certainly work well for readers and seekers, both of these men were incorrect in assuming any section of the Word of God is more—or less—about Jesus than another.

This will be illustrated first through a personal testimony of one of these authors, Donna Howell, and then we will discuss a few terms that are essential to approaching the Word of God. (For the next section, until the header that reads "Progressive Revelation and Supporting Evidence," Donna Howell is the sole writer. The first-person "I" references are to her, and then the book will resume under the authorship of the collaborative work.)

In Donna's Words:
The Prayer That Hit Me Like a Freight Train

I discovered on my own, only recently at the time of this writing, how true the previous statements are regarding Christ throughout the entire Bible. It isn't that I wasn't already aware of that as a fact, but one incident sparked an epiphany. In order for me to tell you about what happened at the stop sign in my car in the middle of the night, I have to first describe a radical event from years ago.

It was the summer of 2016. Allie Anderson and I were at a conference in Arizona, tending to meetings and trying to manage our regular jobs remotely. I had just completed a major writing project, and there had been a pretty unfortunate miscommunication between myself and a member of our production staff that resulted in the work landing at the printer before it was supposed to. Though it only took a couple of phone calls to sort out, one of the conversations involved some uncalled-for frustration on the other end of the line that was… well, "unpleasant" would be a kind and discreet way of putting it. When the call was over, I returned to the meeting hall for the remainder of a presentation I had almost entirely missed. My mind was abuzz with the recent stress of it all, and I couldn't hear anything the speaker was saying. Afterward, Allie and I went back to the hotel, and I wandered out to the balcony alone, pacing, replaying, processing the morning, wondering if I should have handled things more firmly on my end, trying to imagine what long-term damage I had potentially caused by being too lenient…on and on my mind spun.

As out of the blue as anything I have ever experienced—and, as far as I know, it wasn't from any internal focus-shifting power of my own: Right in the middle of my stress-looping, a thought crammed its way into my head, evicting any thoughts of my coworker and the production schedule, and jerking me into a very real and sober reflection that played out like a short conversation between me and God.

"It's boots-on-the-ground Gospel time," the words in my mind spoke. "When you get back home, the second you get off the plane, you are to hit the ground running and never look back. You need to be about the work of the Gospel. Be confident that you are called and equipped, and don't slow down."

"Is that You, Holy Spirit?" I asked. "Are you telling me You are going to start the next Great Awakening just as Tom Horn, Larry Spargimino, and I predicted a couple of books ago in *Final Fire?*"

"The Great Awakening has already begun," was my answer. It came almost before I was finished asking the question, and it landed with blunt-force clarity and confidence. "It's in the beginning phases. Only those with eyes to see and ears to hear will see it and hear it. It's starting with My people, My *true* people, while a good portion of the Church and the world around it are asleep and unaware."

If I am correct in believing this was God, there was much more in the sudden "download" of His words, though His follow-up statements will be included at the end of the third volume of this work.

"What do I do?" I asked silently. I waited a few seconds, and when my thoughts started to drift into a fog, I tried to hold on to the moment with additional promptings: "What do I need to know? What's the first move? Tell me what I'm to do and I'll do it!"

Once again, there was no answer.

I leaned over the balcony in the Arizona sun, looking down at the parking lot, taking in what I thought *might* have been a legitimate exchange between me and God. I tried to process it further, bounce some ideas around, and make a responsible conclusion based on my intellect (which is how I roll; I don't always believe it's God every time a random thought pops into my head, even when that thought comes out of nowhere and bulldozes away all others like this one did). I attempted, over and over, to elaborate within my own means, imagining what else might have been said had the conversation continued. I concentrated and contemplated for a couple minutes, wishing to reinitiate the dialogue that had first come upon me so urgently and insistently, but it was useless. I couldn't think. I wanted answers and illumination on what precisely was expected of me if those words had in fact come from God, but it was as if I had taken some kind of brain-mush drug that shut off the efficiency of my reasoning to the point that I was effectively catatonic. Everything in my head seemed to turn to putty as I watched a few strangers on the asphalt below exit their vehicles and head with their luggage to the hotel entrance. My eyes landed on a grate with hundreds of discarded cigarette butts while I continued to pray for clarity that wasn't coming in that moment.

Reeling, but unable to evaluate how and why, I mechanically made my way back into the hotel room while my thoughts were still camped out on the balcony railing. Allie glanced up, saw my disoriented expression, and asked what was going on. I briefly told her about the occurrence, including the strange way it all ended.

"It's like I was tuned to the right frequency of a radio channel," I explained, "getting a perfect signal and hearing everything as clear as day, and then, just like that, I lost the signal, fell out of the frequency, and couldn't get it back. I really can't explain it in any other way. It's like someone—or Someone with a capital *S*—got through to me and then turned the channel so I couldn't add to or take anything away from the conversation. And now I don't know what it was all about or what I'm supposed to do with it."

Even as I write this, the event and my reaction to it are as clear as a photograph, like it happened yesterday. I can still count the approximate number of cigarette butts in that grating (somewhere around seventy-five or so on the bottom left, where the largest collection was, and around a hundred others in a semi-circle edging the rest). It is so vivid! Yet I'm struggling to find words to explain how bizarre it was. However, this was the first time in my life I had thought to phrase it in radio-frequency terms, and I have spoken of this phenomenon since over television and in person with some believing friends who have had similar experiences.

"So, lemme get this straight," Allie said, trying to put it all together. "You went out to the balcony to pray, and—"

"No!" I interrupted, shaking my head. I hesitated, having to really try hard to remember what had been going on before all of this. "No, it wasn't about prayer. I... Wait a sec. What *was* I doing?" It wasn't until then that I retraced my steps aloud and remembered the whole ordeal about the book-production schedule and the dramatic phone call. "That's part of what makes this so weird, Allie. If it had come during prayer, I might be more inclined to think that, in my own human excitement or earnest desire to hear God's voice, I imagined the whole thing, but I was seriously looping some major drama. This voice or this...thought-conversation or whatever it was...literally blasted through and interrupted what was already an all-consuming list of troubles on my mind. It came from nowhere and demanded precedence to the point that I forgot about this morning's blow-up until this very moment."

"Yeah," Allie said in reference to the phone call. "That would have distracted me, too. I see what you mean about this interruption."

Allie and I agreed I should take the directive to some folks back home whose counsel was trustworthy. As soon as we returned from the trip, I met with several and received great advice, but the two top answers I needed were these: 1) whether the words that popped into my head were from God; and 2) if they were, what I was supposed to do about it.

First, as I touched on earlier, I have good reason to believe it's dangerous to assume God is speaking any time something randomly comes to mind. I have seen scenarios like that play out in others' lives before, even hearing a few Christian associates say things like, "I was just standing there, and all of a sudden this super-powerful idea came to me out of the blue, and now, by this time tomorrow, I will be on a boat to Africa! We're gonna be missionaries!" Without proper planning or preparation (spiritual, financial, emotional, cultural, lingual, and so on), moments like these tend to invoke a honeymoon-phase ministry that fizzles into nothing, but not before entire lives have been disrupted, houses have been sold, jobs/careers have been severed, and so on, making the whole incident a very expensive, impulsive mistake. I had to know before I did anything that something more than mere imaginings had rattled me on that balcony.

Second, assuming it was God, I felt the extreme need for clear direction. Was He telling me to hit the ground running in a brand-new ministry and abandon the one I was in? Or was He telling me that Skywatch TV *was* the platform upon which He might use me to accomplish "boots-on-the-ground Gospel time"? If the former, then I needed to know right away if I should quit my job and stand on a street corner with Bible tracts and preach…or whatever the plan was. If the latter, then I needed to get over my fears, get into those television studios, and preach my heart out over the broadcast tools we've been given.

Part of my concern with trying to be so careful about discerning God's voice has been because the content of SkyWatch TV is about prophecy, discovery, conspiracy, supernatural worldview, ancient civilizations, and other similar topics that "fish" for men and women, stimulate their minds, and help train and strengthen the faith of believers across the globe, but it's not in the same wheelhouse as other ministries like James Dobson's Focus on the Family or Billy Graham's Evangelistic Association. So when I heard the phrase "boots-on-the-ground Gospel time," I wondered if I was being taken away from my ministry in cutting-edge media to become something else, such as a missionary or a church-planter.

As history attests, after much deliberation and advice-seeking, I decided to stick around and just give it my all, taking every opportunity to be about the Lord's work right where I was (which is why I suddenly became super visible on television and over the radio right about that time). However, I never knew for certain if what I heard that day was the voice of the Spirit or just my deep, internal psychology escaping the drama of a bad day.

Fast forward to about a year and a half ago. My husband, James, and I began to hold private, pre-planned gatherings outside church buildings with those we felt led to reach out to or bless. The reasons for this change are lengthy (the long version is told near the end of *Dark Covenant*, a book Allie and I wrote in 2021); one of the main reasons was that I was still wrestling within myself, trying to figure out whether the voice I heard that day on the balcony was calling me to something more than my role at SkyWatch TV.

We saw immediate positive results of those gatherings in our home church. For example, within just a few months, a couple of people got saved; others released long-stored, long-fed baggage of their past, leading them to recommit to God; one person asked to be baptized in the river; and one marriage was possibly saved. James and I were reaching people with the Gospel now, and the proof was in the results all around us!

One couple, whom I will refer to as Benjamin and Anika, spent a lot more time with us than anyone else. Both were struggling with their faith, which they initially articulated to us in words like, "I don't

really know if I buy all this stuff about there being a God out there."
Right away, it was evident that their issues stemmed mostly from a
heavy trust in demonstrable science (that tends to be cited as proof
against Creationism) and a massive load of religious abuse in their
pasts. Neither had gone out of their way to provoke or offend us—
they were respectful in airing their doubts—but they didn't hold back,
either. James and I shared many knowing glances and nods between
ourselves in those first days, always so grateful we could host company
like these two, who never would have (seriously, *never*) attended a
church, and who would therefore not have had a place where they
could process their hurt, disbelief, and skepticism or ask beefy questions that many churches would consider inappropriate (or simply
not be prepared to answer). Because we chose to meet in a somewhat
unorthodox way, defensive walls came down, and this couple was let
loose to speak freely. Benjamin and Anika spent the first couple of
meetings with us just venting, and we only listened. We didn't quote
Scripture, redirect casual chatting back to the subject of God, or try to
lead them into any prayers, because we felt it was simply their season
to be in the presence of Christians who had nothing but time and no
interest in anything but hanging with friends.

But after a while, we had a meeting one night when everything
clicked: It wasn't that Benjamin and Anika didn't believe in God, they
just couldn't believe in the "God" they had previously been indoctri-
nated to believe in. For them, "faith" had always been there, hovering
right at the edge of "relationship," but the way other Christians had
walked out their faith in front of them presented a terrible image of
who God is and how He thinks of them. (Ironically, they did *not*
come to this conclusion because James and I cornered them and force-
fed them our theological and scientific opinions until they caved in;
they concluded this because they had finally been allowed to breathe
and process openly. This approach to friendship really should be a far
more important goal than it is in these times...)

Shortly after this had surfaced, Benjamin admitted (indirectly) how little he knew about the real, historical Christ. To him, Jesus was a blue-eyed Caucasian male who walked around in a white robe with a purple sash and clean sandals, touching people on the shoulder and saying "Bless you, My child" on repeat. He was worshipped and praised everywhere He went, and apart from one confusing story about how He made wine ("which surely must have been nonalcoholic grape juice or something, right?"), He never sinned, which means He hung out with uber-spiritual people and remained calm and composed at all times. Oh, also, He knew He was going to die on a cross, so He must have had a sad and reflective demeanor, always gazing off into the distance with His long, curly, blond hair gently swaying in the breeze while His perfect disciples tore their clothes in agony, chanted like monks, and gave money to charity.

I'm sure you've heard similar ideas before, and I wish I could say the Church is right where it should be in making sure young and curious minds are getting a proper description of the Man we follow, but Benjamin's concepts are actually quite common. Jesus is a mystery, and the only "facts" many hear about Him are whatever the next cultural joke about Him tells.

Still feeling the timing wasn't right to go in with guns blazing and blast Benjamin with what we know of Christ, James and I simply made some mental notes, did an exorbitant amount of nodding, and, when appropriate, laughed with him as he regaled us with funny accounts of some of the bad religious experiences he'd had. (Like many, humor is Benjamin's defense mechanism, so to join him in laughter was to endorse the *purging* of his pain, not the pain itself.) Over the next few months, we would have small opportunities to dispel some of his incorrect beliefs about this fantastically inaccurate Christ—such as briefly stating that Jesus actually hung out with oddballs, sinners, tax collectors, and fishermen—but the substantive "Jesus trail" that would matter most in these meetings would require trickier timing.

Then, a week or so later, we had a breakthrough.

During one of our casual meetings, I happened to let it out of the bag that I find the arguments of the "old earthers" fascinating. Neither Benjamin nor Anika had heard the term, so I explained that it represents a group of Christians who believe the Creation account is absolutely true, precisely as the Bible describes, but that science is also a sensible means through which God could have conducted Creation, possibly based on some interpretational theories such as the Gap Theory and several others. Neither of them could hardly believe there was a community of Christians out there who would accept the evidence of Scripture and science at the same time.

Our conversation went on for hours, and, since the iron was hot, I also explained a number of other, less-than-mainstream biblical topics: fallen angels, Nephilim, the "great men of renown" from Genesis 6, and the possible link between those "men" and the gods of the Greco-Roman pantheon; giant bones with double rows of teeth in ancient, Native American burial mounds the Smithsonian covered up with the so-called Powell Doctrine; gargantuan stones carved from quarries in and around Baalbek and dropped miles away that no man-made technology at the time could have moved; unidentified flying objects that Jesuit priests within the Vatican openly talk about tracking from their "Lucifer" telescope on Mt. Graham; the curious and inexplicable mysteries of the Great Pyramid; theories of astral catastrophism and what that might mean for certain anomalies viewable in space. We talked about many of the subjects I had researched for SkyWatch TV in the past, and the longer I talked, the more Benjamin and Anika wanted to hear.

Oddly, the more I talked, the more the subject kept naturally coming back to what Bible scholars have to say…and the more the Bible had to do with the topic, the more Christ came back into the discussion.

Christ was linked to *everything*!

Unlike before, when my mouth uttered Jesus' name and Benjamin and/or Anika would exchange nervous glances, this time, they were begging to hear about the Bible, eating it up like starving canines sitting before an all-you-can-eat steak buffet and competing with each other to be the next one to ask a question.

Eventually, the night had to come to a close when it got ridiculously late (between two and four o'clock in the morning). However, because our friends had caught the fever on all this new discussion, we (Benjamin, Anika, and I) agreed to meet at their place the next night.

When we got together again, we revisited some topics because it had been too much to take in the first time; such dense conversation needs a break and a recap. But lo and behold, when I mentioned that Jesus fulfilled the Passover feast in ways no ordinary human could have orchestrated (discussed in the "Exodus" study shortly), neither Benjamin nor Anika balked. On the contrary, their expressions brightened: They were intrigued. Anika slid forward in her seat, elbows on her knees, eyes wide with expectation, and Benjamin blinked dramatically, as if to say, "Really? There's actually something *to* that?"

And I launched.

For the next hour, I talked as fast as I could and tried to cover everything about Christ's role in the Jewish feasts—stopping here and there to tackle interesting tidbits like the Day of Pentecost and the relationship between that event and its precursor at Mt. Sinai—showing incredible, supernatural links to prophetic fulfillment throughout the whole Word of God...*all of it having to do with this Man who died for our sins*. The topics touched off a colossal shift in our young, precious friends' attitudes. Their eagerness to learn more was palpable. They wanted to hear about the Savior, His Father, and the Spirit He sent, and to learn about the unexpected scenes throughout the Bible that we don't initially "see" Jesus in. This Messiah really is, as the scholars say, "in every book of the Bible," from Genesis to Revelation—and our friends were realizing this! When we had begun our visit, we were dog tired from our late night before...but I was so jazzed when James and I left their place that you could have canned my adrenaline and cancelled coffee for a year throughout the West.

On the drive home—we had again talked until late in the night—

on a back road with no other traffic, I immediately began to pray about my relationship with our friends, and I suddenly said something out loud that "hit me like a freight train" (that's a Donna-ism for having a radical epiphany). See, because of my experience on television and over the radio, I try to make it a habit to never speak aloud without carefully thinking about my words. Although I haven't perfected it without question, even in my private prayer life, I take care to say exactly what I mean and never carelessly blurt. That's why this prayer floored me: It came right out of my mouth without warning, and I wasn't aware of what I was saying until it had already been said.

"Lord, give me the *weird* stuff. Give me the stuff that no churches or ministries really talk about."

That very second, the memory of a day on the balcony of a hotel in Arizona came back to me. The last several years of wondering if I'm where I'm supposed to be had new light. I crept up to a stop sign and my car idled as it all connected and sank in…

Oh my goodness, I thought. *I literally just asked to be given what I have already received. Everything I have studied truly does point to Christ! He's in every single book of the Word!*

When I got off that plane from the Arizona conference years ago, I *did* hit the ground running—putting myself into increasingly vulnerable and uncomfortable positions, allowing myself to be stretched in the media (an outlet I never wanted anything to do with because I prize privacy and anonymity)—and I *did not* look back. I've been studying "the weird stuff" all this time, using it as an ice-breaker with people like Benjamin and Anika who otherwise have nothing in common with "church people"…but I've also been wondering if I was legitimately accomplishing what God might have said to me on a balcony years ago because my ministry doesn't always fit into the box our culture thinks "Gospel work" is packaged in. (Even the meetings we have with people are outside the church building, which has tremendous advantages, but approaches "churching" from an unconventional angle in today's world.) Now, in a single instant, I was able to believe the Holy Spirit was breaking through my drama that day to get my attention. But far more important was the second layer of what had just been confirmed...

From out-of-place artifacts of the ancient world all the way to obscure and little-known theology—it all traces back to biblical evidence with Jesus eventually appearing as the main character. From Genesis to Revelation, the whole Bible's heartbeat is the revelation of progressive redemption through one Man. Jesus is not more available to humanity as a human Baby in a manger than He was to Israel in the Old Testament through the Father that gave His people a Someday Redeemer to hope for and look forward to during unprecedented seasons of tension with surrounding pagan territories. He is not the promised Messiah of Genesis "more than" He is the Savior of the Synoptic Gospels. In each of the sixty-six texts of the Holy Bible, Christ is in it, through it, intrinsically sewn into every page, and irreversibly linked to everything touched by His story in the world since the dawn of time.

By the way, there's a term for that phenomenon...

Progressive Revelation and Supporting Evidence

Theology students hear, very early on in their studies, the term "progressive revelation." (This is *not* to be confused with "progressive Christianity," a current trend that, for the most part, represents tweaking the Bible to accommodate today's culture and flatter modern social movements. It does this by slapping God's name and authority upon any secular endeavor—including those the original biblical writers would never have endorsed.) "Progressive revelation" encapsulates the concept that the Bible, with its sixty-six books, is *one story* of God's plan—presented cohesively as one narrative rather than as a random collection of narratives and lessons God wanted to share with humanity. Choosing to accept progressive revelation involves accepting that the story of Christ is present throughout all books, even while the collection of documents is incredibly diverse! It is the "unity" of Scripture existing harmoniously within the "diversity" of Scripture. It is tracing elements and themes to a central character and redemptive purpose—documented over the course of approximately fifteen centuries by about forty authors whose backgrounds were wildly varied: from lowly men with no money or education to wealthy kings and everything in between, including physicians, lawyers, shepherds, fishermen, tax collectors, prophets, priests, and at least one now-famous tentmaker.

Initially, it seems unbelievable that the Word of God would have one central message, one fundamental revelation of God's plan, yet was compiled by such a wide assortment of people. Under no normal circumstances would a tax collector (Matthew) tell the same story of the same Messiah as a zealous Jewish theologian (a traditional description of John). Under *normal* circumstances, these men would be natural enemies whose backgrounds and experiences would paint completely different portraits of a personal Savior. We would also never expect each author to remain consistent in his approach to the subject of God, both within his single books—and within multiple books and letters. This is because the authors were human, and therefore experienced God from many divergent periods of their own lives during the writing process. Their perspectives of the Divine were shaped by differing seasons of maturity and understanding. Yet, in a way that is initially quite mystical, this very kind of unity is precisely what happened among about forty men over a span of fifteen hundred years...*sixty-six times*!

To toss out another theological term, this is known as the principle of internal consistency: the standard that demands that no part of the Bible disagrees with any other part; there are no inconsistencies or contradictions within Scripture, *even though* its human authors had unique personalities, came from differing cultures, employed varied worldviews, and lived in extremely different periods of history.

(As a quick note: Some skeptics claim there are inconsistencies and contradictions within Scripture, but they usually say this without considering the proper context of passages. One example, as shared in our recent release, *Misfits: Learning from Our Inner Outcast and How It Can Empower Us to Find Our Destiny*, relates to the passages from Deuteronomy that atheists claim are God's instructions on how to beat one's slave.[1] But, as *Misfits* goes on to point out, we can "look to chapters 15–21 for a wider and more accurate context... that, when read altogether, [describes] 'God's instructions on how much and what kind of punishment will be enacted upon slave own-ers who beat their slaves'—and the 'slave,' of course, in this context, is a Jew of the same race who has taken a *paid position* to work under a housemaster voluntarily as his full-time job [much like recent his-tory's indentured servitude]."[2] That said, when context *is* responsibly applied to Scripture, we arrive at the miracle of internal consistency: one God, immutable and unchanging forever, consistently portrayed in the writings of many men from all over the world who experienced Him differently in their lifetimes, which occurred over a period of a millennium and a half.)

Internal consistency as a principle, and that alone, argues well for the authenticity of the Bible as a truly divine (God-breathed, God-directed) document. Scholars and mathematicians have pondered throughout history the probability of this kind of unity occurring over sixty-six times by happenstance, and they've calculated some unbelievable numbers. One example is found in the computations of famous mathematician, Peter W. Stoner. Stoner is the former chair-man of the math and astronomy departments, as well as Professor Emeritus of Mathematics and Astronomy, at California's Pasadena City College in the early '50s. Immediately following his tenure there, he chaired the science division and served as Professor Emeritus of Science at Westmont College, California, for the second half of the decade. *Science Speaks*, his magnum opus in the field of probability estimates and calculations as related to biblical prophecy, has been cited countless times for decades by secular and Christian scholars.

Despite some minor criticism (much of which pulled Stoner's numbers out of their immediate context), Stoner's work remains a leading, reliable source of honest, transparent mathematics. Stoner's opinion, therefore, becomes crucial in the question of whether this Book, this Word of God to humanity, is internally consistent. The "odds" (or lack thereof) that Jesus accidentally or coincidentally fulfilled the prophecies about His birth, life, death, resurrection, and ascension are ruled out by even secular logic and unbiased numbers, if today's mathematician is being honest. But, to use Stoner's calculations as an example: If Jesus had satisfied only eight Old Testament prophecies in His New Testament coming, it would be by "one chance in one hundred million billion" that it occurred outside the realm of divine guidance and intervention.[3] He goes on to stipulate that "the probability of [Jesus] fulfilling forty-eight prophecies [by coincidence] was one chance in a trillion, trillion, trillion, trillion, trillion, trillion, trillion, trillion, trillion, trillion, trillion, trillion, trillion!"[4]

As well-known, former Jesus skeptic and *Case for Christ* journalist, Lee Strobel, attests: "Our minds can't comprehend a number that big. This is a staggering statistic that's equal to the number of minuscule atoms in a trillion, trillion, trillion, trillion, billion universes the size of our universe!"[5] This, for obvious reasons, makes the *three-hundred-sixty-five-plus* prophetic utterances of the Messiah prior to Christ's arrival almost unfathomable to even attempt calculations for in similar terms...

And, unbelievably, many of these numbers do not take into consideration the odds that Jesus would have "accidentally" fulfilled the Jewish feasts and extrabiblical traditions the way He did. An intense study of His fulfillment of the Passover involves a rarely studied ritual of the Passover feast called the *afikomen*—involving an unleavened matzah cracker that is broken, hidden away in the household, and located by family members who then break the matzah into smaller pieces and partake of it. This represents the search for and discovery of the Jews' future Messiah. (Sound familiar? Kinda like, oh, say, communion?) Jesus, on the night of His arrest, carried out a Passover Seder meal with His disciples and involved the *afikomen* ritual, though He deviated from tradition for a grand reason. He took the unleavened matzah bread before the meal and broke it into pieces, but skipped the hide-and-search portion of the ritual to illustrate that the Messiah was now found. It would be His body that would now be broken for humanity, fulfilling the purpose of the Passover ritual that had been carried out by the Jews for thousands of years before Jesus was born on the earth. In this, He became the Passover Lamb who was slain once for all. (The two men on the road to Emmaus recognized Jesus by the way He broke bread [Luke 24:34]. Unless Jesus had some mystical way of tearing bread apart that distinguished Him from every other bread-eater of His day, this account shows that He likely handled the messianic "cracker" in a way that tipped them off to His identity. For a detailed, faith-building journey through this and other feasts/traditions fulfilled in Jesus' time—and the religious authorities' attempt to cover all of it up—get a copy of *The Messenger: It's Headed toward Earth! It Cannot Be Stopped! And It's Carrying the Secret of America's, the World's, and Your Tomorrow!*, available at SkyWatchTVStore.com.) But, though this is all true, we are so far removed from the culture of the ancient Jews that, in order to completely comprehend Jesus' fulfillment of the feasts and traditions, we need extrabiblical research to fill in the blanks—and that is enormous territory. As a result, calculations of probability are usually based only upon clear Scripture and its mainstream interpretations, which leaves the brain-bending numbers noted earlier as the sole representation of the "odds" of Christ accidentally/coincidentally fulfilling prophecy. Imagine if we could take *all* we know about Christ and add that to the mix as well. The odds would certainly be impossible…yet one Man did it all!

In addition, the archeological evidence alone is astounding. The Word of God will never (as far as we know) be "provable" enough to place even the strongest skeptics in a position to believe, and we think this is because God wanted His Word to be accepted on faith, not based on science. There were, however, pieces of otherwise unexplainable leftovers from the ancient world that can strengthen the faith of those with eyes to see. Despite those who have, throughout time, tried to debunk or disprove certain historical details in the Bible, we can point to extrabiblical evidence, including: the census at the time of Jesus' birth that led Mary and Joseph to the stable; thirty-two countries, fifty-four cities, and nine islands in the book of Acts situated on the map precisely as the Bible describes, without error (that's a lifetime of travel for Luke just to show his book is geographically accurate in a day when nobody could have hopped online to challenge the accuracy of his maps); kings, rulers, government officials, and prominent leaders who served at the time the Bible indicates (which, again, would be easy for a creative fiction writer to get the who, when, what, and where confused); ancient extrabiblical documents—papyrus fragments, cuneiform tablets, and the like that relate many of the same facts, people, and stories included in the Bible; massive ruins still existing of the buildings, castles, and military structures mentioned in the biblical narrative; areas of land or soil that appear to have been, in ancient times, affected by something unnatural and unexplainable unless we consider them in the light of biblical miracles (the Flood, for instance); and so on. The purpose of this book isn't to prove the authenticity of the Word, however, the closer we get to admitting that there is something too astounding about the Word to ignore, and the longer we pore over the pages of this life-giving Book, the more clearly we see that it's all pointing to one progressive story of redemption through Christ.

So you see, the Bible is not a collection of marginally important, random notes and narratives recorded by a bunch of Jewish guys that climaxes in the record of the arrival of what we're *really* interested in: a Savior…who doesn't appear until the fortieth book. Nor does it simply build on the "more important" earlier Scriptures that foretell the coming Jewish Messiah, ending with the inconvenient, peripheral, and supplementary teachers' notes by Jesus' buddies called the

"New Testament." If progressive revelation (alternatively, the "revealing of God's plan for all of humanity") is going to coincide with the unswerving principle of internal consistency (one of the first and major rules in dependable biblical interpretations), then we arrive at a necessary convergence of the two concepts mentioned by the Pentecostal preacher and the YouTube rabbi at the beginning of this book.

The unity of the sixty-six books that outline progressive revelation is so astounding that, once understood, it seems even more bewildering than even the incomprehensible probability statistics and calculations of Stoner. Not one part of the text is better than another, and each portion depends on the others for a complete picture.

It's kinda like a perfect steak:

1) God's plan is cut out even before the beginning of the universe and the human race, involving Creation and the miraculously preserved bloodline of the Messiah (Genesis).

2) God's plan is seasoned in the spiritual preparation of God's people, Israel (Exodus–Song of Solomon).

3) God's plan is marinated in the message of the prophets who foretold of the Messiah's arrival and the circumstances of His redemptive work (Isaiah–Malachi).

4) God's plan is seared and sealed as the Messiah arrives, fulfills the prophecies of His coming, completes the work of redemption, is raised from the dead, and ascends to His Father's side (Matthew–John).

5) God's plan is browned and heated as the Messiah sends the Comforter (the Holy Spirit) to equip His disciples to carry the Good News of salvation to the ends of the earth and leads His disciples to proclaim His message dependably to the fledgling Church (Matthew–Jude).

6) God's plan is finally cooked to perfection and full flavor in the consummation of the redemption plan: His future return in the ultimate concluding demonstration of God over all evil (Revelation).

The real, beefy, meaty steak of the Bible keeps feeding perpetually.

In short, the integrity of Scripture is well supported throughout history, both by the world's proof (what was shared earlier is only the beginning of mountains of other proofs), as well as by countless other apologetics materials by brilliant scholars who have documented other mind-boggling evidence that the Bible is authentically the God-breathed Word—the self-revelation of God to humankind.

The Massive Importance of the Biblical Narrative

By now, it seems silly to stipulate this, but please note: The most responsible and effective Christology (the study of who Jesus was and what He came for) comes from the Bible's narrative about the historical Jesus.

Duh, guys… Where else would we derive our concepts about Jesus?

It sounds like a ridiculous stipulation, all things considered. However, some readers would be surprised to know that many wise and famous men of Church history, from antiquity through today, have sought to explain and understand Jesus from pools of thought other than from the Bible. It's human nature to try to understand enigmatic concepts from within the powers of our own mind (such as philosophy), rather than rely on the testimony of a book, no matter how sacred. Sometimes we make the mistake of considering the Bible as a thing to debate rather than as the Great Commission directive of Christ; and, more often than not, the debate takes place within the Body of Christ.

Where and How Some Went Wrong

Key Christian theologians, though often sincere in their work, traded the simplicity of New-Testament-narrative Christology in favor of "a more abstract, propositional view"[6] due to the championing of philosophical debate and analyses in the Greco-Roman culture. These discussions centered on the ontological nature (or "substance") of God (otherwise coined the "Immanent Trinity," how God exists within His own intra-divine nature) instead of the historical Jesus operating in the Spirit to complete God's redemptive plan (known in some theological circles as the "Economic Trinity": God's redemptive plan to reconcile humanity to Himself). Such emphasis on the intra-divine reality of God contributed to the more speculative and philosophical view that the Father is a different substance than the other members of the Trinity.[7]

Yet, even after that was largely settled through the early councils, "the Western theological method that prioritizes ontology as a substance over ontology as a relation was set on its course"[8] and would remain a trend for centuries.

The early Church was fractured with division as sincere men of God debated who Jesus was. Over time, Jesus' mission to reconcile God with humanity was traded for complicated theologies or a marriage of Church and politics, which led to a neglect of spreading the Gospel in its biblical simplicity. For some who might be new to the history, the Church councils were efforts of the early Church to resolve disagreements and establish consensus about beliefs by sending bishops to debate conflicting theology and establish creeds. Let's take a brief glance at the development of Western Christology from portions of the early Church forward.

Arian of Alexandria believed and taught (circa AD 318) that Jesus and God the Father were of a different, yet similar "substance," Jesus being *a creation of* the Father, instead of *always existent with* the Father. This belief—termed "Arianism"—denied the eternality that Christ and the Father shared; in simpler terms, it introduced the concept that Jesus' divinity was less potent than the Father's. The debate became one of whether Jesus was *equal to* the Father or *similar to* Him. This heresy reduced the salvation impact of His death on the cross.

So, the first ecumenical council—the Council of Nicaea in AD 325—met to, among other things, bring closure to the controversy of Arianism. To make a super long and complicated story short and simple: Arian's use of the Greek word *homoiousios* ("of *similar* substance") as a descriptor of the *Logos* (Jesus) and the Father was rejected by the majority of scholars equally learned in Scripture and Greek, and it was replaced with *homoousios* ("of *the same* substance"). This acknowledged Jesus in His rightful place—in a state of eternal existence with the Father, as described in the Gospel of John and supported by 1 Corinthians 1:24 (i.e., the biblical narrative). The Nicene Creed that resulted from the council reads, in part: "We believe in one God, the Father Almighty.... And in one Lord Jesus Christ, the Son of God... very God of very God...being of one substance with the Father."[9] The bishops then proceeded to "affirm twenty canons, or doctrinal propositions, thus laying a foundation for canon law."[10]

Awesome. Heresies silenced, Church united, canon established. Things looked good for a while.

Then, the Council of Chalcedon met in AD 451 to address more deeply the relationship between Christ's two natures—His humanity and His divinity—when new heresies popped into the picture. Archbishop Nestoria of Constantinople claimed Jesus' divine nature and human nature were separate, creating a "two Sons" theology (a "human Son" and a "God Son"). Comparably, Apollinaris of Laodicea held that Christ's body was *only human*, while His soul was *only divine*, thereby cancelling the fully human-mind rationality Jesus would have used to make the choice to submit to the cross. Apollinaris maintained that Jesus' human side was subordinate to His divine side. This meant "Jesus the person...[was] divine and only materially human in appearance."[11] Alexandrian bishop Cyril, who argued against Nestoria at the Council of Chalcedon, adopted a form of Apollinarianism, teaching that Christ's divinity dominated His humanity, "virtually swallowing it up."[12]

In a sense, this idea helps our finite brains make sense of how Jesus could have been the only perfect human who was tempted in all the same ways we are and yet never sinned (Hebrews 14:15), because He had a "God side" that mechanically controlled His human side and forced Him, like a robot, to remain in line with the Father's will. However, again, it does not fit the biblical narrative of Jesus being fully human and fully divine and, inadvertently of course, promotes the heresy of Docetism (a popular theology in opposing world religions that states Jesus' human body was a phantom or shadow—a mere "appearance" of flesh and blood—while His mind and consciousness were operating through the ghostly illusion). Just a glance at Scripture (see Luke 24:39; 1 John 4:1–2; 2 John 1:7; 1 Corinthians 15:17; John 20:27; and others) shows how these man-made notions fall short of the truth about Jesus' wholly-human, wholly-God existence during His time on earth.

The council rejected these "two Sons" heresies on the basis that redemption through the sacrifice of the cross would be impossible unless Jesus was fully human and simultaneously "undiminished deity."[13] The Chalcedonian Definition therefore affirmed that Christ's "hypostatic union" (the union of Jesus' two natures into one being) was "without confusion," "without change," "without division," and "without separation."

During the Middle Ages, Christology took on a bizarre, meta-physical emphasis under the teachings of Anselm, Abelard, Augustine, and others who confused the purpose of Christ even further.

Anselm developed the "substitutionary atonement theory," which viewed Christ's sacrificial work on the cross as a judicial transaction that paid a debt to the Father for the sins of humanity. Anselm's error was in his objective approach that Jesus, through His redemptive work, accomplished all that was necessary for salvation within the intra-divine nature of the Immanent Trinity. It thereby required little to no action on the part of the human recipient but to acknowledge within his or her rational mind the work that had been done on their behalf. Put in simpler terms, Anselm's teaching made salvation a thing of intellectual assent instead of an internal heart transformation for the saved Christian. (One only needs to *agree* to Christ being God to be saved, as opposed to *living for* Him.)

Abelard contrasted this with the subjective moral influence the-ory, which claimed that the purpose of Christ's work was to set a behavioral example for followers, that His death on the cross was only as an expression of the love of God (as opposed to expiation for sin), and that "there is no obstacle on the part of God which would prevent Him from pardoning their sins," because God is only love always.[14]

Augustine Christianized Neoplatonism: In short, the human soul reflected the Trinity and the image of God within itself already, to the point that knowing one's self completely equaled drawing nearer to God. The soul of a human had "fallen" into a body—the "lower part" of the inner person was the flesh, while the "higher part" of the inner person could comprehend God. Salvation in this theology requires people to look "in, then up" within themselves until they find Christ and salvation.

These are only a couple of examples of how the early Church had to gather to weed out false teachings by theologians, scholars, and others who made studying Scripture the main purpose of their lives for hundreds of years. Much can be said for the personal integrity of most of these precious men of God who meant well and only ever attempted to make the Bible and Jesus easier for us to grasp. Unfortunately, what is remembered of many of them today is that they were heretics, because they *did not follow the biblical narrative* of Scripture when they began to teach the multitudes their various philosophies. The malady that follows this grievance is not limited to what is taught about Jesus' divinity. As we will briefly show, abandoning the biblical narrative is also often the cause for the misguided marriage of Church and state. (Please note that these authors believe wholeheartedly in Christians engaging in responsibly following their nation's national administrations, legislations, and voting processes. We certainly should try to reflect our moral convictions upon those in governmental leadership so that we do our part in attempting to make our lands pleasing to God. However, that's different from interpreting the Bible to say we should focus on creating a theocracy, because Jesus' Kingdom is "not of this world" anyway [John 18:36], and our chief focus is to reach the lost, not establish world governments [Matthew 28:16–20].)

The "Constantinian arrangement"—which could be reworded as the merger between the Church and state from the time of Constantine through the next thousand years—assimilated the Roman Catholic Church with the secular Roman Empire to the point that the two were nearly inseparable. The era began when Constantine (and Augustus Licinius), through the Edict of Milan in AD 313, legalized Christianity and formally ended persecution of believers.

This event is documented in encyclopedias as "an era of the utmost importance in the history of the world" for its impact upon Christian freedom.[15] That's understandably true, as it legalized Christianity everywhere, allowing anyone in a previously hostile region to follow Christ without peril. However, there was a negative impact upon the Christian theological method as well.

What first began with the Constantinian arrangement further bled into the longstanding marriage of Church and state, resulting in corruption of Church leadership and practices. In 800, Pope Leo II oversaw the coronation of Emperor Charlemagne, which "blurred the jurisdictions of church and state," exalting Charlemagne above the pope as "the highest authority figure in the church."[16] By the mid-sixteenth century, following this trend, King Henry VIII replaced Christ as representative over the whole church and the secular, political world.

This religio-political pact allowed for new extremes of exploitation of the poor and desolate. As one example: The sale of indulgences (money in trade for a shorter time in purgatory during the afterlife) was instigated by the papacy to raise money for projects—such as St. Peter's Basilica in Rome financed by the indulgence-fundraiser of Johann Tetzel in 1506.[17]

However, Jesus was anointed to help the "poor," "brokenhearted," "captive," "blind," and "bruised" (Luke 4:18). He frequently expressed that these were the folks *we, too,* should feel called to help (Luke 6:20–21; 12:16–21; 14:12–14; Matthew 25:34–36; Mark 10:21–22; 12:41–44). In regard to world government, He expected us only to pay our taxes (Mark 12:17).

Thus it is shown how the resolute inseparability of Christianity and world government can lead to accomplishing the opposite of Jesus' instructions and therefore the opposite of the Church's missions. The Reformation was, in part, the passionate resistance to this tragedy. Nevertheless, some of the most popular voices against these developments still missed the mark and created another form of the same problem.

The Anglican Church took the most theocratic approach of all churches that split from the Catholic Church during the Reformation. Though the Christology of the Anglican Church reflected that of the Roman Catholic Church, an early goal was for the king to be chief leader over the whole Church of England in place of the pope.

The Reformed movement under Huldrych Zwingli positioned Christ as the ultimate example of moral, Christian living. Zwingli also held that Church and state were inseparable, that the Church could have intense sway over society and politics and, therefore, believers would get involved in national reform as evidence of Christ doing an inner work.

Reformer John Calvin's doctrine of predestination claimed God revealed Himself to only select humanity through the Incarnation, making Jesus "a category of study. A person needed only to recognize himself or herself as one of God's elect in order to be a Christian."[18] Calvin believed a Christian's purpose is toward ordering society, which naturally merges Church and state.

We said all of that to say this: When even the sincerest Christians move away from the biblical narrative in their thoughts, theology, or actions, human nature takes over and produces an imperfect gospel that confuses the reason Jesus came in the grand picture of progressive revelation.

We will visit on a book-by-book basis how Jesus is central to the overall progression of redemption and humanity's reconciliation unto God. However, as we've illustrated, it's "just that easy" for anyone—even the most highly educated biblical scholars and theologians in the world—to get away from the basics regarding Christ and make Him and His mission different than they should be.

Biblical Narrative Christology: The Basics

In that interest, here we'll pause for a crash course of Jesus' role in the whole Bible, as it may help the bigger picture "click" more effectively later.

The original Hebrew states God created humans in His "image" (Genesis 1:27) and they became a living "breath" (Genesis 2:7). By this, we were created to be a "viceroy or representative" for God on earth and a "participant in God's ongoing care" in our dominion over creation.[19] From this unique relationship, God intended an order: God over people, people over animals, and animals subject to both. The original sin was an inversion of this order, as the serpent convinced Adam and Eve they could be like God if they ate from the tree of the knowledge of good and evil—an action that violated God's instructions.

After eating the forbidden fruit, humanity lost its state of perfection and acceptance in the eyes of God, yet gained knowledge that initiated a more driving desire to be like God, while the shame and death introduced through sin would make knowing God by one's own efforts impossible. There would be only one way of overcoming this disaster: The curse would have to be God's reversal plan of salvation and reconciliation with humanity.

God's reconciliation plan began with Abraham, who had been called out of the existing nations to resettle in Canaan and establish God's nation, Israel. These people were to stand in sharp contrast to the wickedness in the world—as people of priestly service rather than people in the outside world wrought with demonic warriors and kings who dominated with bloodshed.[20] This would be an enormous task, achievable only through faith in God's promises. From this early moment, God's intention of blessing all people of the earth through Abraham's family line was promised (Genesis 12:2–3) and it soon began with his son, Isaac (Genesis 21), who fathered Jacob, who was renamed "Israel."

The subsequent centuries of judges, kings, and prophets rendered both ends of the extreme—unwavering-faith highs and idolatrous lows—for the Israelites toward God, illustrating the continual need of a Savior despite that they were given the Law through Moses.

Rapid-fire fast-forward to the Savior's (physical) entrance into the story…

In the Synoptic Gospels (Matthew, Mark, and Luke), Jesus was conceived in Mary's womb by the Holy Spirit (Luke 1:35; Matthew 1:20), rendering Him the Son of God, literally. Mary, in the song she sang while she was with child, recognized that this Baby Boy was the promised help to Abraham and his offspring (Luke 1:54–55). Mary's cousin Elizabeth called the unborn Jesus "Lord" (Luke 1:43)—kurios in Greek—a reference that "overlapped" Christ's identity with Yahweh, showing that the Spirit's conception of Christ constituted Jesus' existence as the Son of God and a member of the Trinity.

Matthew wrote of the Spirit coming upon Jesus at His baptism, which resulted in the Father's audible, public announcement that this was His Son, in whom He was "well pleased" (3:16–17). Through this baptism, the Father began His work to reverse the human condition of sin. Jesus' ministry began with the temptation in the wilderness (the Spirit led Him directly there; see Matthew 4:1). Afterward, Jesus announced Himself as the Messiah at the synagogue in Nazareth (Luke 4:18–21).

The Gospel writers concur that, toward the end of Jesus' life, more demonstrations of His divine Sonship fulfilled Old Testament prophecies, such as the crowd's response as He rode a colt (Luke 19:38; Matthew 21:9). Another example is the cleansing of the Temple (Luke 19:46), which illustrated, among other things, the transition from the physical structure of the Jerusalem Temple to "another kind of temple" in the Kingdom that was never going to be "of this world" (John 18:36). But the culmination of Jesus' life in the Spirit was exemplified through His ultimate obedience to death and suffering on a cross for the reversal of sin.

During His ministry, Jesus illustrated that God's Kingdom was different. It didn't look anything like what even the most pious Jews expected. Righteousness, goodness, and holiness under this superior Kingdom order inverted the Jewish perception, as shown through Jesus' radical reversal-teaching of religious standards (Matthew 8:10–12). Those God would accept into His kingdom and allow to accomplish His work were sharply increased beyond the comfortable borders of Jewish expectation, as seen in Jesus allowing "outsiders" to cast out demons in His name (Luke 9:49–50), and in His extending the salvation invitation to non-Jews (such as Zacchaeus; Luke 19:1–10). At seemingly every turn, Jesus showed that the Kingdom of God was a deep contrast to the world's system. It was not for earthly, political relief on behalf of an elect few devoted Jews that He came, but for spiritual freedom and the reconciliation of *all* sinners to God through the reversal of sin on the cross.

Because "everything about Jesus' life and mission was accomplished in the Spirit," His coming in this way was "for the sole purpose of establishing the kingdom of God."[21] Jesus' life example, therefore, defines the Spirit-filled life.

And, yes, you read that right: Being a Christian means more than just believing *in* something like a child believes in the boogeyman. The Bible says even the demons believe in *that* way (James 2:19). The very word "Christian" means "little Christ."[22] Therefore, the paramount responsibility of Christians today is to conform as closely as possible to the character of Christ, in every way He lived His Spirit-filled life.

However, there is also the good news that the Spirit who conceived Jesus in Mary's womb, carried Him through His life and ministry years, and equipped Christ for radical obedience to the Father is the same Spirit that walks with confessed believers today.

Before His ascension, Jesus promised to send His followers the Holy Spirit for the purpose of spreading the Gospel (John 7:33; 14:16–26; 15:26–27; 16:7–11). According to Numbers 11:29, the people of God had anticipated the glorious day when the Spirit of God would be poured upon them. Following the ascension, the Day of Pentecost was the fulfillment of this hope, which took place just as Jesus had said (Acts 1:9; 2:3–22; Luke 24:51; Mark 16:19; John 16:28; 20:17). This gift of the Spirit created the potential for followers of Christ to do all the works Jesus had done—and more, if you can believe that (John 14:12)!

Without this historical Jesus—the fully human being who was also paradoxically wholly God—the doctrine of salvation becomes a product of internal reflection or rational assent, as opposed to a heart transformation. Western Logos Christology (the typical theology in the West regarding who Jesus is and what He came to do) fails in expressing the importance of Jesus' earthly works and is "most closely related to certain wisdom motifs in Alexandrian Judaism."[23] Spirit Christology is the study of how God related to the human Jesus and, therefore, "God's redeeming work in Jesus."[24] This is where the West must return in its theological endeavors: back to the original, scriptural narrative to reprioritize the spread of the salvation message.

The Christological focus of the New Testament Church was born of the simplicity of having witnessed either Jesus, Himself, or the movement that came about as a result of His life, miracles, death, and Resurrection. To these, the Church was a perilous but simple activity of spreading the Gospel throughout every region they could travel. Self-denial became a heavily adopted theme among followers of Jesus (Luke 9:23; Matthew 16:24; Mark 8:34), and they embraced the understanding that some may be martyred for their cause. In fact, such a fate was considered the seal of a life lived *and* sacrificed for the Lord. The New Testament Church first approached Christology from the narrative of Jesus' life as it naturally showed the fulfillment of God's revelation and salvation plan throughout the Old Testament and subsequent history. The earliest approach identified all three members of the Trinity at work in this way: God the Father sent His Son to earth to carry out His plan of redemption through the empowerment of the Holy Spirit (the Economic Trinity).

With this as a central method, the goal of Christology does not lean on our intellectual comprehension of and connection to God, but on proclaiming the Good News of Christ by allowing Christ's identity and person to be revealed through His life. This proclamation first identifies the lost, sin-nature of humanity, then provides the narrative of how God arranged for the salvation of humanity through the Son, without being pigeonholed into our cultural, ethnic, or religious boxes. It is with this in mind that we write this book.

Before We Proceed

We're almost ready to dive in and see how Jesus' many appearances throughout the Word align with this ultimate progressive plan, but we need to address a few things before we begin in order to streamline the flow later on.

"Traditional" Authorship and Dating

This work isn't intended to discuss each book of the Bible in the same way as historical criticisms; we won't be deeply discussing authorship or the dates the books of the Bible were written beyond what's indicated by tradition. (Note that "criticism" isn't meant as a synonym for "disapproval" or "condemnation." It merely refers to looking at books' origins and trying to reliably show who wrote them, when, and in what context.) We fully understand and submit to the examination of authorship as other scholars and historians have done, and we believe such work to be crucially important for many works today.

We're likewise familiar with many of the arguments surrounding the traditional delegations, such as whether King Solomon really was the author of Proverbs, Ecclesiastes, and the Song of Solomon (or Song of Songs). Scholars throughout history have looked at internal and external evidences that ultimately question these attributions in responsible ways. But because such an investigation would detract from our goal of tracing the footprints of our Savior throughout each of the sixty-six books of the Bible, we've chosen to allow the traditional designations to hold steady in this work unless a discussion of authorship, canonicity, or dating will have a significant bearing on our topic.

The Word "Sage"

A quick note here about terminology—specifically, the word "sage": In today's usage, the "sage" is sometimes associated with pagan or New Age ideologies, or is seen as synonymous with "guru." For the reader today, "sage" may even inspire imagery of a robed mystic trained in religio-philosophy burning dried plants to "cleanse evil spirits" from a haunted house, a graveyard, or an old church property. (In fact, one of the authors of this book just days ago saw the word used with that very connotation in a documentary about the paranormal world.) However, in this study, we use the term in its most basic historical application: "Sage" simply means "wise man" and refers to one who sought the wisdom of the elders of Israel—whether personally or through their writings—and taught from the experience of that knowledge. In fact, many scholars refer to Jesus Christ, Himself, as the supreme Sage, due to His expert retorts against His agitators while He walked the earth.

What Is a Theophany/Christophany?

It's easy to assume that, although there might be symbols and typographies of Christ in the Old Testament (and there is an abundance!) there is no literal, physical, observable "appearance" of Jesus (or even the Father) in the Old Testament. "The only way God is literally or physically present," one might say, "is by the observable effects of His power, such as the parting of the waters. We can observe waters climbing into a giant wall, but we can't observe God pushing the waters back. As far as the other two members of the Trinity, there's a confusing reference about the Holy Spirit hovering over the waters of the earth in the opening passages of Genesis, and then the Son shows up in Matthew."

However, scholars from all over the world and from every culture and background have long acknowledged that the Greek and Hebrew languages of the original biblical manuscripts frequently describe appearances of the Father and the Son throughout the Old Testament in a form that, to the people standing there at the time, would be corporeal—physically touchable and seen by the naked eye. In the case of Christ, this would be prior to His human birth. *Baker Encyclopedia of the Bible* simplifies this complicated idea: "The human-form theophanies in the OT [Old Testament] are often referred to as Christophanies on the basis that these appearances of God are best explained as pre-incarnate manifestations of the Second Person of the Trinity. These appearances thus anticipate the incarnation of Christ and provide an OT glimpse into the triune nature of the Godhead."[25]

In a work like this one, where Christ appears in an Old-Testament narrative ages before He was born to Mary in the flesh, the subject becomes important to tackle from the beginning. Allie Anderson and Donna Howell addressed this in *Encounters: Extraordinary Accounts of Angelic Intervention and What the Bible Actually Says about God's Messengers* while they were ironing out how Jesus could have been the Old Testament "Angel of the Lord":

The word "theophany" is derived from the Greek words *theos* ("god") and *phainein* ("show" or "reveal"). A theophany within the context of the Holy Bible, therefore, is a visible appearance of God, Himself, to mankind.... A "Christophany" is essentially the same thing, but specific to an appearance of Christ, much like the Apostle Paul's "Road to Damascus" experience. Most theophanies describe God in human form, but some are more mysterious and complicated, such as when He appeared to Moses in the form of a burning bush (Exodus 3:2 and 4:17)....

Sometimes we needn't look far for the proof that an "Angel" is, in fact, a theophany, since near the verse in question, another passage clarifies it in no uncertain terms. For instance, Genesis 31:11 says, "And the Angel of God spake unto me in a dream, saying, 'Jacob': And I said, 'Here am I.'" Initially, it's not certain that this is God, Himself. But two verses later, this same "Angel of God" says, "I am the God of Bethel, where thou anointedst the pillar, and where thou vowedst a vow unto me." Nobody needs to wonder whether a mere messenger [angel]...is "the *God* of Bethel" (or the "God of" any place, for that matter). Beyond this, pillar anointings and vows would not be made to a spirit-being *servant* of the Almighty instead of the Almighty, Himself....

At times, Scripture distinguishes a theophany when a passage describes the Angel performing an act, service, miracle, or all-powerful character trait that only God, Himself, is capable of....

[As one example:] God is the *only* power in the universe that can create life (Genesis 1; Isaiah 40:28; Acts 17:24), and even more importantly, He is the only power that can create life out of *nothing* by the sheer force of His command (Colossians 1:16).... Yet in Genesis 16:10, we read: "And the Angel of the Lord said unto her, I will multiply thy seed exceedingly, that it shall not be numbered for multitude." Here again, a "messenger" [the literal translation of the Greek word for "angel"] of the Creator wouldn't have the power to multiply offspring.

Elsewhere, Joshua "fell on his face to the earth, and did worship" the Angel; immediately after Joshua's worshipful expression, the Angel told Joshua—in the same flavor as He had told Moses earlier—that Joshua was standing on "holy ground" (Joshua 5:14–15). Within the boundaries of healthy Christian theology, angels are *not* to be worshipped. This kind of error led to the evil/fallen angels in the first place. Any "holy angel" of the Lord's Celestial Order would not accept worship, as is proven by John's account on Patmos [Revelation 22:8–9; see also Matthew 4:9–10; Romans 1:25; Colossians 2:18]....

Therefore, we know the Angel in the Joshua account was a theophany, as he openly accepted worship and spoke in the same terms as God.[26]

Thankfully, Allie and Donna saw that some eyebrows would be raised if a "theophany" was explained as the appearance of God, but the "Christophany" wasn't addressed, and in short order, they go on:

By now, you might be wondering why so many scholars are convinced that some of these theophanies are Christophanies, specifically referencing an appearance of Jesus in the Old Testament ages before He would come in human flesh. A couple of factors contribute to this calculation.

First, scholars consider the attributes and characteristics of each member of the Trinity and find Christ the most likely candidate to appear corporeally. The Word is clear that "no man hath seen God at any time" (John 1:18), yet *many* have seen Christ while He walked in the flesh. This conundrum has confused a great number of Bible students throughout the years, because verses like these are scattered throughout Scripture:

"And he said, 'Thou canst not see my face: for there shall no man see me, and live'" (Exodus 33:20).

But wait a second...*Jacob* saw God and lived: "And Jacob was left alone; and there wrestled a man...[and thereafter said:] 'I have seen God face to face, and my life is preserved'" (Genesis 32:24, 30).

On the other hand, *nobody* can see God: "[God] only hath immortality...which no man can approach unto; whom no man hath seen, nor can see" (1 Timothy 6:16).

But on the *other* other hand: "And Manoah said unto his wife, 'We...have seen God'" (Judges 13:22).

Whereas it appears quite clear in Scripture that no man can see God and live, it's quite obvious that Jesus—God in human form—was "seen" by mankind everywhere He went. He was corporeal, touchable, and physical....

Second, the "Angel of the Lord" mysteriously disappeared after Jesus Christ was born in the flesh. If the Angel was, in fact, the preincarnate Messiah, then it explains why the theophany/Christophany didn't take place during the years He was going about His Father's business in human form. In a time as spiritually and eternally significant as Christ's ministry years, one might find the absence of theophanies a notable oddity, until we allow that the same God behind the theophanies was walking with the disciples, challenging the Pharisees, etc. It is during this time when God's chief messenger was identified as Gabriel, *not* the "Angel of the Lord."

Third, although we know that Christ is "much better than the angels" (Hebrews 1:4) who in turn "worship Him" (Hebrews 1:6–7)...Malachi's prophecy (Malachi 3:1) about the future Messiah specifically identifies Christ as God's *mal'ak*, which, as we discussed earlier, is Hebrew for "messenger" and by extension "angel." This is key language that links Christ, Himself, to theophanies.[27]

Note that some translations—the KJV is one example—attempt to deeply analyze which moments recorded in the Word are Christophanies referred to as the "angel of God" or "angel of the Lord," and the term is capitalized: "Angel." So if you're reading your Bible and an "angel" is given a surprise capital letter, you know you've stumbled upon what the translators and scholars behind that translation believe to be a Christophany.

As thoroughly as this explanation was handled by Allie and Donna in their work, it's only the beginning of what could be a ton of evidence that Christ was corporeally present in the Old Testament, typically as a human male. Some instances where the form of this theophany/Christophany does not reflect human design can be mind-boggling. At times, it's so strange that we feel tempted to skip over it, shrug, and assume it will all become clear in the afterlife. However, as our good friend and paramount theologian, Dr. Michael Heiser, often says, "If it's in the Bible and it's *weird*, it's important." We won't spoil it here, but there were times either Christ types or Christ, Himself, appeared in bizarre manifestations early on that, once understood, will flip that switch of comprehension even further regarding Christ's identity in the New Testament and how it miraculously links to God's redemption plan from the beginning.

Typology and the Word "Type" in This Work

Moving forward, you'll note we use the word "type" quite often. In the realm of theological study, this is a doctrine and/or theory that links the Old Testament to the New Testament in regard to people, places, objects, events, and so on, that foreshadow things to come (but always in some relation to the Messiah). In other words, it is used to refer to a foreshadowing of Christ prior to His coming.

A multifaceted example of an Old Testament type is in the account of Abraham, when he was sent to sacrifice his only son, Isaac. The boy asked his father where the lamb for the sacrifice was, and Abraham answered that God, Himself, would provide the animal (Genesis 22:8). When Abraham was provided with a ram caught in a thicket as a provision that saved Isaac's life, we see layers of Christ in the story: Abraham was asked to sacrifice his only son, and it was God's only Son who would be the one sacrifice for all; Isaac lived because the ram was his substitute, and Jesus was the New Testament Lamb substitute (more on this in the material on the Exodus later on) who is slain for all so that all might live; the ram was "crowned" with a thicket, and Jesus was crowned with thorns. To reiterate, the ram in this story is a "type" (a prophetic prefigure) of Christ, because he is the lamb God provided for a sacrifice, as Jesus was the Lamb God provided for the ultimate sacrifice. Another example is Jonah. He is a type of Christ because, as Christ was dead for three days and reemerged to life, Jonah was swallowed by a whale, where he remained for three days before he reemerged to the living, appearing to rise from the dead.

One final note: This book doesn't read like some studies, beginning each book of the Bible by explaining its contents (though that is closer to the format we follow from the Epistles forward). Instead, this book is a *companion* to the Word. We suggest you keep your Bible handy and consult it often while you read this book.

The Word of God is a love story, from beginning to end...and it all begins in Genesis, where our Savior is first mentioned to the human race as the seed of the woman. That seems as good a place as any to start, yes?

OLD TESTAMENT

The English word "Testament" we see in the two major headers of the Bible is translated from the Greek *diatheke* (dee-ath-ay-kay), and it has a triple meaning, all quite legally binding. First, it means what it sounds like, as regarding evidence, a witness, or proof (think of a "witness testament" in court). Second, the word represents the "will" of someone, similar to the "Will Contract" document arranged that designates one's personal property to beneficiaries. Last, especially in the context of the Word, it denotes a "covenant."

Some define "covenant" as "a promise," but it involves much more than that. Promises can often be made and easily broken with little consequence apart from a single individual or small group getting their feelings hurt or their hearts broken. A covenant is far closer to the concept of a contract, and in the Bible, that's precisely what it is.

God gave us His self-revelation, a contract in writing, and His signature appears on each page of the document. He is bound by what is stated within it, and we are given a choice: We can "sign" it and agree to live by its terms to reap its eternal benefits, or we can refuse to "sign," it, with the understanding that our temporary existence on this planet will conclude with death—without the afterlife profits the contract stipulates to us as beneficiaries.

What we must *never* do is "sign" the contract and then be found in breach of its conditions and clauses, saying we're Christians and living like heathens or the ancient Israelites who swore oaths to "be married to Yahweh" and then "cheated on Him with other gods" (the nuptial language used in both Testaments to describe this "contract" as a marital arrangement).

With that said, the Old Testament is not called "old" because it's irrelevant or defunct. Two humans can write a contract and later update it, but the new one is still based upon the stipulations of the first. In that regard, as we proceed, keep it in mind the Old Testament could alternatively be called the "Evidence of God in the Beginning," the "Will of God before His Anointed," or simply, the "First Contract."

Genesis

THE WORD "GENESIS" MEANS "BEGINNING," and the first book of the Bible is so named because it records the literal beginning of all things in existence—the planet, along with the animals, plants, and ecosystem, etc. It also details the creation of the first man and woman—the first intelligent beings of free will—and the misuse they make of that gift. The reality of the first sin that took place when Adam and Eve ate the forbidden fruit recognizes mankind's need for a Savior as early as Genesis 3:6. Jesus comes into the picture as that very future Savior in verse 15, which reads: "And I [God] will put enmity between thee and the woman, and between thy seed and her seed; it shall bruise thy head, and thou shalt bruise his heel." The "it" said to bruise the serpent's head here is the Hebrew *hu'*, which does translate to "it," but it is a demonstrative pronoun of the third person (singular), so it equally could translate to "he" (or "she") depending on the context. In this sentence, since it's a prophecy of a male in the offspring line of Eve who will defeat the enemy, the word obviously becomes "he." Many at this point jump to the (precious and correct) conclusion and acknowledge they already know this pronoun refers to Jesus. But don't lose the power in the moment by assuming you've heard all this before.

Many folks who read Genesis feel the impact of the first sin. Upon hearing the title of the book, the first image that pops into mind is the fruit in Eve's hand—something beautiful, nearly irresistible, but carnal and depraved; a prohibition, broken from the lust for illicit indulgence; perfect innocence defiled; and the closest relationship with God that mankind has ever known traded for a taste of forbidden knowledge. We see a tree with two completely nude, yet guiltless and pure, people standing under it, listening to the deceitful and misleading words of the enemy who will in only moments trick them into ushering the first evils into the world...upon which their handsome nudity will be made perverse and illicit, stripped of its otherwise innate beauty through virtuous Creation. We see a colorful garden paradise, branches drooping low with every kind of organic, nutritious fruit within reach, tending to itself and reproducing without any human toil—then we see the fiery swords of the angels who stand guard at its gate lest any stained man or woman ever again attempts to enter this utopia.

But this doesn't need to be our first or only thoughts about this book. We should be able to think "Genesis" and hear the words of our Father, during the edict of His salvation plan, directed to *us*, today: "And I will put enmity between thee and the woman, and between thy seed and her seed; it shall bruise thy head, and thou shalt bruise his heel." The very moment that we, the kiddos God created and loves like a papa, got into trouble for the very first time, He intervened with a plan to save us all! We're careful to steer clear of ever overusing the "daddy" idea of God, because it can quickly start to sound too casual, but take a second to think about this paramount, historical moment: God formed people, male and female, even in His very own image, which He was gracious enough to share with mere mortals (Genesis 1:26). This was done for His glory (Isaiah 43:7; Romans 11:36), as He finds pleasure in the humans He made (Revelation 4:11), and wants to be near us whenever we need and seek Him (Acts 17:27). He would now watch us enjoy life and multiply (Genesis 1:28), so He might see His workmanship walk in goodness upon the earth—a goal He ordained for His people from the beginning (Ephesians 2:10) so we all might be exalted in due time because He cares about us so much (1 Peter 5:6–7). And all of this arrangement He acknowledged as very, very good (Genesis 1:31)!

Adam and Eve really blundered a beautiful thing, didn't they?

Well, yes, they goofed. In fact, they more-than-goofed. This was a cosmic sneeze that would blow the world off course forever—a toe-stubbing of epic proportions humanity would never stop limping from. But before we grip the pitchfork and blame every historical woe upon these two folks, consider the circumstances behind their actions and try to see them as God would have seen them: as tragic victims of the foulest trickery most of us today can't identify with when we stumble over far smaller blocks of sin.

At this time in the Genesis narrative, the first two humans are creatures of free will, while they were not yet creatures of experience. Without a human history for them to relate to, there was no record compelling them to fear repeating the raw, infantile decision to go against something God said. All Christians, who often sin every single day (even if "only" in our thoughts [Matthew 5:28; Proverbs 24:9]), should look upon Adam and Eve with grace and forgiveness for this original sin, especially because the enemy's words were partly true and, therefore, held far more power to deceive. American theologian Albert Barnes, in his *Barnes Notes on the Whole Bible* commentary, agrees:

> Let us remember that this was the first falsehood the woman ever heard. Her mind was also infantile as yet, so far as experience was concerned. The opening mind is naturally inclined to believe the truth of *every* assertion, until it has learned by experience the falsehood of *some*.

There was also in this falsehood what gives the power to deceive, a great deal of truth combined with the element of untruth. The tree was not [immediately] physically fatal to life [as the serpent said], and the eating of it really issued in a knowledge of good and evil [as he promised it would].[28]

If Barnes, alongside countless scholars and several psychologists who have weighed in on this moment, are accurate in understanding what this first-human naivety would have been like up against the purest of all evil persuasions in world history, then we should admit most of us would have made the same mistake under those circumstances. This wasn't just a bully behind a dumpster at the back of the playground offering his buddies a cigarette because all the cool kids are doin' it. Adam and Eve were confronted with the temptation to commit the ultimate, supremely intelligent original sin while they were more morally green and untested than any humans have been since.

With that in mind, we can see the genius of the deceiver in all he stole from them in that moment, and with compassionate sympathy we reconsider the weight they must have felt after the irreversible deed was done. It wasn't just that they, because of taking a bite of a knowledge-tree fruit, suddenly became aware a thing called "evil" existed, as God had already told them it did when He had warned them to stay away from the tree of the knowledge of good and *evil* in the first place (Genesis 2:17). That tree could have been named the "tree of the *experience* of good and evil," because *partaking* what was forbidden yielded the *experience* of evil; in other words, disobeying God and going against His will always produce evil. Barnes likewise understood the unique relationship in this initial interlock between knowledge and experience, profoundly stating "it did not make [Adam and Eve] know good and evil altogether, as God knows it, but in an experimental sense, as the devil knows it. In point of knowledge, they became like God; in point of morality, like the tempter."[29]

That "in point of morality, like the tempter" status is what the rest of us inherited from the sin nature after the Fall. In that, we are like Adam and Eve. Many easily admit this is because we're born into the consequences of the grave-separation error they made in the garden, while many others don't even consider whether we would have taken a bite also, had we been there, had our minds been as new and vulnerable, and had we been as titillated by the most convincing and tempting deceiver ever known. Either way, under far less powerful temptation and often as a matter of convenience, there are sins we commit on the daily that we don't consider a big deal—and, regardless of the form of the temptation and what voice is pitching it as a good idea, we do far more than eat off-limits fruit. The most fairminded and unbiased approach to this story is that we do—by nature and by free will—share in the sin of Adam and Eve, making us "in point of morality, like the tempter."

Yikes. We all are in need of this Savior! Let's therefore place ourselves in the narrative alongside Adam and Eve going forward.

So here's God, only moments prior to the Fall, rejoicing over the beautiful world He has made and the sweet people He delights in. We can see Him in our imagination, filled with joy overflowing to join us in Eden, walk with us like companions through the gorgeous flora, take in the jubilant sounds of the water in the nearby brook that splash off the rocks like laughter bubbling up from the ground, and look out over the animals with us as they peacefully graze on the surrounding greenery. Everything is perfectly peaceful. God engineered countless brilliant species, brought life to all of them, and rested, seeing that all of what He had done was good: just good always; nothing bad or ugly, ever. Purity, light, joy, fun, wonder, rapture…just goodness everywhere.

Then in one instant—one invisible, horrible, tragic, and staggeringly upsetting instant—we humans choose to go against our closest and greatest Friend because we believe a lie…and nothing *we* do can reverse the mistake. We're doomed, forever, to separation from His presence because He is all holiness and can't coexist in the same space as someone or something that has been spotted by evil.

We, his kiddos, have ruined it. We hurt Him when we mar the beautiful things He has made. (The Word makes it clear in Genesis 6:5–6 that, when humanity eventually became only evil always, it broke His heart. We're aware the context involves a dark and sinister evil related to the Nephilim of Genesis 6:4. That is the subject of another book entirely, but the essence of God's pain in Genesis 6:6 is a result of a wicked humanity. Therefore, if God is immutable—that is, if His nature and characteristics are consistent—then the grief He feels in 6:6 would logically be present in 3:6, the moment Eve's teeth sink into the fruit, instantly separating Holy God from sinful man.)

Again, we're all for the responsible use of theological anthropomorphism (describing God with relatable, human traits) because it helps us understand His otherwise incomprehensible nature. Old-Testament writers attribute God, who is technically a Spirit (John 4:24), as having human body parts and movements for this same reason. The psalmists said He crushed Rahab and scattered His enemies with His "mighty arm" (Psalm 89:10), and that His "eyes" are on the righteous and His "ears" listen for their cry (24:15). Even God, Himself, said He would deliver His people from the Egyptians with His "outstretched arm" (Exodus 6:6). Yet, we try not to feel too comfortable thinking of Him in "daddy" terms, as stated before, because we never want to over-humanize or make casual how we view the Almighty. But in this narrative, when humanity is fresh, new, and perfect, then so suddenly soiled by the perversion of sin, we see God as a papa looking over His children, His loving, fatherly heart tearing in two—not out of surprise or shock, for God the Omnipotent sees and knows all, but out of despair for the closeness with Him we steal from ourselves when we sin, and what we humans, on this fateful day, *have taken from Him.*

Many books, classes, Bible studies, movies, programs, and other media formats out there take a long look at what happened in the

Garden that day. Most focus on the Fall of Man, what that meant theologically, what occurred in the supernatural, and how, from every angle, it has affected mankind from that day to this: Why do we go through what we do as a result of the Fall? What did we lose in the Garden? How we should feel about it? Too few resources encourage readers to consider what God went through that day. What about *Him*? What about *His* loss? He showed us nothing but love and the greatest care in forming us, then He befriended us in a literal paradise, yet we turned against Him at the first sign of temptation.

We broke His heart.

To put it in childlike-faith terms: We hurt Him really, *really* bad. In the midst of this—the worst, most hurtful form of catastrophe inflicted against God—instead of owning what we did and showing remorse...we hid.

And then, when it looked like Papa had every right to declare us unredeemable, blow up the world, scrap it all, start over, kill us all, or punt-kick the planet into the universe in rage and watch it ping-pong about the cosmos like a magnificent pinball table in space, He suddenly didn't.

What *did* He do?

He informed the two sinners that *He* was going to reverse the mistake by sending His one and only Son through the womb of a virgin to declare victory over the consequences of their sin. He would make a way through whatever sin would block mankind from the presence of God!

Behold, the Christ of Genesis! Yes!

See, Genesis does give us bad news about sin. But for those who miss the phenomenal promise of restoration in the narrative, a closer look is in order. For just as one act of disobedience in the Garden caused all of us to be sinners, ironically, one act of divine obedience by the Son made all righteous (Romans 5:19).

This is the first time in human history and in the Bible God mentions a salvation plan, the beneficiaries of which are human. (Actually, it's the first prophecy in the Word of God.) The theological term for this mention of the salvation plan is "protevangelium" (sometimes "protoevangelion"), or what commentator and Old Testament scholar Derek Kidner calls "the first glimmer of the gospel."[30] Right here, just a skip over from the creation of humanity, we see God's intervention in the damnation of humans.

Interestingly, though most of the genealogy passages in the Bible (and in ancient culture) are ever focused on seed and offspring as being passed through *males*, in this instance, God notes that it is through a *woman* that this future bruiser-of-the-heel would come. The Hebrew word translated "seed" here is *zera*, a masculine noun, with one of its definitions as "semen." We see it used that way in several places in the cleanliness laws of Leviticus 15, where it refers to the act of procreation, as does the use of "seed" near "woman" in Numbers 5:28. Yet in Genesis, while God is speaking to Adam and Eve about the someday Savior of all the world, a *woman* has a seed. How is that so?

Today, because we have the rest of Scripture, we're not surprised by this outcome. But to any student of the Pentateuch (the first five books of the Bible, traditionally believed to have been written by Moses) any time prior to approximately 740–730 BC (the period including events recorded in the book of Isaiah), this would have sounded exceedingly odd. Many must have pondered to themselves: *Why in the world wouldn't God instead tell us about the* man *He will use to father this future child? Why did He just pass straight over Adam in this moment? Is he not standing right there? And why does "woman" suddenly have "seed"?*

The literal fulfillment of the Genesis 3:15 prophecy of the crushing and bruising between seed lines can be ambiguous outside the context of the Hebrew and without the explanation the New Testament innately gives. Because our goal is to briefly visit all sixty-six books of the Bible, specifically examining how each one relates to or involves Christ (the "crusher" in this prophecy), the big-picture fulfillment will be throughout this work. So, briefly, the question that arises for some is why the enemy, or his seed line, would ever have the power to bruise Christ, and what exactly that injury becomes later.

Surprisingly, the Hebrew *sup* is used for both "crush" and "bruise" here (which is why some translations have "bruise" twice), and the term is complicated enough that not all scholars agree on what it describes, though one common conclusion is that it is a verb indicating a pressing or hitting against the skin to the point of injury. Some alternative words suggested by Hebrew linguists include "bite" or "strike," or even "batter," which denotes a repeated striking motion—which, here, would indicate a back and forth between two parties, good and evil. If the latter is true, then the word picture in Genesis 3:15 could be of two forces fighting a continual war throughout the ages, which is certainly true of good and evil and the chief characters over each. Initially, an injury to the point of death is not implied in this violent term, but once the location of the wound in this context is brought into the equation—the "heel" against the "head"—it seems pretty obvious that head injuries can be a great threat to mortality.

When this narrative is brought into a clearer perspective with the events described in the Gospels and in Revelation, we can more easily see why scholars largely agree on the translation of the Hebrew *sup* to indicate a fatal crushing wound to the serpent's head through Christ's foot, while Christ only suffered a bruise to His heel in stomping out the enemy. After all, though Christ will always be the ultimate victor over evil (Revelation 20:7–10), He also did suffer injury and die, as recorded in the Gospels. Symbolically, this would be the "bruising" of Christ, but in that very act, things suddenly didn't bode well for the serpent.

Therein lies the entire Gospel narrative from Genesis 3:15 alone: Eve's lineage, continuing through Abraham (Genesis 12:1–3; 15:5), produced a human being who would not and could not stay in the grave. *Through the very wound* the evil one inflicted upon the Christ, the serpent's head was crushed by the Christ, who raised up and out of that grave undefeated and unfazed. No harm upon Jesus could be enduringly fatal, while the whole defeat of the serpent and his lineage is made clear and complete by the end of the book of Revelation.

Damnation started with Adam and Eve, who "took" and "ate" what God the Father had forbidden them to touch lest they die. Redemption started with Christ, who instructed us to "take" and "eat" of His body, something God has sent us so we might live forever (Mark 14:22–25, Luke 22:18–20, 1 Corinthians 11:23–25).

The complete reversal of what was caused in the Garden, as well as the restoration of what was lost, began right here, in the protevangelium, in the first book of God's Word.

…and it carries on in the second book.

Exodus

THE OVERALL THEME OF EXODUS is without doubt the deliverance of God's people from slavery in Egypt. Most reflections on the book are primarily concerned with its main character, Moses, leading God's people away from the angry pharaoh after he refused to let the people go despite ten devastating plagues. *Our* focus here, however, is on Christ, which brings us to the night of Passover. It will take a minute or two to tear down incorrect (but mainstream) concepts around that night in order to provide a grander and more accurate idea of who the Jesus of Exodus is, so bear with us while we explain a few things about the ritual that was *really* performed that night.

As some may already know from one of our earlier projects, *The Messenger*, the word "passover" has nothing to do with an angel "passing over [or around]" the blood-marked doorposts of the Israelites. That's poetic, which is why history has latched onto that explanation and will probably never let it out of its tentacles, but it's not really what the word means. In fact, the ancient Hebrew word *pesach*, what the feast is actually named after, predates the tenth plague (and therefore predates the angel of death in that plague) by uncountable generations and involves not only the Israelites, but all of the ancient world as far as we know.

Wait a second...what? Did this book just say that Passover involved pagan nations and was some kind of event that existed long before the night the Jewish Passover feast was inaugurated?

Yes, it's true. (Seriously, if you don't have a copy of *The Messenger*, you'll want to get it and read it, even if only for the sake of digesting what the Passover feast was *really* about, as it's not what many people think, and the research backing it up is immense. However, we will cover at least some of the mind-blowing details here.)

The quickest way of explaining this is to state that the *true meaning* of *pesach* is not "to avoid something," but literally "to cross over and into" something (essentially, it's paints a picture quite opposite of an angel passing by a blood-marked doorpost).

Rewind to the ancient world, to as far back as we can trace humanity, before worship structures like synagogues or temples were built. Even at that time, humans were inclined (and even were intelligently designed) to reach out to someone or something spiritual, something larger than themselves, and to revere, worship, respect, and pay homage to that deity or supernatural force. Because blood is the common symbol of life—and, at its loss, death—it has been deemed sacred by the first human cultures and onward. As such, the life blood shed from a perfect animal sacrifice as a symbolic stand-in for a human has been a central element of deity tribute from the beginning, inside and outside of any Jewish or Christian religious ceremony. We are then led to ask: What did the earliest sacrificial altars look like, and where would they have been kept, stored, found, or even erected?

The short answer is right inside the doorway of a person's home— or, primitive domicile.

See, people didn't have to worry about whether or not the blood of animal sacrifice would stain the carpet, whether the meat from the prepared offering was going to attract mice or other critters, or any other such modern-day hazards. In the earliest lean-to-style shelters, most of which sprang up in nomadic people groups and were therefore transportable anyway, animal sacrifices were carried out right at the doorway of the home. Although the deity being honored or worshipped varied from one territory to another, the purpose of the doorway sacrifice was universal in its symbolism: the threshold of a home or dwelling is where people or spirits come in or out bearing blessings, curses, or whatever else might be their agenda. To sacrifice a perfect animal at the front door to a favored deity, then, symbolized the residents' appeal for that deity to enter and guard that household against bad spirits or other potential harm from the outside world.

Appropriately, historians and anthropologists today refer to this as the "threshold covenant," but that's not what the ancients called it. In Hebrew, as stated earlier, it was *pesach*, as it described the act of crossing over something. In this case, that would obviously be a home's threshold, but it would *also* be the blood of the sacrifice that had just been made. To as many primordial human cultures as we can tell, the life blood that fell to the floor of the threshold was far too sacred to be trampled on, and if that grievance were to be committed—whether accidentally or intentionally—the agreement between the person and deity would be dissolved (or worse, disrespected, possibly to the point of incurring the deity's wrath, some believed). So any entity (human, spirit, etc.) that came in or out while the blood remained had to "cross over" or "pass over the top of" the life blood.

Also, remember that "bowl" or "basin" of blood from Exodus 12:21–22 the Israelites were told to dip their hyssop branches into before they spread it over the door? That's an anachronistically (historically out of correct time) translated word, even while the KJV was being translated. If we look up the root word *sap* in a Hebrew lexicon, it will acknowledge "bowl" or "basin" as its use in *younger* books of the Bible (for example, 1 Kings 7:50 and 2 Kings 12:13), while in *older* books (see, for example, Judges 19:27), the exact meaning of this word is "threshold." From *The Anchor Yale Bible Dictionary*, we read the noun "*sap*...belong[s] to the architectural vocabulary of ancient Israel and denote[s] an essential component of an entrance, whether gate or doorway. In the Hebrew Bible, that component is always the threshold, with the one exception of Ezek 40:6–7, where a gate chamber may be indicated."[31] (Part of the reason the word became "basin" or "bowl" eventually was because it was generically a "place where blood flows," so when the Israelites began letting the blood flow into a bowl, the word for "threshold" became synonymous with a liquid-carrying vessel.)

Exodus is one of the older books, before *sap* would not have been a vessel, so the instruction given in Exodus 12:21–22 is, more accurately, for the Israelites to dip their hyssop branches into the blood on the threshold...the threshold of their homes where they would have literally just sacrificed the perfect lamb whose blood was now sacred in its symbolic invitation to a deity to enter, "cross over" the blood, and stand guard at the doorway to stave off spirits that could otherwise do harm.

Are you starting to get the picture? *Pesach* wasn't about the angel of death. Way before the angel of death, it was about a human culture—*any human culture*, not just Israel—bringing human and deity together at the door of a home in a contract bound in sacred blood. When God told the Israelites to enact this *pesach*, He, *Himself*, the omnipresent God of the Jews, was going to be the deity that stood guard at the doorways marked in the lamb's blood in response to this covenantal deed. Ironically, He would be protecting His own people from the angel of death He was responsible for sending. Why? So all of Egypt could see this miracle and know without doubt that the God of the Jews was who He said He was, and that He was immensely stronger than any of the pathetic gods in the pagans' own pantheon.

No way... There is no way I'm going to believe that Yahweh, the God of the Israelites, would lead His people into participating in a pagan ritual!

Neither would we, and that's not what He did. (As usual, the contextual details are enormously important here.) What God did was rebrand and trump a universal, familiar ritual known to the ancients of the world (including the Egyptians) by showing Himself far more powerful than any standard "doorway deity," so to speak. He used a preexisting idea the pagans would have recognized from their own practices and the practices of neighboring heathen civilizations, then He outperformed it—involving blood not only on the threshold, but all around the door—by sending *His* angel of death, not just weakly protecting them from other random, wandering spirits. By this, He was eclipsing every other threshold covenant that had ever been performed for/with other little-"g" gods, putting the heavenly smack-down on the Egyptians for their cruel and murderous treatment of the people He chose to preserve upon the earth.

(By the way, that kind of "rebranding" wasn't as unusual as we may think. Even the moment when Abraham took Isaac up the mountain to sacrifice his own son at God's command has roots in paganism, as Donna Howell frequently teaches and has spoken about on her web-exclusive show, *Chalk Talk*. Before he was a follower of Yahweh, Abraham had been from Ur, and those in his home territory had engaged in all kinds of spiritual weirdness, including human sacrifice. Then suddenly we happen upon the awkward, hard-to-read moment recorded in Genesis 22 when *our* God—the God who, according to His character as it is revealed throughout Scripture, would never agree to human sacrifice—ordered Abraham to sacrifice his son. Isaac wasn't just any ol' kid, either. He was the *promised* child. Today, we can find comfort in that "Whew, that was close! God provided a ram instead!" part of the story, seeing that our God never intended for Abraham to carry out the killing of his own son. However, we still feel uncomfortable seeing God even hint at the concept of human sacrifice, which contradicts His nature, *until* we understand this: God was taking Abraham through the old, familiar pagan ropes, we might say, to bring him to that very moment when Yahweh would rebrand the former sacrifice ritual into something better that *He* had ordained with heavenly oversight. Then, it's as if God said, "Stop! You will follow *My* ways now. See that ram in the thicket? *That's* the suitable sacrifice. For I am your God now, not those gods of old from your past in Ur. You are finished forever with the old ways." The message was imprinted in Abraham's mind for good: "Followers of Yahweh don't sacrifice *people*, and we never will." And, of course, we never have. But it took the buildup to the human sacrifice—followed by the illustrative shooting down of that practice with a spiritually suitable replacement—for that to have become firmly established in the mind and practices of Abraham and his future generations all the way down to us. Simply put: God never intended a human sacrifice; He intended the aforementioned "almighty smackdown" of a human sacrifice using a "rebranding" of a pagan idea to outperform it.)

The founder of the Institute for Hebraic-Christian Studies and author of *Celebrating Jesus in the Biblical Feasts*, Dr. Richard Booker, acknowledges this historical threshold connection to the word *pesach*. Before the Exodus, Booker says, the word meant "to come under the protection of a deity by crossing over, jumping over, stepping over, or leaping over…the threshold" and into the protection of a home sprinkled with the animal's blood.[32] Academic genius of Yale Divinity School, Henry Clay Trumball, also speaks about this in his work, *The Threshold Covenant or The Beginning of Religious Rites*. While addressing "the beginning of religious rites, by which man evidenced a belief, however obtained, in the possibility of covenant relations between God and man,"[33] he openly ties the threshold covenant to the universally practiced *pesach*, which took place at the "threshold, or door-sill, or entrance-way, of the home dwelling-place."[34] From there, he notes that, "in Syria and in Egypt…every such primitive covenant in blood includes an appeal to the protecting Deity to ratify it as between the two parties and himself."[35] So, the Egyptians were accustomed to performing their own *pesach* to their own protecting deities. Then, Yahweh appears on the scene, and to the Egyptians, He effectively says: "Because you will not let My people go, I will send My own angel of death through your doorways and into your homes, across your threshold. You think your own cross-over covenants will protect you, but there will be no stopping this, as I am mightier than your gods." Trumball goes on:

> How the significance of the Hebrew passover rite stands out in the light of this primitive custom! It is not that this rite had its origin in the days of the Hebrew exodus from Egypt, but that Jehovah then and there emphasized the meaning and sacredness of a rite already familiar to Orientals. In dealing with his chosen people, God did not invent a new rite or ceremonial at every stage of his progressive revelation to them; but he took a rite with which they were already familiar, and gave to it a new and deeper significance in its new use and relations.
>
> Long before that day, a covenant welcome was given to a guest who was to become as one of the family, or to a bride or bridegroom in marriage, by the outpouring of blood on the threshold of the door, and by staining the doorway itself with the blood of the covenant. And now Jehovah announced that he was to visit Egypt on a designated night, and that those who would welcome him should prepare a threshold covenant, or a pass-over sacrifice, as a proof of that welcome; for where no such welcome was made ready for him by a family, he must count the household as his enemy.
>
> In announcing this desire for a welcoming sacrifice by the Hebrews, God spoke of it as "Jehovah's passover," as if the pass-over rite was a familiar one, which was now to be observed as a welcome to Jehovah. Moses, in reporting the Lord's message to the Hebrews, did not speak of the proposed sacrifice as something of which they knew nothing until now, but he first said to them, "Draw out, and take you lambs according to your families, and kill the passover"—or

the threshold cross-over; and then he added details of special instruction for this new use of the old rite.[36]

In Exodus 12:13, the original Hebrew language documents God saying "I will [*pesach*] you" to any Israelite who has obediently painted the blood of an innocent lamb over and around the doorposts. Once we understand that *pesach* means "cross over and into [something]," it changes the entire narrative of Exodus in our mind's eye, because now we see God recognizing the blood and deliberately entering the home and spending the evening with His people like an honored guest, instead of just allowing His angel to pass by it. But *pesach*, in proper context, doesn't mean an awkward lunging over blood. The emphasis is upon the end-game, the purpose behind such a stepover—to gain protection. *Pesach*, then, in light of all we've discussed, means "protect." In fact, the translators of the KJV and other early translations rendered Exodus 12:13 to read, "I [God] will pass over you," but the English translation of the Septuagint (LXX) has it as, "I [God] will protect you"!

A shift took place in the unseen realm between God and man that night. A key element of the Old Covenant—one of the most important—was established on the night of the tenth plague, when the threshold covenant marked the moment of intervention, protection, and deliverance of God's people who came out of Egypt. What that has to do with Jesus might trigger tears…

Consider this passage in Jeremiah that refers to the Exodus narrative:

"Behold, the days come," saith the Lord, "that I will make a new covenant with the house of Israel, and with the house of Judah: Not according to the covenant that I made with their fathers in the day that I took them by the hand to bring them out of the land of Egypt… But this shall be the covenant that I will make with the house of Israel; After those days," saith the Lord, "I will put my law in their inward parts, and write it in their hearts;

and will be their God, and they shall be my people. And they shall teach no more every man his neighbour, and every man his brother, saying, Know the Lord: for they shall all know me, from the least of them unto the greatest of them, saith the Lord: for *I will forgive their iniquity, and I will remember their sin no more.*" (Jeremiah 31:31–34; emphasis added)

Through His prophet Jeremiah, God was announcing that something He had started when He took His people by the hand and led them out of Egypt would find its perfection and completion through the New Covenant. The sacrificial death of a Passover lamb (the animal, lowercase "l") would *cover* the sins of God's people. The sacrificial Passover Lamb (the Messiah, uppercase "L") would make the sins of God's people "no more" (Jeremiah 31:31–34). This Lamb, John the Baptist said, is Jesus (John 1:29).

Before we look at Jesus in Exodus any further, consider what shows up immediately at this point:

- The Israelites spread a perfect lamb's blood on the door to establish a threshold covenant between God and them; B) Jesus is the Perfect Lamb, whose sacrifice of blood established the New Covenant between God and all people.
- The threshold covenant involved all Hebrews inviting God into their homes through belief in the lamb's blood on the doorpost; B) The New Covenant involves all believers inviting Christ into their lives through belief in the saving power of the Perfect Lamb's blood on the cross.
- The threshold covenant saved the Israelites from the plague God sent upon the land; B) The New Covenant saves all believers from the judgment of God upon sin.
- The threshold covenant ultimately led to the Israelites' deliverance from bondage in the hands of the Egyptians and onward to the Promised Land; B) The New Covenant immediately made

possible our deliverance from the bondage of sin and onward to the Kingdom of God.

- The lamb's blood marked the doorway of a common house, where the Israelites invited God the Father; B) Jesus' blood marks the doorway of His Father's house, where God the Father invites His children.[37]

That's just the tip of the iceberg, and it goes much, much deeper. This perspective sheds new light on a lot of Christ's words and helps us understand on a more intimate level why His blood was central to His redemptive work on the cross: "This is my blood of the new covenant" (Matthew 26:28; Mark 14:24; Luke 22:20). Christ was telling His disciples, essentially, "This is My blood of the threshold"! Read His words in John:

"Verily, verily, I say unto you, He that entereth not by the door into the sheepfold, but climbeth up some other way [some way other than the door/threshold], the same is a thief and a robber. But he that entereth in by the door [meaning Himself] is the shepherd of the sheep [the sheep are the believers of Christ].... And a stranger will they not follow, but will flee from him: for they know not the voice of strangers."

This parable spake Jesus unto them: but they understood not what things they were which he spake unto them.

Then said Jesus unto them again, "Verily, verily, I say unto you, I am the door [threshold!] of the sheep [believers]. All that ever came before me are thieves and robbers [because they didn't establish a threshold covenant]: but the sheep did not hear them. I am the door: by me if any man enter in, he shall be saved, and shall go in and out, and find pasture. The thief cometh not, but for to steal, and to kill, and to destroy: I am come that they might have life [through a blood sacrifice on the cross], and that they might have it more abundantly. I am the good shepherd: the good shepherd giveth his life for the sheep." (John 10:1–10)

A couple of chapters later, we read that Jesus stated for clarification, "I am the way, the truth, and the life: no man cometh unto the Father [into His eternal dwelling], but by [through] me [as the new doorway and therefore threshold covenant]" (John 14:6). The writer of Hebrews was well aware of Jesus as the threshold-blood Lamb, as well as the cancellation of a threshold covenant in ancient times if blood were trodden upon: "For if we sin wilfully after that we have received the knowledge of the truth, there remaineth no more sacrifice for sins… He that despised Moses' law died without mercy under two or three witnesses: Of how much sorer punishment, suppose ye, shall he be thought worthy, who hath *trodden under foot the Son of God, and hath counted the blood of the covenant, wherewith he was sanctified, an unholy thing*, and hath done despite unto the Spirit of grace?" (Hebrews 10:26–29; emphasis added). Further, Jesus told His disciples on the night he was betrayed, "With desire I desired to eat this Passover with you before I suffer: For I say unto you, I will not any more eat thereof, until it [the *pesach*/Passover] be fulfilled in the kingdom of God [which was later accomplished through His sacrifice]" (Luke 22:15–16). Because of the New Covenant established through Him (Luke 22:20; Ephesians 2:11–13), He became the Passover Lamb, "our passover [who was] sacrificed for us" (1 Corinthians 5:7) on the threshold of His Father's Kingdom, fulfilling the purposes of the Passover feast even as it extends into heaven and eternity.

We're still only barely scratching the surface…

An excerpt from *The Messenger* reveals some staggering details that have always been there, but that aren't always obvious:

Recall that, in Exodus 12:46 (see also Numbers 9:12), the Israelites were commanded to prepare the Passover lamb in a way that wouldn't break a single bone….but do we all know how the

Israelites had to prepare the Passover lamb in order for no bones to break? Do we know how they carefully roasted the animals in such a way that the entire flesh could be accessed and devoured (Exodus 12:10) without breaking any bones?

The process isn't one we will go into in great detail, because those with weak stomachs may not appreciate it. Put simply: Once the lamb's organs were removed, a pole (or branch from a sturdy source such as a pomegranate tree) was inserted horizontally to splay open the chest and upper arms of the animal, guaranteeing even and thorough roasting. Then another pole was inserted vertically and driven into the ground in order to hang the animal upright near the fire. The removed entrails were coiled atop the lamb's head, an ancient tradition called the "Crown Sacrifice" or the "Crown of the Passover Lamb." The result was literally a blood-crowned lamb hanging on a cross...a visual foreshadowing of Christ's death. No regular human imagination could have planned that element centuries before He was crucified.

We could explore countless other parallels on this trail to understanding how Christ fulfilled the Passover. Here are just a few more that we can mention quickly:

- Jesus was thoroughly examined by the Pharisees, Sadducees, and scribes for four days and found to be spotless (1 Peter 2:22), just as the Passover lamb for Seder was continuously examined for four days to ensure perfection before the sacrifice.

- After the building of the temple, when the Jews would gather en masse, preparations took more time to complete, and all the Passover lambs would have to be gathered and tied to their altars at 9 o'clock in the morning in order for the families to assemble to sing the Psalms. Nine in the morning was the same time Jesus would be nailed to the cross.

- In order for the lamb to be prepared in time for the feast, however, it needed to be slain at 3 o'clock in the afternoon—the same time of day Jesus died.
- At 6 o'clock in the evening, the Passover meal is complete and a new day begins. This is the same time Jesus was laid to rest in the tomb.
- When the temple's high priest had completed the ritual killing of the lamb on the altar, he lifted his hands apart in the air and said, "It is finished." This was the position of Jesus' body on the cross when He spoke those same words and then gave up the Spirit.

The list goes on and on, detailing hundreds of intricate links and connections between the manner in which Jesus died and the feast that had been established or ages before He was born, many of which (like the timing of His crucifixion and death) couldn't have been planned to symbolically align so perfectly....

The best writers in Hollywood can't produce a more poetic drama...[38]

Ladies, gentlemen, behold the Christ of Exodus, our gentle, selfless, Passover Lamb!

Leviticus, Numbers, and Deuteronomy

THOUGH THE LAW, BIBLICALLY SPEAKING, is determined to be the Pentateuch (again, that's the first five books of the Bible written by Moses),
we've already highlighted the major points of how Christ appeared in
Genesis and Exodus. Exodus explains the deliverance of the Ten Commandments, which develop into a more complete legislative system for
God's people as outlined in great detail in Leviticus, Numbers, and Deuteronomy, which is why these three books are handled together here.

As the Law is further explained, we see the role of Christ peppered throughout. "Leviticus" is Latin for "of [or relating to] the
Levites," and stems from the Hebrew *vayikra*, which translates "the
Lord called," in reference to the descendants of Levi called by God to
be priests over Israel. (If you're wondering why the Levites were chosen above the other tribes, it traces back to Exodus 32:19–29, when
the Levites rallied together and put three thousand of their brothers
to the sword for worshipping the golden calf.) As such, we could view
the book of Leviticus as a "manual for the priests" as they performed
their duties in the tent or Tabernacle and later the Temple. For the

most part, the book is made up of regulations explaining how acts of consecration, cleanliness, purity, offerings, sacrifices, vows, and other rituals were to be carried out by the priests and the rest of Israel; how the priesthood would operate and what governance guidelines/procedures applied to the management of their office; how the Tabernacle was to be furnished and cared for; and judicial laws for civilization. (Note, however, that there is a small amount of historical narrative in Leviticus recorded in chapters 8–9, 10:1–7, 10:16–20, and 24:10–14.)

But far from it being a mere collection of rules, Leviticus marks a moment in history when God's people were completely set apart from the rest of the pagan world, spiritually as well as physically. Without Leviticus, the human race wouldn't have the instructions needed to fully appreciate and respect either our relationship with God or the immense level of respect His house would need to be given while generations of His people followed and interacted with Him. We would never have grasped what is or is not moral, because we wouldn't have had the handbook that identified what this mysterious thing called "sin" even is beyond what was provided in Exodus and what was illustrated in the mishap of the Garden. Further, without Leviticus and the ancients' willingness to follow its parameters of conduct in relation to cleanliness, sanitation, and hygiene, we can assume the Bible may have ended right then and there when all of Israel died off as a result of disease.

Critical to understanding the angle of Christ's involvement, however, is noting the parallel of the priests as the people God appointed to uphold the holiness standards of the Jews, thereby making them a people God could cohabitate with, protect, bless, direct, and—most importantly—save!

Every law the Levitical priests had to follow ultimately contributed to the spiritual wellness of people who have an inherent sin nature toward being presentable and acceptable to God. Each animal sacrifice was a covering of sin—a sign that sin had been paid for. Only then could the Jews find forgiveness and be seen as whole and clean in God's sight. Sin is a *serious* offense to God, an act of direct rebellion worthy only of death, and it is only by fully comprehending how horrible sin is that we realize how badly we need to have a means of separating ourselves from it. A priest was a mediator and intercessor for the people and during the services rendered to God, but he was also one set apart as holy to perform the services needed to assist the covering of sins for the people. His lifestyle was pious to the extreme, and although it was considered a privilege and honor to be a priest of God, it was a great weight and responsibility as well.

Within the group of priests, one would be chosen to be the high priest. He was considered the most consecrated, devout, and righteous among priests. He, alone, was deemed worthy to enter the Holy of Holies (or Most Holy Place) of the Tabernacle—and only once per year, on the Day of Atonement—to place the blood of the sacrifice on the Ark of the Covenant as a covering for the sins of the people.

This would be the practice until the Messiah came. Then He, through His once-and-for-all blood sacrifice for all sin, would become not the mere replacement of this rite, but its fulfillment from both perspectives: Jesus would become the Sacrifice as well as the High Priest who offered the Sacrifice to the Father on the day He bled and died. The writer of Hebrews identified this transformation beautifully. Let's reflect on the following passage, with brackets added for clarification:

For the law [at the time of Leviticus] having a shadow of good things to come [looked forward to a better way through the Messiah to come], and not the very image of the things [though it did not directly show what that better way looked like], can never with those sacrifices which they offered year by year continually make the comers thereunto perfect [the sacrifices of the Law could never completely present a people as perfect unto God the way the Messiah could].... But in those sacrifices there is a remembrance again made of sins every year. For it is not possible that the blood of bulls and of goats should take away sins [no matter what, the blood of bulls and goats—even perfect ones—could not completely remove sin]....

Then said he [Christ], "Lo, I come to do thy will, O God." He [Christ] taketh away the first [He took away the first kind of sacrifice], that he may establish the second [so that He could establish Himself as the second, perfect, and effective kind by which a true *removal* of sin, and not mere covering]. By the which will we are sanctified through the offering of the body of Jesus Christ once for all [no more annual sacrifices]....

[And God said:] "And their sins and iniquities will I remember no more." Now where remission of these is, there is no more offering for sin. Having therefore, brethren, boldness to enter into the holiest by the blood of Jesus [no longer needing a human priest, we now enter the Holy of Holies or Most Holy Place through the blood of Jesus on the cross once for all], By a new and living way, which he hath consecrated for us, through the veil, that is to say, his flesh [His flesh became the new and living sin-removing way by which we are *all* able to come into the Holy of Holies or Most Holy Place so we can enter into the presence of God as perfect and spotless]; And having an high priest over the house of God [by this, Jesus is our High Priest!]...

Wherefore in all things it behoved him to be made like unto his brethren [Jesus saw fit to become human], that he might be a merciful and faithful high priest in things pertaining to God [so that He might now become our Intercessor and Mediator], to make reconciliation for the sins of the people [in presenting Himself as Sacrifice, He reconciled people to God]....

Wherefore, holy brethren, partakers of the heavenly calling, consider the Apostle and High Priest of our profession, Christ Jesus. (Hebrews 10:2–4, 9–10, 17–21; 2:17; 3:1)

Though the Jews wouldn't completely see and understand this for what it really was, Jesus' role as we see it in the book of Leviticus was to become the High Priest mediator and intercessor for all.

Here's a bit of homework. Read through the book of Leviticus, taking in the nearly countless rules and regulations the Levitical priests had to follow. Next, imagine those priests as they enter the Tabernacle with the blood of atonement, humbly approaching the Mercy Seat of God where the Father's presence dwelt, so that their Israelite brothers and sisters outside could be made whole. Now imagine all of that as foreshadowing the steps Jesus would take to do this very thing for us. In Leviticus, therefore, Jesus was the High Priest.

The book of Numbers in English is named after the Greek Septuagint title of this fourth biblical book, relating to the numbering of the tribes of Israel in the first four chapters. Its original title— Hebrew *Bemidbar*, meaning "in the desert [or wilderness]"—was perhaps more suitable to the book's narrative beyond just the count-ing. It opens at the foot of Mt. Sinai as the Lord delivers the Ten Commandments and closes forty years later as Israel is finally pro-ceeding into the Promised Land. (Is it perhaps a bit unfortunate that many today see a biblical narrative devalued by a title that references only its numerical status? We digress…) Our goal herein is not to discuss the numbering of the tribes, but to focus on our Savior's role in each book of the Word, so we will proceed with Numbers' "wilder-ness" theme in focus.

Deuteronomy confuses folks sometimes because, at the onset, it appears to repeat many laws and events recorded in the first four books. The very name of the book insinuates that as well. Originally called *Devarim* (Hebrew for "words," which is ambiguous), the name "Deuteronomy" was later assigned in Greek translations—and though the etymology of the title is complicated, suffice it to say that it does *not* mean "second law," as many believe, but actually "repetition" or "copy." In other words, it's not a "second" to anything, but a "copy" of the first, as it pertains to what was covered in the previous books. As to *why* it was included in this way, it might be assumed that Moses felt the need to readdress specific issues with his audience that were not being given the proper attention prior, as well as to leave them with some parting words that didn't appear in the other documents. Since "words" was the original title of the book, that theory is not far-fetched.

(Interestingly, the narrative closes in part by describing Moses' death and burial on a mountain by the hand of God, which causes some to wonder how he could have been the author toward the end. Scholars have taken generally two stances on this: 1) Moses personally wrote this book, ending it near the time of death, and the beginning of the book of Joshua actually begins near the end of Deuteronomy before it would in our contemporary Bibles; 2) Deuteronomy was not penned by the hand of Moses and was actually recorded at a slightly later date in Israel, but he was accredited as the author since the record was a "copy" of pieces of his original work [with the obvious exception of his death account].)

The overall outline of the Numbers and Deuteronomy narratives (as well as blips from the other three books of the Pentateuch) can be frustrating to readers who appreciate the idea that promises should be kept. It kinda goes like this: Israel promises to obey God and then doesn't; Israel is grateful to the Lord for His mercy and provisions, then moans and complains about the circumstances they, themselves, created (often through idolatry); Israel begs for mercy again, promises again not to repeat the offense, then disobeys or worships false gods all the more the next time the temptation presents itself. Truly, it's a wonder Israel *ever* inherited the Promised Land. That they did proves that even when people don't keep their promises, our Heavenly Father keeps His. However, the wilderness story is also evidence that going against God again and again results in the *delay* (not the dismissal) of the blessing we might have otherwise been given beforehand, as well as the punishment earned for disobedience:

But as truly as I live, all the earth shall be filled with the glory of the Lord. Because all those men which have seen my glory, and my miracles, which I did in Egypt and in the wilderness, and have tempted me now these ten times, and have not hearkened to my voice; Surely they shall not see the land which I sware unto their fathers, neither shall any of them that provoked me see it. (Numbers 14:21–23)

A generation of disbelieving forsakers of the Lord had to die out so that their sons and daughters could inherit the Promised Land.

Meanwhile, however, they were more than cared for with all they needed to survive, including the miraculous water and bread from heaven that kept their bodies nourished, their throats satisfied from the dryness of the desert, and their bellies fed. The Lord even kept their shoes and clothes brand new (Deuteronomy 8:4; 29:5)! But through the bread and water, God was preparing a parallel that would later become undeniable through the words of His Son. Consider this New Testament passage:

Then Jesus said unto them, "Verily, verily, I say unto you, Moses gave you not that bread from heaven; but my Father giveth you the true bread from heaven. For the bread of God is he which cometh down from heaven, and giveth life unto the world."

Then said they unto him, "Lord, evermore give us this bread."

And Jesus said unto them, "I am the bread of life: he that cometh to me shall never hunger; and he that believeth on me shall never thirst." (John 6:32–35)

This is God, Himself, in the flesh as the Son, accomplishing three things in order. He: 1) identifies that it is literally the bread and water in the story of "Moses," so there can be no interpretation that Jesus may have been referring to some other historical moment or symbolism other than the wilderness epic by which He would now be identified as the character "appearing" in Exodus through Deuteronomy; 2) explains that the bread (and water) was sent from heaven by the Father in the same way the Son was sent from heaven by the Father; 3) states plainly that "the bread of God" in this New Testament time "*is* he which cometh down from heaven [Jesus]," irrefutably linking Himself to this same miracle—but this time, instead of temporary, physical sustenance, He will give "[eternal] life unto the world." In case His listeners were still confused, He states succinctly that anyone who comes to Him in faith will never hunger or thirst (spiritually), because He is the wilderness bread and water in the flesh. If we stopped here, it would be enough to see quite powerfully how Jesus was foreshadowed in the desert. However, the next part involves an oft-missed and obscure detail that, once seen, cannot be unseen, and is therefore sure to widen the eyes of some of the most devout readers of the Word.

One of the most iconic intervention accounts we read about from Exodus through Deuteronomy is the Cloud by day and the Fire by night that leads Israel and the tent (the portable Tabernacle) as they wander, as well as provides shade during the day and light at night. (Why do we capitalize these terms? You will see in a moment...) We are including a lengthy excerpt of Numbers to highlight the repeated mention of this provision:

And on the day that the tabernacle was reared up the cloud covered the tabernacle, namely, the tent of the testimony: and at even there was upon the tabernacle as it were the appearance of fire, until the morning. So it was always: the cloud covered it by day, and the appearance of fire by night. And when the cloud was taken up from the tabernacle, then after that the children of Israel journeyed: and in the place where the cloud abode, there the children of Israel pitched their tents. At the commandment of the Lord the children of Israel journeyed, and at the commandment of the Lord they pitched: as long as the cloud abode upon the tabernacle they rested in their tents. And when the cloud tarried long upon the tabernacle many days, then the children of Israel kept the charge of the Lord, and journeyed not. And so it was, when the cloud was a few days upon the tabernacle; according to the commandment of the Lord they abode in their tents, and according to the commandment of the Lord they journeyed. And so it was, when the cloud abode from even unto the morning, and that the cloud was taken up in the morning, then they journeyed: whether it was by day or by night that the cloud was taken up, they journeyed. Or whether it were two days, or a month, or a year, that the cloud tarried upon the tabernacle, remaining thereon, the children of Israel abode in their tents, and journeyed not: but when it was taken up, they journeyed. At the commandment of the Lord they rested in the tents, and at the commandment of the Lord they journeyed: they kept the charge of the Lord, at the commandment of the Lord by the hand of Moses. (Numbers 9:15–23)

It's clear Moses *really* wanted his readers to see that the Cloud and the Fire Pillar were directly responsible for leading the people. It's likewise obvious by the end of the passage that the movements of these elements are "the commandment of the Lord." But is it possible that this is a theophany? Is it possible that God, Himself, *is* the Cloud and Pillar?

Exodus 13:21 clarifies the answer in no uncertain terms: "And the Lord went before them by day in a pillar of a cloud, to lead them the way; and by night in a pillar of fire, to give them light; to go by day and night." All the while the Israelites were seeing clouds and fire, they were viewing a theophany. Now, observe what happens several verses later, in Exodus 14:19: "And the Angel of God, which went before the camp of Israel, removed and went behind them; and the pillar of the cloud went from before their face, and stood behind them."

Whoa…wait a second. This doesn't *just* identify that the Cloud and Pillar of Fire is a literal appearance of God. It states it is "*the* Angel of God"! (Refer to the section, "What Is a Theophany/Christophany?" under the header, "Before We Proceed" if you need a reminder as to why this term often identifies a Christophany.) Therefore, if an impressive number of scholars are correct in their interpretations, Israel is here being led through the wilderness by Jesus as Cloud and Fire! It changes how we view the journey quite a bit, doesn't it?

To be fair, scholars aren't necessarily unanimous in concluding the Cloud and Pillar are Christ. Whereas nearly all reputable scholars allow for the interpretation that the Cloud and Pillar are certainly God, in at least a theophany, some believe that dubbing it as a Christophany is taking interpretational liberty. The reason for their hesitation in this reference isn't always clear, since these same learned men often treat other passages with identical language and syntax as "Christophanies." But internal evidence by the Apostle Paul strongly leans in this direction. In fact, in his address to the Corinthians, he even takes it a step farther, linking Jesus to the Rock that miraculously produced water for their thirst:

> Moreover, brethren, I would not that ye should be ignorant, how that all our fathers were under the cloud, and all passed through the sea; And were all baptized unto Moses in the cloud and in the sea; And did all eat the same spiritual meat; And did all drink the same spiritual drink: for they drank of that spiritual Rock that followed them: and that Rock was Christ. (1 Corinthians 10:1–4)

Jesus is the Bread, the Water, the Cloud, the Pillar, and the Rock—*all* vivid symbols directly out of the Exodus–Deuteronomy Scriptures! (And actually, though it does seem awkward for our finite minds to imagine, we might question how literally Paul meant his words when he said that Jesus was the Rock in this scene. It seems absurd at first to imagine Jesus Christ in an Old Testament Christophany embodying the form of a stone, but if He did, or even if it is a symbol of Him, it may explain why Moses striking it in anger would result in his being prohibited from entering the Promised Land. Moses was ever faithful and obedient to God even as he lived in a nation of folks who repeatedly disobeyed God, so it's hard to see why his decision to hit a rock with his staff would cause him to be kicked out of the land his people would inherit. But if we realize that what he struck was Jesus or an Old Testament type of Jesus because of the life-giving water the stone then produced, suddenly we imagine Moses ramming his holy tool into it and our minds collectively scream, "No! Don't do it Moses! That's Jesus!" Interesting brain candy, at the least.) It would be shameful, then, to overlook how He is typified by what occurred in Numbers 21:8–9. Consider briefly:

And the Lord said unto Moses, "Make thee a fiery serpent, and set it upon a pole: and it shall come to pass, that every one that is bitten, when he looketh upon it, shall live." And Moses made a serpent of brass, and put it upon a pole, and it came to pass, that if a serpent had bitten any man, when he beheld the serpent of brass, he lived.

When Jesus was speaking to the intelligent Nicodemus in John 3:14–17, He said:

And as Moses lifted up the serpent in the wilderness, even so must the Son of man be lifted up: That whosoever believeth in him should not perish, but have eternal life. For God so loved the world, that he gave his only begotten Son, that whosoever believeth in him should not perish, but have everlasting life. For God sent not his Son into the world to condemn the world; but that the world through him might be saved.

This passage, of course, includes the ever-popular John 3:16 verse believers have since relied on for salvation through faith. In fact, many have it memorized and quote it often. But, in our experience, few grasp that this eternal-life promise directly follows Jesus' mention of the fiery serpent of Moses. Jesus, Himself, in this conversation with Nicodemus, identifies the bronze snake as a type of His forthcoming cross—a prophetic description of how He would go on to save the entire planet. Galatians 3:13 states: "Christ hath redeemed us from the curse of the law, being made a curse for us: for it is written, 'Cursed is every one that hangeth on a tree.'" The word "tree" here is translated from the Greek *xylon*, which alternatively translates to "pole." In fact, the NIV translation ends the verse like this: "Cursed is everyone who is hung on a pole." God told Moses to set the serpent upon a "pole" (Hebrew *nes*), and those who had faith enough to look upon it and accept the miracle of its saving power would live, despite the fatal venom of a snakebite. Jesus hung upon a cursed pole, and those who have faith enough to look at the cross and accept the miracle of its saving power will live eternally in the presence of God, despite the spiritual fatality caused by the poison of sin.

This brings us to a final thought regarding how Jesus' death on the "cursed pole" is foretold in the final book of the Pentateuch. Though it is largely a continued record of the Mosaic Law, it's interesting to note how important the book of Deuteronomy was to Jesus; He quoted from it more often in His teaching and conversation than from any other book of the Old Testament. Asked which of the Commandments were the most important, His answer came from the words in Deuteronomy: "The first of all the commandments is, 'Hear, O Israel; The Lord our God is one Lord: And thou shalt love the Lord thy God with all thy heart, and with all thy soul, and with all thy mind, and with all thy strength'" (Mark 12:28–30; cf. Deuteronomy 6:4–5). When He went into the desert to fast and prepare for the three temptations of Satan, *all three* of His rebuttals against the tempter originated from this final book of Moses (Luke 4:1–13). How poetic, then, that the most important and life-giving act in world history would be one Jesus identified as His own curse from this area of Scripture.

Deuteronomy 21:22–23 explains that anyone who has committed a sin grave enough to justify being put to death by being hung on a pole is cursed, "for he that is hanged is accursed of God." This sentence allowed the offender to be on display as a sign of judgment and as a warning to the rest of Israel. This passage also mentions that the offender's "body shall not remain all night upon the tree, but thou shalt in any wise bury him that day." Though unbeknownst to the Israelites during the time of Moses, the long-awaited Messiah would someday willingly take the curse of sin from the whole world upon Himself, and His body would even be buried during the day (Matthew 27:57; Mark 15:42).

How can a person *not* love Jesus after seeing the miracle of what He accomplished…for *us*! It's a gift of life that never stops giving, it will always be true, and it came at a cost we will never have to pay. A death by cross-hanging was humiliating, horrible, and shameful—not only for God's people, Israel, but for Rome and the rest of the ancient world as well. Jesus' coming, His death, and especially the resurrection proved He was precisely who and what He said He was: the Almighty, the All-Powerful, the Son of God who loved and taught from the Law, and whose death on the Deuteronomic, cursed pole fulfilled every letter of that Law (Matthew 5:17–20)!

Let's recap where we're at super quick: Up to this point in God's progressive revelation story, we have had in Genesis the account of Creation, as well as of the Fall with its first prophecy of the Someday Savior. In this book we also see record of the first covenant between God and Abraham—and by extension, his descendants—establishing that a nation from his seed would eventually inherit the Promised Land.

Exodus details the enslavement of God's people (Abraham's offspring through Isaac and Jacob, who became Israel) and their deliverance through God's servant, Moses. Meanwhile, the Christological approach to Exodus shows how the early laws were set up to be fulfilled by that Savior, and the Passover foreshadowed how that would happen.

The books of Leviticus, Numbers, and Deuteronomy continue with the record of laws that would be fulfilled by the Savior, as well as provide some interesting narrative moments where we get a "sneak peek" of the Messiah before His Incarnation (meaning before He walked the earth as a man).

However, at the end of Deuteronomy, we are still waiting for God's people to inherit the Promised Land. This brings us to Joshua.

Joshua

THE BOOK OF JOSHUA IS, of course, named after its central character, the appointed leader (both spiritually and militarily) over all of Israel during wartime who is on a quest of settling God's chosen people into the Promised Land, Canaan. Joshua, himself, is an Old Testament type of Christ.

We can look at a few passages of Scripture to see this typography in motion from the beginning. But first, consider what is said of this strong leader a couple of books back, in Numbers 27:16–23:

> Let the Lord, the God of the spirits of all flesh, set a man over the congregation [a leader over all Israel is meant here], Which may go out before them, and which may go in before them, and which may lead them out, and which may bring them in; that the congregation of the Lord be not as sheep which have no shepherd.
>
> And the Lord said unto Moses, "Take thee Joshua the son of Nun, a man in whom is the spirit [meaning the Holy Spirit], and lay thine hand upon him; And set him before Eleazar the priest, and before all the congregation; and give him a charge in their sight. And thou shalt put some of thine honour upon

him, that all the congregation of the children of Israel may be obedient."

And Moses did as the Lord commanded him: and he took Joshua, and set him before Eleazar the priest, and before all the congregation: And he laid his hands upon him, and gave him a charge, as the Lord commanded by the hand of Moses.

The book of Joshua also begins with this charge: "Now after the death of Moses...the Lord spake unto Joshua...saying, 'Moses my servant is dead; now therefore arise, go over this Jordan, thou, and all this people, unto the land which I do give to them, even to the children of Israel. Every place that the sole of your foot shall tread upon, that have I given unto you, as I said unto Moses'" (Joshua 1:1–3). Let's look at some comparisons between Joshua and Christ:

- Joshua was the chief servant of God over all of His people, whose selfless actions on the battlefield resulted in his role as the savior over their earthly bodies. Jesus was/is the absolute, ultimate Chief Servant of God the Father over His people, whose selfless actions throughout His life and on the cross (a spiritual battlefield, if there ever was one!) resulted in His role as the Savior of souls.
- Joshua accomplished all he did because he was "a man in whom is the spirit" (Numbers 27:18). Jesus accomplished all He did because He operated within the Spirit, as prophesied in the Old Testament (Isaiah 42:1) and fulfilled in the New (Acts 10:38).
- Joshua was "magnified" (Joshua 3:7) before all of Israel at the Jordan River, where the flow of the water stopped for the Hebrews to cross to Jericho. Jesus was magnified publicly as the Son of God upon His emergence from John the forerunner's baptism in this same river (Matthew 3:16–17).
- Joshua led God's people to inherit the Promised Land, and the most notable battle was won with a peaceful demonstration,

followed by a shout and a trumpet blast (Joshua 6). Jesus leads God's people to inherit the Promised Land after the conclusion of this life (heaven and eventually the New Jerusalem in Revelation); notably, He accomplished this first through a peaceful demonstration at trial and on the cross, followed by: a shout, the sound of the Temple veil tearing in two, the rumblings of earthquakes, and the very raising of the dead from the tombs (Matthew 27:50–53).

Oh, and then there's this interesting "coincidence." The name "Joshua" is the same as "Jesus," but spelled differently—like "Hailey" and "Hailie" or "Caiden" and "Kayden." Both "Joshua" and "Jesus" mean "the Lord saves." Therefore, it's not hard to see where Jesus may be presented here. It's like asking, "Does Jesus show up in this book of Jesus?" Yeah. He's all over the place!

Evidence also points to the conclusion that Jesus was the literal, corporeal "Captain of the Host of the Lord" who shows up as a mysterious figure with a sword to speak with Joshua in person early on in his career. Watch this:

And it came to pass, when Joshua was by Jericho, that he lifted up his eyes and looked, and, behold, there stood a man over against him with his sword drawn in his hand: and Joshua went unto him, and said unto him, "Art thou for us, or for our adversaries?"

And [the mysterious figure] said, "Nay; but as captain of the host of the Lord am I now come."

And Joshua fell on his face to the earth, and did worship, and said unto him, "What saith my Lord unto his servant?"

And the captain of the Lord's host said unto Joshua, "Loose thy shoe from off thy foot; for the place whereon thou standest is holy." And Joshua did so. (Joshua 5:13–15)

Did you catch that this figure who showed up was God in the form of a human male? As He stated, He was merely the "Captain of the Host of the Lord," which could be referring to a messenger angel or archangel of God in the highest form of celestial leadership...*until* the man allowed Joshua to fall down and worship Him. Angels—true angels of the One and Only God, that is—will never accept worship because they know God forbids the worship of both angels and of humans (Exodus 20; Deuteronomy 5–8; Revelation 19:10; 22:8–9; Matthew 4:9–10; Luke 4:7–8; Romans 1:25; Colossians 2:18). If this was not an appearance of God, the worship would have been stopped. Furthermore, the presence of God at the burning bush experience of Joshua's predecessor, Moses, was also referred to as "holy ground" that required the removal of footwear (Exodus 3:5), and angels elsewhere make no such command. It's clear that we are dealing with a theophany here, at least.

It's not unusual that God the Father would show up and speak directly to anyone at any time and in any form He pleases because, well, He's God. Yet, scholars who have worked long and hard to separate which theophanies are the Father from those that are the Son conclude that the evidence here, based on the allowance of John 1:1–18 (where it is explained that Jesus is the "Word" [more on this later]), is stacked in favor of a Christophany. The *Bible Knowledge Commentary*, compiled by multiple respected theologians who undergo sharp peer review before they are considered collaborators, states: "As with...the two disciples at Emmaus, there was a flash of revelation and Joshua knew he was in the presence of God. It seems clear that Joshua was indeed talking to the Angel of the Lord, another appearance in Old Testament times of the Lord Jesus Christ Himself."[39] Other commentators, such as Matthew Henry, author of *Matthew Henry's Concise Commentary on the Bible*, think the conclusion of a Christophany is so obvious in this Joshua account that they state it as a fact without the need for much elaboration: "There appeared to him one as a man to be noticed. This Man was the Son of God, the eternal Word."[40]

Perhaps this was the belief of the writer of Hebrews also, as the internal evidence of the Jesus/Joshua parallel suggests: Joshua was the captain of the armies of Israel, but Jesus is literally the "Captain of Salvation" in Hebrews 2:10.

In addition to these ruminations, try to remember the importance of the man's introduction. Joshua immediately wanted to know if the warrior was on his side or the side of the enemy. The answer was neither. He stated he was for the Lord only—as should be Joshua and the rest of the God's nation. The implication is clear that Joshua should place the Lord and His will into a position of far grander importance than even his own human brothers and sisters readying for Promised-Land inheritance. Only then would he be completely receptive to the sometimes odd ways God would conduct battle, such as through a shout or trumpet as central weapons, which incidentally would become the best and only way Joshua's brothers and sisters would be saved. We should all follow this warrior's example.

Behold, the Christ of Joshua! The Captain of the Host of the Lord!

Before we move on, note that Jesus, our Savior, descended from the bloodline of the "scarlet thread" savior-ess, Rahab, in Joshua 2. Many remember her for being the harlot of Jericho. Though that might be true, her story is a brightly shining example of redemption that illustrates how God will use any willing believer to carry out His miracles and will. Rahab's maneuvering (marking her house with a scarlet thread) saved the Israelite men from certain capture and death so they could retreat to their Hebrew camps and inform their tribes of enemy status. In trade, they promised (and then kept their promise), Rahab would not be harmed. This not only ensured victory for the Israelites in conquering the land of Jericho, it resulted in Rahab joining the tribes of Israel, from whose offspring the Savior Messiah would be born.

And that brings us to the Promised Land. Finally, after generations of pain, the people of Israel arrived—home in the land God had prepared for them. This event is paramount in Israel's history, as it solidified the relationship between what God says and what He does, as shown in the long-awaited journey to and settling in the territory He had promised to bless them with and protect them in.

Jesus is preparing a Promised Land for us (John 14:1–3), too— and He, too, does what He says He will do.

Judges

UNFORTUNATELY, THE LAND the Israelites finally secured was eventually lost because of their wickedness. The generations following Joshua's death did not honor God in raising their sons and daughters in the way of Yahweh as they had vowed, and soon they fell into worshipping pagan gods. Their repetitious, idolatrous rebellion against God resulted in the invasion of enemy troops, and when the enemy won, a conquered Israel came under the domination of pagan nations.

Following this, for what feels like an eternity, the storyline settles into a most infuriating pattern (similar, but not identical, to the pattern discussed in the books of Law): The people cry out to God for deliverance; He sends a judge to deliver them; the judge eventually passes away and Israel forgets about God again; Israel then gets into trouble with its enemies and cries out to God...who sends a judge... who delivers Israel...who turns to idols and cries out to God... Seriously, the whole book outline could be: cries, deliverance, rebellion, cries, deliverance, rebellion, and on and on (Judges 2:18–19). For the modern, believing reader, this book is a history of how human nature continues forever to fall into the worst behavioral patterns as a result of the Fall. It makes the woman who continues to date abusive men, the kid who won't stop lying, and the business executive who keeps cheating on his taxes—all despite echoing promises that it's the last time—more relatable. But this pattern of human weakness, as expressed in Judges, is an extreme example that just keeps giving.

Note that references to judges in the Bible don't indicate anything like the judges of our time and culture. This term doesn't even refer to the pre-nineteenth century judges wearing white horsehair wigs and black robes, wielding wooden gavels in court. Instead, imagine a biblical judge as a heroic soldier, military commander, chief political executive, spiritual leader, savior and deliverer, and the top judicial officer—all wrapped into one person presiding over all of God's people. Judges of these ancient days carried heavy responsibilities, no doubt, and they weren't in office because of birthright or by election, but by selection. He or she was chosen by God, Himself, appointed to lead His people. (And yes, even during these days when patriarchy was the guiding system, there *was* a female judge over Israel. Not only was Deborah a powerful and well-respected judge, she was an appointed prophet of God as well! Her bold, fearless, Joan of Arc-style march to the battlefield ensured Israel's immediate victory followed by forty years of peace.)

Here is what Judges 2:16–19 states about the nature of God presiding over His people:

Nevertheless the Lord raised up judges, which delivered them out of the hand of those that spoiled them. And yet they would not hearken unto their judges, but they went a whoring after other gods, and bowed themselves unto them… And when the Lord raised them up judges, then the Lord was with the judge, and delivered them out of the hand of their enemies all the days of the judge…because of their groanings by reason of them that oppressed them and vexed them. And it came to pass, when the judge was dead, that they returned, and corrupted themselves more than their fathers [children of future generations were even more wicked than their fathers!], in following other gods to serve them, and to bow down unto them; they ceased not from their own doings, nor from their stubborn way.

This is only one tiny section of Judges, though elsewhere this pattern is illustrated repeatedly: God *wants* to bless, protect, and ultimately save His people, and that remains His nature, character, and will regarding them despite their painful, recurring rejection. No matter what corndog ideas they kept getting in their stubborn heads about how bowing to a false idol would result in the out-performing of Yahweh (that must have been what they were thinking, or else they wouldn't have worshipped a pagan entity at the risk of incurring God's wrath in the first place), they continued to fail while He continued to show up in a big way. It's in His very nature—regardless of *human* nature—to reconcile with the humanity He has become estranged from as a result of both the Fall and the continual whoring after other gods.

Some people (usually nonbelievers, if we're being honest) love to see the book of Judges as an account of our Lord capriciously "delivering Israel into the hands of her enemies" (see, for example, Judges 2:14), and the offense of the repeated behavior is in *God's* failure, not man's. But often, misunderstood and misinformed statements like these come from folks (whether respectful or not) who haven't studied the nature of sin, how it contrasts to holiness, and the relationship of whether (or how) those two elements may or may not coexist. It's a theological mountain with a billion peaks at least (and we've already addressed it somewhat back in our Genesis reflection), but as a short reminder: Humans are born into a fallen species, and though we share the likeness of God from the Creation event (Genesis 1–2)—which is where we inherit that inexplicable but universal, constant, and internal draw toward being and doing good—we also have a share in the sin nature, which is where we inherit that weakness to give into sin and temptation. Therefore, we daily experience the ever-present dichotomy of both natures, good and evil, within us. We *so* understand this on a collective level that even secular cartoons depict characters struggling to know whether to follow the advice of the little devil perched on one shoulder and the little angel on the other. But when we read Scripture and ponder God, we have to remember He is only holy always. As "only holiness," He cannot sin or have anything to do with it (He cannot occupy the same space as sin).

Therefore, when Israel falls into sin, an oil-and-water reaction happens. The distance between God and Israel increases, just as it was between the Creator and Adam and Eve in the Fall account. In fact, that is a story of how the ugly, black thing called "distance" between humans and the Almighty first came about. Similarly, Judges provides the account of people attempting to bring God (and His protection from enemies) closer to them with cries of penitence and "we'll-never-do-it-again"-isms—and then failing, with an Adam-and-Eve flair, to obey God, which forces Him to back off and deliver Israel to her enemies because it's the fate they seal in their own sin and rejection of God.

This is paramount to understanding God's actions in Judges.

God is not *against* His people; He is *for* them!

Judges is not an account of God turning *His* back on Israel over and over; it's an account of God's people turning *their* backs on Yahweh over and over—and He, our precious, sweet, Creator God, continues to show mercy and love by providing one savior-judge after another. That is the nature of God. It's giant leap to the opposite edge of what the skeptics have made it. A slightly tweaked wording of the cycle in Judges could be: They shove Him away; He retreats; they invite Him back; He comes back with an embrace in the form of protection and a judge He has raised up from within the tribes to save them all; they shove Him away; He retreats; they invite Him back…

With that point clearly made, we are now able to see the resemblance between the judges (plural, as in what their office stands for—not as in any individual judge [because some of them blundered badly]) and the Judge-Savior the Father sent to save us all at a later time. You see, Jesus' act on the cross was foreshadowed not just by the events in an Old Testament book and the similarity to its heroes, but in the very nurturing nature and character of His Father, *who was always going to provide a savior/Savior no matter what His children deserved!*

Considering their job description responsibilities, in the most glaring sense, we can view any biblical judge who did right in the eyes of the Lord as a type of Christ. Jesus was and is the Supreme Deliverer, sent as Savior of an idolatrous, sinning people. In that sense, even though some of the judges in this book didn't always serve as the ideal role model that Jesus was, they foreshadowed Christ and revealed the nature and will of God—that His people will be saved, delivered, *always.* What each of the judges in this book were chosen to do militarily and politically, Jesus was chosen to do spiritually.

But in Jesus, there would never need to be another cycle, because He is the Perfect Lamb, the spotless sacrifice who died one time for all and forever. Jesus, as He is archetypically presented in the book of Judges, is the Last Judge and the Last Lawgiver. Every battle the judges fought on Canaanite soil was a precursor of the battle the Judge fought both on the soil of Golgotha's mound outside Jerusalem as well as in the invisible realm. Every law-giving decree the judges pronounced over the nation of Israel was a prototype of the Lawgiver's New Covenant sealed in the flesh and blood of the Last Judge.

Here's the other whammy hidden within the parallels between the book Judges and the Covenant of Christ: The Covenant sealed in the blood of Christ on the cross was given in the same nature as the grace in Judges: No matter what today's people do, no matter how constantly we fail to obey God, no matter how "over and over" we force Him away with our idolatrous ideas or unfaithfulness, the Judge the Father raised once and for all will *always* be victorious in extending salvation to every child of God. Unbelievably, the free gift of salvation belongs to every human on the globe, including the Gentiles whose heritage may not be in any way linked to the people who cried out for the intervention of judges in the beginning.

It's sobering to think about. God is so good. Each time we think we have Him figured out, we come face to face with another layer of His salvation plan, His progressive revelation as played out first in Israel's history and finished in the days of the Christ, and we're confronted all over again with the implications of all He has done for His people.

For those who still may not be convinced of the parallel between Jesus and the judges of the Old Testament, there's one interesting character we would like to take a closer look at: Samson. This particularly popular judge (Judges 13–16) is without doubt a type of Jesus. Both Jesus and Samson were born in miraculous ways following an angel's announcement of their arrival, and the resemblances continue to climb.

- Samson was chosen by God before his birth to deliver Israel from the Philistines (Joshua 13:5); Jesus was chosen by God before His birth to deliver all of mankind from sin (Matthew 1:21).
- The Spirit of the Lord came upon both men powerfully (Judges 14:6–19; 15:14; Luke 4:18; Matthew 12:28).
- By the power of the Spirit of the Lord, both Samson and Christ were victorious over the enemies of God's people.
- Samson was betrayed for money by his companion, Delilah (Judges 13); Jesus was betrayed for money by His companion, Judas (Luke 22).
- Samson and Jesus were both beaten and bound near the end of their lives.
- Most astonishingly: Samson defeated more enemies through his death than he did while he lived (Judges 16:30)...and so did Jesus (Colossians 2:15).

Pretty neat, huh?

There are more parallels, but if you haven't already noted them, we don't want to give them away just yet. More about Jesus as a type of judge will be covered in the discussions of 1 Samuel through 2 Chronicles. Many scholars who separate sections of Scripture by theme see Judges, 1 and 2 Samuel, 1 and 2 Kings, and 1 and 2 Chronicles in a bundled arc (and some put Joshua at the front of that list). We are *sorta* following that idea here, which is why more about Judges will appear in that subsequent section.

However, we have one major problem with that bundled-theme concept that a lot of scholars follow: It minimizes Ruth.

For reasons we will now take necessary time to explain, we just can't do that with this book! As short as it may be, we simply can't grasp the fullness of Christ's work without it.

Ruth

IN A NUTSHELL, the book of Ruth follows the story of a young girl from a pagan city who marries into a Hebrew family, faces the death of her husband, follows her mother-in-law to Bethlehem (where Jesus was later born), and meets and marries a kind-hearted man named Boaz.

Oh, I know this one, some readers may be thinking. *It's that age-old, "Jesus' bloodline through the obedient daughter-in-law" thing, right? That's how Jesus "appears" in the book of Ruth?*

Right!

Except, uh, not entirely.

It's true that the bloodline of Christ moves directly through the womb of this former pagan, but Ruth is often overlooked when it comes to exploring the significance of the Christ type. In fact, many might recall hearing terms like "kinsman" and "something about Boaz being a redeemer," and they might know these concepts link to Christ, but it's likely they haven't seen how the pieces of the big picture all connect. One major eschatological (end-times) scene of Jesus in the book of Revelation draws its sweet and beautiful roots from this endearing, four-chapter book named after a young woman many folks largely don't understand (or pay much attention to). The story needs to breathe to be fully appreciated, as opposed to being dropped once a year into a twenty-minute sermon about being willing to abandon a former life in pursuit of a new one (although that is a great message also!).

The narrative begins with a woman whose first marriage was on a rocky foundation. Some might even say her marriages were... *forbidden.*

Once upon a time, there was a pagan city called Moab. It sprang from the incestuous seduction of Lot's eldest daughter, who bore a son from her intoxicated father's seed (Genesis 19:30–38). The child of this deplorable union, Moab—meaning "from my father"—grew to become the father and founder of the city that, for Israel, sat like a blight on the map as a constant reminder of sexual indecency between Abraham's nephew and great-niece.

But that wouldn't be the only shameful thing associated with this dark place.

Jewish tradition acknowledges that Chemosh, the national protector-god of the Moabites, is "developed out of the primitive Semitic mother-goddess Ashtar"[41] (also spelled "Astarte" and appearing in the Akkadian counterpart as "Ishtar"), the goddess of war and sex, as well as the "queen of heaven" whom the Canaanites worshipped. From the Moabite Stone—a stone tablet documenting parts of the city's history ordered by then-reigning Moabite King Mesha—we read that the local worshippers considered Chemosh to be synonymous to certain early manifestations of the Canaanite god Baal, also. In fact, the Moabite Stone, according to lines 30 and 31, state that when Baal is pleased with King Mesha, Chemosh "speaks to Mesha," or channels his knowledge into his servant directly: "Chemosh, therefore," the twelve-volume *Jewish Encyclopedia* states, "was in general a deity of the same nature as Baal."[42]

The *Encyclopaedia Biblica: A Dictionary of the Bible* from 1899 acknowledges that back when ancient cultures believed the gods and goddesses were heavenly bodies or meteoric phenomena (basically, objects in space), Chemosh was considered to be the sun by some, and by others, "Milcom-Moloch-Saturn."[43] Sun worship was common for countless early civilizations, but Moloch (who is alternatively known as "Milcom" or "Saturn") was the widely known Canaanite god of child sacrifice. This could explain why, as documented in the Word of God, this bizarre mishmash of Chemosh and Moloch/Saturn would accept child sacrifice to "secure his favor."[44] In 2 Kings 3:27, we read that this same King Mesha—who was accepting channeled oracles (translation: weird, demonic downloads) from Baal—sacrificed his eldest son and heir as a burnt offering to Chemosh in the middle of a war with Israel. Likely out of righteous indignation, disgust, or pity at the sight of the young crown-prince of Moab burnt and displayed atop the wall as a greeting, Israel retreated. Though the Bible verse doesn't fully explain the retreat in those terms, historians, scholars, and linguists have ruled out most other motives for retreat, such as fear. In support of this, Jewish historian Josephus says everyone who approached the sight of the crown prince's remains "were so affected, in way of humanity and pity, that they raised the siege, and everyone returned to his own house."[45] But regardless of what shock the sight of a charred, smoking prince would have had on the neighboring nations, King Mesha's choice to sacrifice his son to appease the eerie Moloch/Saturn/sun-god/Chemosh deity who apparently lived in his ear wasn't a surprise to Moabites. On the contrary, it was "done in accordance with the fierce fanaticism of the Moabite nation."[46] Rather than lead a public mourning of the prince who had to be burned to mollify the blood-hungry god, the king instead spent his attention and energy compiling the Moabite Stone that would document the victory and elevate his name in history—that is, until he was defeated shortly thereafter. The Moabites who lived in subjection to this king didn't appear to be offended by this form of worship, either. They would be known in the Old Testament by the pagan-god-fearing moniker, "the people of Chemosh" (Numbers 21:29; Jeremiah 48:46).

Needless to say, even though these events happened after the time of Ruth, these were the people she belonged to, and this is the child-sacrificing, incestuous-religion climate she grew up in. The inhabitants of Moab were so loathsome to the people of God when they first came from Egypt that even the heavy enforcement of the Mosaic Law sought to exclude them from the assembly at all costs:

> An Ammonite or Moabite shall not enter into the congregation of the Lord; even to their tenth generation shall they not enter into the congregation of the Lord for ever: Because they met you not with bread and with water in the way, when ye came forth out of Egypt; and because they hired against thee Balaam the son of Beor of Pethor of Mesopotamia, to curse thee. Nevertheless the Lord thy God would not hearken unto Balaam; but the Lord thy God turned the curse into a blessing unto thee, because the Lord thy God loved thee. Thou shalt not seek their peace nor their prosperity all thy days for ever. (Deuteronomy 23:3–6)

Can you imagine what the Israelites would have thought of Ruth? She was a woman from "one of *those* kinda nations," a natural enemy to the chaste youth of the Hebrew tribes! It's likely she didn't look like she does in Sunday school coloring books.

This raises the question: How would an Israelite's (and later Boaz') marriage to Ruth, a Moabite, not be an affront to the Law of God during that era? Some say it would have been allowed because the prohibition of this Deuteronomic law would have naturally been upon the male Moabite procreating with Hebrews, not the female marrying into their tribes, for various reasons related to the preservation of the Jewish bloodline through the sons of Israel. (This is a likely possibility, actually, as such exceptions are recorded in the Mishnah.) Others can argue that God would have allowed it because He had a special plan for Ruth (which is true) or because Ruth became a convert to Judaism (called a "proselyte"). We can assume this is true based on her story's narrative (Ruth 1:16), even if her moment of conversion was not documented. And technically, there was no *direct* law against an Israelite marrying a Moabite (as there was for, say, a Canaanite [Deuteronomy 7:1–6]). But eventually, if they're not even allowed to enter the assembly of Israel, common sense (if nothing else) indicates a union between Ruth and an upright Israelite man would be forbidden at least socially. That would have been true for other epochs scattered about the early days of Israel, as Israel and Moab were constantly at each other's throats (see Numbers 22; Judges 3:12; 2 Kings 1:1; 3:4, among others).

So, there you have it: a slightly more intimate introduction to this brief book that will help you grasp the importance of its later events.

The book opens by explaining that it wasn't happenstance or a flippant decision that caused a few families from Israel to flee to Moab for shelter and food during the famine. Elimelech, Naomi, and their two sons were one such family that had little choice but to move into pagan territory and place their fate in the hands of a city that would, off and on, wage war with their own. (Israel and Moab were not at war when Elimelech settled there.) Early on, Elimelech died and his two sons married Moabite women, one of whom was Ruth. Ten years passed, and both of Elimelech's sons passed away, leaving Naomi and Ruth alone (the other son's wife, Orpah, went back to her family in the city). Naomi, who was returning to Israel upon receiving word that the famine had ended, couldn't convince Ruth to stay behind with her Moabite mother, family, or people. In an odd turn of events, Ruth repeatedly refused to leave her mother-in-law's side, boldly pronouncing one of the most oft-recited verses in the Bible: "Thy people shall be my people, and thy God my God" (Ruth 1:16).

Pretty brave, all things considered. It may not be the Moab-vs.-Israel tumult we see just after Ruth's story in 2 Kings, but since the day

Moses descended from Mount Sinai, Israel *did not* like the Moabites. There was almost always bad blood between them. So Ruth determinedly staying beside Naomi as a young, widowed proselyte with the tainted, evil-city blood and human-sacrifice religious background marching into a camp of *Yahweh* (of all places!) says a lot about how much she loved Naomi.

Back in Bethlehem, Ruth learned of a wealthy kinsman of Naomi's on Elimelech's side and offered to go to his fields to gather some corn for food. Boaz spotted her from a distance as she was pathetically picking up the scraps of the field and upon discovering that Naomi was a Moabite (the Moabites' wicked reputation alone could have ruined any chances Ruth may have had of appealing to Boaz' mercy and charity), the kinsman urged her to gather freely from his harvest, told her to enjoy the company of the other Israelite women at the site, and informed her that he had already instructed the men to leave her alone. Ruth, in a wave of extreme gratitude, prostrated herself in humility and asked how she could have found such grace in his eyes that he would acknowledge her, a strange woman (Ruth 2:10).

Some readers might be thinking: *Wow, this is a lot of reflection on these briefly mentioned Old Testament characters, all for the purpose of feeling warm and fuzzy about the lineage of Christ.* If that crossed your mind, you may be missing the parallel here. Go back and read that last paragraph again, paying close attention to the reaction of Boaz to the young woman in need, whose previous sin nature and idolatrous upbringing didn't even appear to cross his mind…

Remind you of anyone?

Such an act of unwarranted, unprecedented generosity left an impact upon Ruth that, without doubt, would never escape her thoughts. She would *never* forget the day she and her hungry mother-in-law were starving in Bethlehem with no food, no providers, no gardens or proper lodging—just her ruddy, willing muscles, rolled-up sleeves, and the courage to wander about on a rich man's private property—and a man named Boaz gave her nothing but kindness. Then, as if it couldn't get any sweeter, his response was over the top:

> And Boaz answered and said unto her, "It hath fully been shewed me, all that thou hast done unto thy mother in law." (Ruth 2:11)

Think about this for a moment: Boaz did *not* say she could only have food from his land if she was willing to pay interest, earn her keep, work extra hours, pay him personal favors, or fulfill any other requirement. He didn't ask her about her former husband or her past in Moab. He didn't seek to find out whether she planned to corrupt his other field maidens with pagan ideas; whether her lifestyle was such that she needed to be under supervision while she drank from the same vessels as the men (which he offered her in verse 9); what hair-raising temple activities she may have participated in back home; if she believed in tithing; if she attended confession regularly; whether she had memorized her denomination's fundamental statements of faith; whether she had ever smoked a cigarette; if she had ever felt *tempted* to smoke a cigarette; how she felt about dying eggs on Easter; how long she'd been a member of her local church and whether she was current on her membership dues; whether she raised her hands during worship in church on Sundays; or whether blonde was her true hair color. Nothing! (And yes, I know this list is sarcastically anachronistic—outside the boundaries of accurate space and time—but to make clear the point: Boaz *did not even care* about her moral codes or reputation, which were huge considerations in Israel's history. Might we learn something from this story about the way we treat people outside the church today?) It's brutally straightforward: Ruth asked Boaz why in the world he would have ever showed her such kindness, acceptance, and grace, and his answer was, quite simply, because she had shown unconditional love for a widow named Naomi.

If you listen real close, you might be able to hear the verse we have in mind, straight out of the mouth of Christ, echoing the end of Boaz' convictions…

Truly I say to you, inasmuch as you have done it to one of the least of these, My brothers, you have done it to Me. (Matthew 25:40)

By now, you've probably picked up on why so many ministers relate Boaz as a type of Christ, although it is usually (and unfortunately) skimmed over so quick that we miss the moment. Again, remember, this is the God-breathed, Living Word we're talking about. Let it *breathe*…

The rest of Boaz' statement showed that he was aware of more than just the kindness offered to Naomi: "and how thou hast left thy father and thy mother, and the land of thy nativity, and art come unto a people which thou knewest not heretofore. The Lord recompense thy work, and a full reward be given thee of the Lord God of Israel, under whose wings thou art come to trust" (Ruth 2:11–13). In other words, he said, "You left everything you've ever known, your family, your people, your city, and you've come here to a bunch of strangers. May the Lord God of Israel give you full reward for this work and shield you under His wings, now that you are His."

Ruth returned to Naomi from her prosperous encounter with Boaz, and Naomi was quick to inform Ruth that Boaz was "one of our nearest kinsman" (Ruth 2:20). As such, Naomi concocted a plan to see Ruth and Boaz married. This brings us to the famous "uncovering the feet while he sleeps" scene. Ruth uncovered the "feet" of Boaz, and he awakened, asking (in the dark, we presume) who was there. Ruth revealed her identity and asked him to spread his "skirt" over her because he was a "near kinsman" (Ruth 3:9).

We may have just reminded some readers of a rumor they've heard. Briefly (and respectfully), we will address this.

There is much speculation regarding what the language used to describe this particular event suggests, as the "covering" or "uncovering" of one's "feet" in the Old Testament is a well-known euphemism referring to a man uncovering his lower region to relieve himself, such as Samuel did when he entered a cave to "cover his feet" (1 Samuel 24:3). Several explanations for this euphemism have been suggested, including the concept that the feet were covered for royalty so the man wouldn't soil them when he "restroomed," or that clothing moved out of the way for a man to relieve himself would naturally drop to the feet. Over time, many scholars agree, the term likely came to refer to certain acts involving women as well, as some commentaries acknowledge that the newborn babies coming from between a woman's "feet" in Deuteronomy 28:57 is one example. David, in an attempt to cover his sin of impregnating Bathsheba, told her husband, Uriah, to go home to her and "wash his feet," with the context appearing to refer to when Uriah refused to "lay" with his wife in response to David's command (2 Samuel 11:8–11). More word studies show the seraphim from Isaiah's prophecy are found modestly covering their "feet" with their wings (Isaiah 6:2). A natural reading of this Scripture, which leaves other clothing articles up for assumption, leaves an awkward visual that begs for further explanation, until we can imagine it's a type of loincloth covering.

Thus, with "feet" possibly indicating below the belt instead of below the ankles in Old Testament terminology, many have assumed Naomi instructed Ruth to go to Boaz at night and uncover what only a *wife* was allowed to see. If this is the true meaning behind the story, Boaz would have been put on the spot, so to speak, to accept Ruth as his wife by obligation of moral code. They had already been intimate with each other to some degree by the time he had awakened to see Ruth by his side, making her request to be brought under his "skirt" a symbol of consummate marriage right there in the moment (even though the narrative doesn't appear to suggest anything further happened physically in that regard). Elsewhere in Scripture—as well as in Hebrew studies and historical accounts of the early Arabs—we know that "spreading a skirt" over someone did represent one person's covenant with and over another, protectively. Observe in Ezekiel 16:8 how the Lord, Himself, refers to this covenantal act: "'Now when I passed by thee, and looked upon thee, behold, thy time was the time of love; and I spread my skirt over thee, and covered thy nakedness: yea, I sware unto thee, and entered into a covenant with thee,' saith the Lord God, 'and thou becamest mine.'"

Thus, two possibilities are in range here: 1) Ruth exposed Boaz' literal feet, the cool night air awakened him, and they further conversed about her becoming his wife; or 2) Ruth exposed Boaz in a more intimate way so that, when he awakened, he would be obligated to marry her *or* react against her in the moment.

Either way, Ruth's proposal attempt, as it might be considered, should not be viewed through a modern lens.

As the Old Testament frequently relates, a man and woman could "go into a tent" and emerge married. So what may appear in today's society to be an indecent move may have been, for Ruth and Boaz, in the visual coverage of darkness (we assume nobody "left the lights on" back then), a marriage proposal and nothing more. It's not like today when a young man gets on his knee to propose, and six months later the promise of marriage is consummated. Had Boaz the mind to, as a single man, he could have consummated the union with Ruth in that moment, and the new dawn would have brought an announcement of marriage. Most scholars agree this was the hope of both Ruth and Naomi, as is seen in Ruth's request: "spread therefore thy skirt over thine handmaid; for thou art a near kinsman" (Ruth 3:9). In other words, "Spread your skirts over me and let's be married here and now because you're the nearest kinsman to me: a widow of Elimelech's son." Placing today's modern ideas into this scene, regardless of the "feet" interpretations, could lead to a corruption of an otherwise pure story. In verse 3:14, Ruth "rose up before one could know another," which speaks of the fact that she rose and left without her and Boaz having consummated their marital plan ("knowing each other" is another euphemism for that particular marital act between a man and woman). Thus, the physical innocence on the part of these two is present in this scene, no matter what "feet" means in Ruth's proposal of marriage.

With that addressed, Boaz' response as recorded in the subsequent verses shows that Ruth's integrity had been under Boaz' watchful eye for some time. All the while she was in a position to consort with other young men, some of whom were rich, Boaz acknowledged, she chose to save herself for Boaz. He honored her chastity, recognized her kindness, called her a "virtuous woman" (Ruth 3:11), and then admitted something that may have been quite a blow: Yes, he *was* her near kinsman, just as she said, and he had every intention of taking her as bride...but one other kinsman was nearer to her than he. In the morning, he would ask this relative if he intended to marry Ruth. If so, then Boaz would bless the marriage; if not, he would take her as his own and their relationship would be official. Meanwhile, he instructed Ruth to go to bed and await his news.

The next morning, as planned, Boaz met with the man he had spoken of as well as the elders of the city. He explained that Naomi's property was for sale...but with it came the obligation to produce off-spring through her son's widow, Ruth. Upon hearing this, the kinsman Boaz consulted stated that he had family of his own to tend to and said he needed to focus upon the inheritance he would leave them; he was not in a position to buy Naomi's land and settle down with the young widow. With witnesses present, Boaz purchased Naomi's land on the spot. Everyone was happy for him, wishing him the same level of prosperity in producing offspring as Rachel and Leah had been for Israel. Ruth and Boaz married, and right away the Lord blessed their marriage with a son. His offspring, too, would be incredibly important.

We've explained the characters and their interactions for more than just a lesson in genealogy or establishing Boaz as a type of Christ—

though he is a beautiful one. In the Old Testament, we occasionally run across the terms "kinsman redeemer" or "nearest relative," though both derive from the Hebrew word *go'el*. In proper context, these terms refer to the passing of property to younger generations. If one fell into rough times financially and the property was out of reach for his sons (for instance, if he'd leveraged or "mortgaged" it to pay a debt elsewhere and couldn't afford to buy it back), then the property owner's *go'el* could pay it off for him. In Ruth's case, Naomi's husband and sons died, leaving two women to manage a property they obviously couldn't afford. Thus, Boaz became Ruth's "redeemer," purchasing her property and restoring it to her.

This type of real estate transaction at the time involved a legal document. When Ruth married her first husband, the terms of the property sale would be written upon an ancient form of parchment, and the back of that parchment would be signed by witnesses and whichever *go'el* was present as a potential future redeemer of the land (see Jeremiah 32:11). The document was then rolled into a scroll and sealed to keep the details private, though the signatures of the witnesses were viewable from the outside. In the case of a lost property, death, or other misfortune, only another kinsman (*go'el*) would be given the right to break the seal to view the contract and see what must be done to keep the property—and its inhabitants (wife, kids, elderly relatives, etc.)—in the family.

Thus far, the image is perhaps a bit underwhelming, seeming like nothing more than an ancient escrow officer notarizing signatures and melting a wax stamp of approval of the purchase. If it ended there, the account of Ruth would be at least a sweet love story of how one morally intact Israelite man took pity on a former pagan for the sake of his relative and loved her regardless of her former beliefs. That, alone, could place Boaz in the role of a Christ type. But if we flip over to Revelation, the parallel becomes a thing of momentary terror for both us and the Apostle John:

And I [John] saw in the right hand of him [God] that sat on the throne a scroll written within and on the backside, sealed with seven seals. And I saw a strong angel proclaiming with a loud voice, "Who is worthy to open the scroll, and to loose the seals thereof?" And no man in heaven, nor in earth, neither under the earth, was able to open the scroll, neither to look thereon. And I wept much, because no man was found worthy to open and to read the scroll, neither to look thereon. (Revelation 5:1–4)

Prior to Christ, no person in history could ever be worthy to redeem humanity. Nor has any human ever been "kin" to God. In "Boaz terms," we were living on a property with no owner, doomed to wander the earth forever as "no man in heaven, nor in earth, neither under the earth" would be "able to open the scroll" addressing our residence to consider any kind of repurchase, redemption, or resale of our property to another caretaker who would see to our provision. It's heart-wrenching to see John in this passage, weeping at what scholars say represented the damnation of a forgotten humankind with no promise or future. We would have wept, too. What a tragic end for all of us…

But in the very next verses (Revelation 5:5–10), we are introduced to the utmost Kinsman Redeemer, Jesus Christ:

And one of the elders [one of the witnesses present at the time this scroll was sealed and therefore one of the only ones who would know what was stated inside] saith unto me, "Weep not: behold, the Lion of the tribe of Judah, the Root of David, hath prevailed to open the scroll, and to loose the seven seals thereof." And I beheld…in the midst of the elders [the witnesses], stood a Lamb [Jesus] as it had been slain… And he came and took the scroll out of the right hand of [God, who] sat upon the throne. And when he had taken the scroll, the…elders fell down before the Lamb, having every one of them harps, and golden vials full of odours, which are the prayers of saints. And they sung a new song, saying, "Thou art worthy to take the scroll, and to open the seals thereof: for thou wast slain, and hast redeemed us to God by thy blood out of every kindred, and tongue, and people, and nation; And hast made us unto our God kings and priests: and we shall reign on the earth."

What follows that passage is a scene of praise wherein every living creature both in heaven and on earth worship the Lamb who was the only Kinsman of humankind with the right to break the seals on the scroll of our planet's fate—the only Lamb whose spilled blood was the currency for the purchase of the land and its otherwise lost inhabitants. Jesus, the only entity in the universe who is literally related to both humanity and God, was willing to take the burden of our fate into His hands, break open the otherwise unbreakable seven seals, and unroll the contract to reveal its details for all to see and for *all* to inherit freely. Christ is our Relative. Without His blood-bought purchase, our destiny would be no more glorious than remaining spiritually lethargic while we wander the damned corners of the earth, belonging to none other than the prince of the power of the air and awaiting death and judgment.

Behold, the Christ of Ruth!

Boaz' gentle, loving interactions with Ruth never once required her to account for the pagan, child-sacrificing, incestuous religious worldview she was raised in as he simply redeemed her in front of witnesses and elders, making nothing of her life before but a distant and irrelevant memory as he bought her and brought her into a new life and new promises. In his loving arms she would remain and *never look back to what the world tried to make of her.*

Jesus' gentle, loving interactions with the human race never once require us to live in the bondage of past baggage or sin. No matter how grievous our wages of sin and death, new life awaits all inhabitants of this property—earth—and Jesus submitted Himself to the cross, paying the price for the redemption contract in blood, without a single person being required first to account for who and what we were before we found Him. In front of the heavenly elders, Jesus tore open that scroll and redeemed us all: We are truly the blood-bought, the Church, the redeemed, as the old hymns say. New life! New promises! And it is into the loving arms of Jesus and the Father that we fall, accepting this generous and gracious gift we could have never earned, while we *never look back to what the world tried to make of us.*

This gift is as free to all sinners who believe in the Kinsman Redeemer—our precious *Go'el*—as it was to Ruth when her precious *go'el* redeemed her. What a powerful picture we so often miss!

But, of course, the end of the story also involves another profound development in addition to the beauty of this scene from Revelation. Ruth and Boaz had Obed, who had Jesse, who had David—*the* David, the one and only boy who would kill giants with a sling and become the greatest king of Israel, the very man whose legacy would point by title of "Son of David" to the Messiah! It is thus twofold, at least: Jesus is in the story of Ruth as the Kinsman Redeemer, foreshadowed by the righteous and kind Boaz; He is also in the story of Ruth through the bloodline that would produce the Davidic King of the Jews—the very One who would later carry out His own "Boaz" story of redemption for all mankind.

Seriously, we couldn't weave these elements together by mere human imagination. The Word is beautiful—so wonderfully, infinitely beautiful—in its extension of love and grace to us from the very beginning. It's worthwhile, in the case of Ruth, to slow down and allow the big picture to come into focus instead of rushing through it the way we often do. And, as hard as it may be to believe, we have one more point to make about how Ruth's life and legacy wind into the New Testament story of the cross. Albert Barnes, in his commentary, notes a detail that would, once again, be easy to overlook: "Ruth, the Moabitess, was undoubtedly one of the first-fruits of the ingathering of Gentiles into the Church of Christ, and so an evidence of God's gracious purpose in Christ."[47]

Wow…Ruth from Moab, a pagan, a Gentile, a girl whose people were listed as off-limits in Deuteronomy to prevent them from spiritually contaminating the tribes of Israel, was brought into the family of Yahweh as one of His own, and she was blessed with a child. Her story would resonate, as Barnes states, with the New Testament message of this same kind of spiritual adoption.

We can't think of a better note to end this chapter on. Praise the Lord for accepting this Gentile, and praise the Lord for accepting us, as well, into the family of God.

1 & 2 Samuel, 1 & 2 Kings, and 1 & 2 Chronicles

THE TWO-VOLUME BOOKS of Samuel, Kings, and Chronicles track the history of Israel from the time of the service of Samuel the prophet through the age of kings and onward through the exiles (the Babylonian and Assyrian exiles; the point when Israel fell into the hands of captors and was no longer a united nation or kingdom). Because these books streamline into one longer story, they are grouped together here. However, here is a snapshot of the focus of each one:

- 1 Samuel: Israel demands the installation of a king, an idea that turns out to be just as bad as God said it would.
- 2 Samuel: David, a crucial character in the history of God's messianic promises, rules over Israel, setting the standard of the ideal king.
- 1 Kings: David's son, Solomon, takes the throne, and Israel enjoys a time of prosperity and peace, but it doesn't last long; the nation splits into two kingdoms: Northern and Southern.
- 2 Kings: Israel refuses to listen to God and ignores the warnings of His prophets, which leads to the exiles.

- 1 Chronicles: From Adam to David, this book starts at the beginning and covers again the history of Israel, spending nine chapters outlining genealogies.
- 2 Chronicles: During Solomon's reign, the Temple is built, but because of Israel's unfaithfulness, the Temple is destroyed and the people are exiled.

Why do 1 and 2 Chronicles simply rehash what has already been described in more detail in the books preceding the accounts of the exiles? The short answer is that the *approach and purpose* are different. The information recorded in 1 Samuel through 2 Kings was written while Israel was approaching and facing the exiles, with a focus on the despair that results from disobedience to God, while 1 and 2 Chronicles were written while Israel was recovering from the exile with a focus on God's grace and the faithful restoration that results from obedience to God. Unlike other history books that simply tell "what happened," one major goal of the Chronicles is to use the histories of the Old Testament up to the exile in such a way as to revitalize hope for Israel's future and tell "what should happen now." By using the nation's brightest moments as models of ideal servitude to God and the nation's lowest moments as warnings to help keep folks in line, the generations of God's people following the writing of these books would have a picture to compare to as they move forward in their faith, awaiting the king promised to one day come through the line of David. It's the *CliffsNotes*, or study guide, of the prior books, so to speak. Therefore, in a way, it resembles an ancient commentary that also happened to be included in the canon.

Many are familiar with most of what's covered in these books, but like many biblical narratives, the robust tension within the text is often overlooked by those who believe they've heard it all before. In order to see—no, in order to *feel*—the Christ of the Samuel, Kings, and Chronicles books, let's see if we can bring a certain scene to life…

You know that moment at a public gathering when one person

starts to chant something rhythmic and everyone else shortly joins in? Sometimes, the message is obvious. If you're waiting for a Michael W. Smith concert to start and people start chanting, "We want Michael! We want Michael!" you know exactly who the people want to see and what he's going to bring to the stage. In the fun of the moment, you might join the chorus as well. But common sense recognizes that if a group starts demanding something you don't fully understand, joining in is foolish.

Here's an illustration. Donna Howell was walking with her husband, James, along a street in Branson, Missouri, recently when they heard a group around the corner from them shouting something that sounded like "All wives matter, too! All wives matter, too!" The Howells needed to get to a destination beyond the crowd, and they were in a hurry, so they reluctantly proceeded on their route, which took them in the direction of the outcries. They simply hoped they wouldn't be delayed by whatever was going on. At first, Donna thought it was probably a social or political demonstration by what sounded to be a female group, but after the group came into closer view, they saw a few animated men pumping signs in the air and making eye contact with uncomfortable passersby who tried to avoid them at the major crosswalk. A step even closer and some lip-reading revealed that the crowd wasn't saying "wives"—despite a distinct "w" sound—but "lives": "All *lives* matter, too." Then, a few of the activists saw the Howells coming and turned their signs toward them. The posters of unborn babies with words scrawled across the top brought clarification, and the message now became clear: "*Small* lives matter, too."

It was a pro-life demonstration.

Until that moment, as far as the Howells could tell, this group of folks could have been communicating their views on anything from battered wives, feminism, racial equality, domestic violence against children, or abortion to any of several other sociopolitical possibilities. It would be more than silly if a person some distance away heard the voices and started chanting in support for "wives" because he or she hadn't investigated the demonstration more carefully. From a "fools rush in" standpoint, even if a person heard the words correctly, joining in on the demands of the crowd would still be ill-advised if a person didn't know: 1) where the group had come from; 2) who they were and what they stood for in other important, related areas of belief; 3) how they arrived at the conclusions they were presenting at the street corner; and 4) what the long-term effects upon the community would be if the demonstration succeeded in provoking societal change.

Generally speaking, if we don't know all the layers behind what we're supporting—if we haven't thought it through—prudence is wise. Otherwise, we could find ourselves making demands that, once satisfied, become costly.

Such a thought was amusing to Donna as she and James crossed the street. *That's kinda what Israel did in First Samuel*, Donna thought. *They had no idea what they were petitioning for.*

As stated before, a judge in ancient Israel was appointed by God, Himself, and became the conduit through whom He iterated His divine will for the people. Essentially, though God's will was spoken through a *human*, the authority on all earthly matters as it was delivered by the judges was the Lord's. This is true whether or not it was followed perfectly by Israel, and regardless of the imperfection of the human vehicle through which God's directives were driven. The emphasis here is that only God, Himself—not voting campaigns or one's bloodline—designated the authorities; every order of the judge was from God. This type of "rule," if you want to call it that, wasn't the same as the governments of Israel's neighbors.

Breaking from this divine-appointment tradition, Judge Samuel decided to appoint his own sons as judges (1 Samuel 8:1). Because this wasn't typically allowed, it has long been a subject for scholarly speculation. Some sources, like the *Faithlife Study Bible* of Logos Software, say that Samuel knew he wasn't supposed to take this liberty but did anyway, which makes it "unsurprising that this move was not successful."[48] Others say he didn't intend for his sons to be "supreme" judges, because Samuel held that office his whole life (1 Samuel 7:15); they suggest instead, he simply meant to have his sons' help as "deputies," of sorts, who would report to him before finalizing any decisions.[49] Whatever his reason, it didn't work out well. Samuel's sons did not inherit their dad's pious nature, and, like other wicked leaders of Israel's past, they perverted judgment and corrupted their positions of power for the sake of lining their pockets with gold (1 Samuel 8:3). This is the backdrop for the launch of 1 Samuel's meaty parts.

Israel then demanded the installation of a king—not God, not another judge, not a brilliant prophet who could utter the mysteries of God and offer guidance…they insisted upon having a *king*, a regular, human man who would sit on a literal throne and lead Israel the way the pagan nations around them did it.

Imagine what this moment would be like today. If you close your eyes and listen hard enough in your imagination, you can hear the crowd of demonstrators rising up from the elders of Israel in 1 Samuel 8:5 shouting, "We want a king! Give us a king!" You can kinda see the picket signs arriving throughout—pumping demands for a human royal the people can see and speak to in person because judges are "old news" and God is incorporeal—as the elders holler their petition: "We want a king! Give us a king!" First peppered here and there, then arriving in droves, signs and voices crunch inward against Samuel, all insisting that he step aside, forget about his sons, and put a king in charge of their holy nation. Never before has a *king* sat over God's people, but the folks in neighboring countries are doing it, so it must be a grand idea (good grief…), and it is now Samuel's job to see to the inauguration of the first crown.

We can imagine Samuel's hasty response: "No, hang on! You don't understand! You don't know what you're asking for! A king sounds good to you, but you don't comprehend the fullness of your demand.

You're joining the chant and waving the signs, but you don't know—
you *can't* know—what this will do to your families, your land, your
national identity under God!"

We don't know, of course, Samuel's immediate response to the
demands—as the Bible only states he was very upset and went to the
Lord with his concerns (1 Samuel 8:6), but we do know God gave
Samuel ample warnings to take back to the people. An earthly king
would take sons away from parents and make them manage his chariots;
take fathers away from wives and children and turn them into weapons
of war and field-harvesters; take young, tender daughters away from
their families and force them to become his palace cooks and Oriental
perfume-makers; steal the best portions of land that rightfully belong
to the people and give it away to his servants; confiscate the people's
food and give it to his officers and servants; rob the people of their own
servants and place them in his own employment; and assume owner-
ship of the people's animals. Generally, Samuel says in his demoralizing
conclusion, the king will see that everyone not covered on the list up
to this point will be socially and politically enslaved. The people will
cry out to the Lord with complaints about all this horrible dictator
has done to them, but the Lord will not answer them in that day,
because it's what they petitioned for—what they demanded—and they
wouldn't listen to reason (1 Samuel 8:10–18).

Keep that image of the picketing elders in your mind and consider
the Israelites' response to such a strong warning:

> Nevertheless the people refused to obey the voice of Samuel;
> and they said, "Nay; but we will have a king over us; That we
> also may be like all the [pagan] nations; and that our king may
> judge us, and go out before us, and fight our battles."
>
> And Samuel heard all the words of the people, and he
> rehearsed them in the ears of the Lord. And the Lord said to
> Samuel, "Hearken unto their voice, and make them a king."
> (1 Samuel 8:19–22a)

In other words, God said, "You may as well just give them what they asked for." Once digested, you can't put potato chips back in the bag. Some decisions are irreversible. The Israelites got themselves a king, and this system of monarchy wouldn't easily come to an end. Israel was about to find out that you can't simply ask kings to step down so the nation can reinstate judges or prophets like the good ol' days. The former system wasn't broken, therefore didn't need fixing, but they "fixed" it anyway and ushered in a new era of leadership that, regardless of its success in the neighboring countries, would *not* function well for Israel.

Furthermore, God said, it wasn't that the request for a king was inherently wrong. It was an issue of internal attitude and heart. To ask that one man in Israel be given the same power as the foreign kings, with the intent that he would use that power to lead righteously under Yahweh's moral codes, could have meant that the installation of kings resulted in strengthening the judicial, political, and social climates throughout the tribes. But righteousness and pleasing Yahweh was *not* the motive behind this king-installation maneuver, which was what made it wrong. God privately shared with Samuel that the internal motive was truly to reject God as King (1 Samuel 8:7–8). The goal of the majority, scholars believe, was to forsake their theocratic and monotheistic government and bring in a human leader who would loosen their moral obligation to the Mosaic Law, forget about the stringent priestly functions that had been such a fundamental part of their daily lives, bring in the blessings of other gods, and act as a military leader who would see to the protection of the people and their land.[50] At no point can we feasibly determine that Israel demanded a king because they wanted to *strengthen* their bond with God. No. Israel saw a human king as a means of booting God from His rightful place as the Leader they already had and raising up a progressive leader who would replace the old ways with a system they believed to be superior and more promising under the gods of a pagan world.

In short, they wanted *a* "king" to replace *the* "King." Their ideas were better than God's...they thought. God saw this, and it appears that He and Samuel were the only ones who ever saw the trouble coming. But, whatever their fate, the damage was done, as God allowed Samuel to grant the request.

Samuel was the last judge who held authority over all of God's people as a united, single nation, and it was now a new era, for better or for worse.

What followed was a short window of reprieve, what some historians and Bible researchers call the "Golden Age" of Israel under the reigns of Saul, David, and Solomon. It's likely that these more peaceful years bolstered the Israelites' confidence that the right decision had been made in replacing Yahweh with men. Those prosperous years certainly weren't without any hiccups (everyone at least remembers the David-and-Bathsheba debacle), but they were smooth enough that Samuel probably heard more than a few "we told you so" comments from some of the elders who had petitioned for a king.

However, the cautionary predictions of God did come to pass as He had warned...and in surprisingly close proximity to the day the warnings were issued. Using only the first warning from God as an example, we can show how His prophetic words started coming to pass even before the end of the Golden Age: In 1 Samuel 8:11, Samuel reiterated that a king would "take your sons, and appoint them for himself, for his chariots, and to be his horsemen; and some shall run before his chariots." Just a skip over to 2 Samuel 15:1, we see that King Absalom—King David's disappointing son who demonstrated his rightful position on the throne by having a public sex demonstration with his father's concubines on the roof "in the sight of all Israel" (2 Samuel 16:22)—had "prepared him chariots and horses, and fifty men to run before him." King David's fourth son was guilty of the same thing: "Then Adonijah the son of Haggith exalted himself, saying, 'I will be king': and he prepared him chariots and horsemen, and fifty men to run before him" (1 Kings 1:5). And King Solomon, despite the good he did for Israel (including his massive contributions to both collecting and the composing the Wisdom literature), had the largest assemblage of men and animals in his horses and chariots department. "Solomon had forty thousand stalls of horses for his chariots, and twelve thousand horsemen" (4:26) "and he had a thousand and four hundred chariots" (10:26). Though these verses appear to be linked to some of the "blessing" verses in the story of King Solomon after he asked God for wisdom, the number of men the king "took" (or "drafted," or "enlisted") in his choice to impose forced labor upon Israel was "thirty thousand men" (5:13). Though we know the "horsemen" included twelve thousand men (4:26), some of the remaining thirty thousand Israelite sons who were absorbed into the forced labor numbers (5:13) may have been given jobs related to building the stalls and chariots, maintaining the buildings, training the animals, and so on.

This more than fulfills the first of God's *many* warnings about the king taking what he wants with little regard to its impact on the Israelites. This one example should suffice to show that God certainly knew what He was talking about when He spoke to His people through Samuel.

There were also warnings God, for whatever reason, did *not* share with Israel that fateful day through Samuel. For instance, He mentioned the daughters of Israel would be taken and turned into cooks, bakers, and perfume-makers (1 Samuel 8:13), but some commentators note there was a far worse fate for *some* daughters, considering the kings' evident penchant for collecting concubines.[51] Yet the Lord didn't see that detail as necessary to state that day (possibly because He knew they wouldn't listen to that bit, either).

To ramp it up to a more alarming illustration, Israel couldn't foresee that, at the conclusion of King Solomon's reign, God's people would face a massive and long-lived split over who the next ruler would be.

Around 922 BC, after the time of King David and King Solomon, the nation of Israel split into what became known as the Northern and the Southern Kingdoms. After receiving a word from the Lord, the prophet Ahijah tore his robe into twelve pieces to represent the twelve tribes of Israel, then gave ten of those pieces to Jeroboam to signify that he would rule over those ten (1 Kings 11:30–33). This prophecy came to pass when the people stoned to death the messenger of the currently reigning Rehoboam and claimed Jeroboam as their king (1 Kings 12:18–20). This became the Northern Kingdom. The remaining two tribes, Benjamin and Judah, remained loyal to Rehoboam, forming the Southern Kingdom (1 Kings 12:17).

This was more than just a political move, and the ramifications would be painful. Benjamin and Judah gave up their inheritance, and the nation they seceded from had always been their family and their national identity. Brother turned against brother, splintering the nation of God in half, weakening their numbers and increasing their vulnerability to the surrounding pagan military forces—all because of the earthly king God had warned them never to install in the first place. And it doesn't end there.

God made sure His people knew from the beginning that they were asking for a dictator (though they didn't listen). They shouldn't have been surprised when their plans went terribly awry. What followed after their decision to disregard God's warnings is an incredibly lengthy, dirty-laundry list of future evil kings who would commit atrocious acts of wickedness, often imposing their sacrilege upon the people, who would therefore share the king's guilt when God's wrath came to knock them down from their profane pedestals. To name only a few on the side of Israel:

- King Jeroboam erected golden calves and forced Israel to commit the ultimate blasphemy by worshipping them as the gods that brought them out of Egypt (1 Kings 12:28).
- King Ahab allied with Phoenicia via the marriage to the Sidonian king's daughter, Jezebel. This ushered in Israel's dark era of

Baal worship, Asherah poles, and the building of Baal's temple in Samaria (16:31–33).

- King Ahaziah led Israel into worship of Baal after Ahab and Jezebel's example. Ahaziah is one of several kings noted to have "walked in the way of...Jeroboam," no doubt referencing the continued practice of worshipping the golden calves as well (1 Kings 2:51–53). Idolatry was now the norm, and Yahweh was only one of many gods they worshipped, all in only a few short generations of earthly kings.

You shouldn't replace a King with a king.

Remember the God-angering cycle from the book of Judges, when the people kept turning their back on Yahweh, falling into despair from their sin, then begging for help until God sent a judge to pull them back into a season of prosperity and peace? The cycle is similar from the Northern-Southern split forward, throughout the two books of Kings and into the two books of Chronicles. The loop in these parts is, basically, "King So-and-So did evil in the sight of the Lord, followed in the ways of [insert wicked ruler's name here] and made Israel sin. And the anger of the Lord was kindled..." Usually, after mentioning the wrath of God, something horrible happened to the earthly kingdom, though, throughout this period of delusional leadership by earthly kings, God remembered His covenant with Abraham and kept His promise to preserve the bloodline, thereby keeping His people Israel from extinction during all the warring throughout this part of history. Despite their being allowed to continue existing on the planet, however, there was *much* death, heartache, and oppression in major seasons of turmoil—all of which might have been greatly diminished (or entirely avoided) had the Israelites simply been happy with God as their King.

Each kingdom offended God repeatedly during the nine hundred years between this time and the arrival of Christ, but the Northern

Kingdom was far more given to wickedness than the Southern, thus was subjected to higher levels of God's wrath than its counterpart. Around 725 BC, Assyria invaded the Northern Kingdom. (After this defeat, the conquerors left their own people stationed throughout the land to maintain Assyrian rule, and subsequent generations interbred with Israelites, resulting in the Samaritan race. This is why, most scholars assert, these individuals were hated by their non-Samaritan peers in the New Testament; they were a reminder of God's wrath bestowed as a result of idolatry, and they were an installation resulting from defeat. Because they often clung to religions on both sides of parental lineage, their practices often reflected a pagan-infiltrated version of traditional Jewish principles, fueling the hatred they endured from surrounding cultures.) Approximately one hundred years later, Babylon rose to power and overtook the Southern Kingdom. It invaded Jerusalem and sacked the Temple, looting its treasures and returning to Babylon with the plundered goods and many captive, enslaved Jews, who were then exiled in Babylon for the next seventy years.

But here is the climax of this arc of books (1 Samuel through 2 Chronicles): God kept every promise He made to His covenant people (Joshua 21:44–45; 1 Kings 8:56). In the face of humanity's ever-increasing spiritual infidelity, whoring after other gods, and disregarding any vow made to Yahweh, God was faithful, always. This divine grace and patience could never have been earned or deserved in the first place, but in light of the people's unfaithfulness, God's gift of grace in keeping His end of the covenant was absolutely, *emphatically*, undeserved.

So why did God keep His word? Why didn't He send a flood or a plague or something that would wipe out everyone and let Him start over with new, more appreciative, loyal people? If your immediate answer is because God is all good and, therefore, only faithful when it comes to His promises, you would be correct as it pertains to the theology of God's immutability (the concept that God's nature and characteristics do not and cannot change). And yes, God's immutability and unquestionable holiness is a solid, reliable, and always-correct answer to this question and many others like it that inquire about why He does what He does. However, at least as it relates to this series of books, there is an additional reason we want to hone in on...so don't miss it.

God was faithful throughout the seasons of the kings and kingdoms "for the sake of David" (read the repetition of this reference in 1 Kings 11:11–13, 32, 34; 2 Kings 8:19; and 19:34; see also God mentioning it again later in Isaiah 37:35).

See, the Lord promised more than just the offspring of Abraham. Though the bloodlines of Abraham were later carried on through David (and therefore represent the same biological descendants, ultimately fulfilling the promise made to *both* of them in the end), a more specific prophetic element in the history of Israel was revealed upon King David's rule, and its theme ran heavily from 2 Samuel through 2 Chronicles. God's promise to David was:

> When your days are fulfilled and you lie down with your fathers, I will raise up your offspring after you, who shall come from your body, and I will establish his kingdom. He shall build a house for my name, and I will establish the throne of his kingdom forever. I will be to him a father, and he shall be to me a son. (2 Samuel 7:12–14a)

Note that this prophecy, like *many* Old Testament prophecies, had a dual fulfillment (discussed again in our discussion of Revelation). Most immediately, the "offspring" from David's "body" was Solomon, and his kingdom was certainly established. Then, midway through verse 13, the emphasis switches from a temporal kingdom to an eternal one, from a soon-to-be-born descendant to a future one beyond the scope of Solomon (but still in his lineage): "I will establish the throne of his kingdom forever." The next words from the Lord are intense: "I will be to him a father, and he shall be to me a son."

This prophecy is, without a doubt, given within the contextual framework of the subject of kings and kingdoms, but the eternality of God's words here shifts meaning to a King and Kingdom God would establish "forever." The King God is alluding to in 2 Samuel 7 is none other than the Anointed One of Israel, referred to in Matthew 1:1 as "Jesus Christ, the son of David, the son of Abraham." Paul, during his sermon in Antioch in Acts 13:22b–23, notes this was directly fulfilled through Christ: "He raised up unto them David to be their king; to whom also he gave their testimony, and said, 'I have found David the son of Jesse, a man after mine own heart, which shall fulfil all my will.' Of this man's seed hath God according to his promise raised unto Israel a Saviour, Jesus." This is even more astounding considering that one devious character, Athaliah, the mother of Ahaziah, attempted to kill the entire royal family (2 Kings 11:1–2). Had this attempt been successful, it would have cut off David's seed forever and there never would have been any Jesus, Son of David. By God's intervention, *one person* from David's line was saved and eight centuries later, Baby Jesus arrived.

But it's so much more than the carrying on of a bloodline just so Jesus could one day be born. God's Son could have been delivered by a stork in an anonymous baby bundle, as could have been His prerogative (and, considering the baby Moses, who was in a basket delivered by river current, it wouldn't even be far-fetched). Jesus could have, in a way perhaps even more grandiose to our finite imaginations, been delivered through rays of sunshine and descending angels from on high whose voices never held a more impressive, otherworldly harmony than the day they brought the wriggling bundle of joy through a brightly lit window of the home housing the holiest man in Israel to raise. For that matter, at the Father's beckoning, the universe could have pulled a *Wizard of Oz* storyline, popping Baby Jesus into a pink bubble that floated gently to the earth, "Glinda style," where the Messiah would have been carried in Dorothy's basket on the yellow brick road to a city of emeralds and raised by a man behind a curtain.

God could have linked the Messiah to any historical origin-story He saw fit. Yet He chose the lineage ties He selected, and these stories are not it. (That would have certainly made for a fascinating ending to the Judy Garland classic, though…)

The Lord linked the bloodline of the Son to the bloodline of Israel's kings. He did this near the same point in history that: 1) His people rejected *Him* as their King; and 2) His people were shown through extreme disappointment, pain, oppression, repetitious cycles of war, death, and dictatorial monarchs, that, just as God and Samuel warned, the kings were *not* better than the King. They had rejected the King and fell into a pit they seemingly didn't have a way out of.

But God!

Right?

Watch this…

The people were unimpressed with the old system of judges or prophets over Israel, so they asked for a king—that much we've covered. But let's take a second, prepare our eyes to be those that *will see*, and look at where this is going.

Historically and biblically, prophets were recognized not by an inheritance of office, through the accumulation of wealth and power, or by any means other than the recognition that the word of the Lord had "come to" them (see, for example, Nathan in 2 Samuel 7:4; Isaiah in 2 Kings 20:4; Jeremiah in his book 1:4; and Ezekiel in his book 3:16.), and they delivered it. In the New Testament, the word of the Father had come to the Son in the same way as the prophets of old (John 7:16; 8:28; 17:8). Jesus prophetically told of events nobody could have guessed would happen (and that signs of the times didn't yet point to, such as we read in Matthew 16:21, wherein Jesus warned His disciples of His upcoming trials and death; these things were fulfilled in Matthew 27–28; Mark 15–16; Luke 22–24; and John 18–20). Jesus not only called Himself a prophet (Mark 6:4), but others also frequently recognized Him as a prophet of the Lord (Matthew 21:11; Luke 7:16; John 4:19). It's pretty clear, then, that Jesus was a prophet because He fulfilled the requirements and duties of the office. But, because He is perfect and therefore is not subject to error, Christ would have carried the words and will of the Father with far superior delivery and execution than even the greatest of Old Testament prophets who appear in the books of Joshua through 2 Chronicles.

The Son of David was, therefore, the ultimate *Prophet* over Israel.

Jesus' New Testament story is often linked to great news of salvation for all, and that is, without argument from us, the main theme of His First Advent (John 3:16). However, another purpose of His coming was to be the Father's definitive Judge. One of the very reasons He was sent to this world was to carry out fair judgment, both upon people (John 9:39) and upon forces of darkness (John 12:31–33). It was prophesied that the Messiah would be a Judge (Isaiah 11:3–4; Psalm 37:6). At the Judgment Seat of Christ, He will evaluate Christians to establish rewards based upon their works of their faith in this life (1 Corinthians 4:5; 2 Corinthians 5:10). At the Great White Throne, He will judge those who never believed in Him (Revelation 20:11–15). At the separation of the "sheep" from the "goats" (the "Sheep and Goats Judgment"), Jesus will decide who the "sheep" (true followers of God) are and who the "goats" (religious fakers) are, and He will determine their respective places in eternity (Matthew 25:31–46). But, again, because He always will be perfect and therefore not subject to error, Christ's role as Judge will be more precise, appropriate, and fair than any that of any of His Old Testament counterparts. Since He is one with the Father, it makes sense that His judgments and the Father's are one and the same, as Jesus stated: "As I hear, I judge: and my judgment is just; because I seek not mine own will, but the will of the Father which hath sent me" (John 5:30b; also see John 8:15–16).

The Son of David was, therefore, the ultimate *Judge* over Israel.

The Hebrew term *hammashiach*, or, *mashiach YHWH* (the lengthier version of the term involving the tetragrammaton, the unspeakable name of God), means "Yahweh's aointed." It is from the truncated appearance of this term, *mashiach*, that we derive "messiah." After the anointing of Israel's first king, Saul, *hammashiach* gained an added layer of meaning. Though there were certainly evil kings—and though Israel most definitely served other gods—*hammashiach* was the moniker for any reigning king of Israel.

When the Hebrew Scriptures were translated into Greek (the translation known today as the Septuagint), the term *hammashiach* became the Greek *christos*, which simply means "anointed." The Greek *christos* did not originally have anything to do with the Risen Jesus of Nazareth…at least not in human history (God was not surprised). It would not be until after the New Testament writers reflected on Israel's back story and considered Jesus in that framework that He would be called "the Anointed," and it's important to remember this name was, for Israel, always linked to Yahweh ("the Anointed of YHWH").

More simply, the Greek *christos* meant "God's anointed one," and this term was a nickname for the king over all of Israel.

In a literal sense, to be anointed for a special office or duty of God meant that one knelt and received a pouring-out of the sacred oil, which was brewed carefully with four fragrant substances. The initial outpouring of the sacred oil appears in Exodus 30:30–32, when Aaron, Moses' brother, became the first priest of Israel:

> And thou shalt anoint Aaron and his sons, and consecrate them, that they may minister unto me in the priest's office. And thou shalt speak unto the children of Israel, saying, "This shall be an holy anointing oil unto me throughout your generations. Upon man's flesh shall it not be poured, neither shall ye make any other like it, after the composition of it: it is holy, and it shall be holy unto you."

Hmmm… It seems odd that God just told the Israelites to pour the oil on Aaron and his sons, and then said *not* to pour it on them ("Upon man's flesh shall it not be poured"), does it not?

This is easily explained: The word "man" in this passage is the Hebrew *adam*, which, *outside* the context of the first man in the Garden of Eden whose proper name was Adam, *adam* simply meant "man," generically. Although priests, prophets, and kings were also "man" in the sense of "mankind" or "human," in the Hebrew context, "man" was a broad word referring to "men" generally. In our own terms, we might see "guy" or "chap" in its place. In other words, and meaning no disrespect to Scripture (just putting together a simplified word-picture here), God basically said, "This sacred oil is *not to* be poured onto the flesh of regular guys." The English Standard Version (ESV) translation renders this: "It shall not be poured on the body of an ordinary person." This special oil was reserved for anointing those God had justified and approved to be His utmost trusted leaders over all His people, acknowledged by all as the holders of the holiest of positions. They were consecrated, which, understandably, means to be declared before all as "sacred."

This act of anointing marked the official beginning of service for priests and kings always, and for prophets sometimes. Therefore, it was done this way in Israel as opposed to a coronation ceremony with crowns and scepters or whatever other imagery comes to mind when we think of the start of a king's reign. The symbolism of the act represented the indwelling of the Spirit of God. We can see this in Psalm 89:19b–21:

> I have exalted one chosen out of the people. I have found David my servant; with my holy oil have I anointed him: With whom my hand shall be established: mine arm also shall strengthen him.

Some may naturally note that not every king was indwelt with the Spirit of God, both because there were wicked kings and, though it wasn't God's plan, the throne was passed to sons who inherited the throne by birthright, not because they were "chosen" by God.

However, when David became king, as this passage shows, he was "chosen out of the people," which was God's plan the first place before the demands of the people messed it up. (Little wonder, when God was no longer doing the choosing, that Israel produced so many terrible leaders.) God's ideal, therefore, is that a man "His hand has established" as king would have God's "arm also" to strengthen his kingship; God would be "with" and "in" the king (so to speak), and the king would be indwelt with the Spirit of God.

This is why, as stated a few paragraphs earlier, *hammashiach* (or "messiah"), and therefore the Greek *christos*, gained an added layer of meaning when kings entered Israel's history. The word "anointed" (*hammashiach/christos*) not only was a term meaning "one appointed by Yahweh to lead His people," it also meant "king," and, by extension of context, it indicated "a king indwelt with the Spirit."

This entire etymological discussion spotlights one powerful fact: "Jesus [the] Christ" responsibly translates to "Jesus the *King*," and unlike one who inherits a throne or is elected, Jesus was *chosen*, and is most definitely indwelt with the Spirit of God, or "Holy Spirit," in New Testament terms (Matthew 3:13–17). (The English word "Christ" obviously derives from *christos*.)

But before we can celebrate Jesus as King, it's important to understand the hope Israel had in relation to a future deliverer through the lineage of David. As discussed previously, in 2 Samuel 7:12–14, God established that there would be a King from David's line who would rule "forever." This is a feat no mere human could ever achieve, as our days are numbered. Now, consider 1 Samuel 16:13a: "Then Samuel took the horn of oil, and anointed him in the midst of his brethren: and the Spirit of the Lord came upon David from that day forward." Of all the rulers in Israel, it's clear that David, a man after God's own heart (1 Samuel 16:13), was, despite his sins and faults, the ideal king whose Spirit-indwelling was always present. (His sin does not negate the indwelling of the Spirit. The Holy Spirit doesn't keep us from sinning nor will it leave us when we do. There will always be a tension between the Spirit and our flesh.) When the New Testament writers reflected on who the "forever king" might be, the significance of David's "from that day forward" spiritual anointing was enormous. It's not a huge leap to see that David was the model of the forthcoming messianic King.

Additionally, we see much beauty in David as a type of Christ. The list of parallels is lengthy, but we will cover a few major comparisons briefly:

- Both David and Jesus were born in Bethlehem, called the "City of David" (1 Samuel 17:12; Luke 2:11; Matthew 2:1).
- David was a shepherd prior to his kingship (1 Samuel 16:11); Jesus is the Good Shepherd (John 10:11).
- David was thirty years old when he became king (2 Samuel 5:4); Jesus was thirty years old when He started His ministry years (Luke 3:23).
- Both David and Jesus were betrayed by one of their closest and most trusted friends (Psalm 41:9; John 18:5). David's friend (1 Chronicles 27:33) hung himself after betrayal (2 Samuel 17:23); Jesus' friend hung himself after betrayal (Matthew 27:5).
- David had many enemies (Psalm 3:1), but he defeated them (Psalm 18:37); Jesus had many enemies (John 19:6), but He defeated them (1 Corinthians 15:25).
- David was the king of Judah (2 Samuel 2:4); Jesus is the King of all, known as the Lion of Judah (Revelation 5:5).
- David was the deliverer of Israel (1 Samuel 17:48–52); Jesus is the Deliverer of Israel (and the world; John 16:33, Romans 16:20).

Jesus was and is the fulfilment of the prophesied Son of David and King over Israel, "the house of Jacob," literally and forever. Thus, the angel Gabriel made this clear to Mary: "He shall be great, and shall be called the Son of the Highest: and the Lord God shall give unto him the throne of his father David: And he shall reign over the house of Jacob for ever; and of his kingdom there shall be no end" (Luke 1:32–33). This messianic kingship was prophesied in ancient times and in no uncertain terms.

Needless to say, however, Jesus' role as King goes well beyond any limitations set by comparing His position with David's. A king, like David, is a ruler, a top authority over his region or land territory. The region or land territory Jesus rules over is any fathomable location in the whole universe. There isn't any higher authority than that mentioned in Ephesians 1:20–22, where we see Jesus seated at the right hand of the Father in the heavens, "Far above all principality, and power, and might, and dominion, and every name that is named, not only in this world, but also in that which is to come: And hath put all things under his feet, and gave him to be the head over all things." Thus, Jesus has undoubtedly proven to be King based on His authority and position. In Jesus, we see not just a ruling King but the One and Only King of kings and Lord of lords, as the Name is written on His robe and thigh (Revelation 17:14; 19:16). He has been given His own Kingdom, but it supersedes this world; it is not a part of this world at all (John 18:36) and it and won't be until the Millennial Reign. To this Anointed One, Jesus the Christ, was given "dominion, and glory, and a kingdom, that all people, nations, and languages, should serve him: his dominion is an everlasting dominion, which shall not pass away, and his kingdom [is] that which shall not be destroyed" (Daniel 7:13–14).

The Son of David was, therefore, the ultimate *King* over Israel.

The people asked for *a* king. Little did they know they were going to get *the* King.

King Jesus is the supreme Prophet, Judge, and King of the universe. Nobody else in Israel's history, all throughout the testaments, has ever been all of these at once.

There is *so* much more to be said regarding how Jesus appears in 1 Samuel through 2 Chronicles. For instance, scholars have given much attention to the genealogies of 2 Chronicles, but it's interesting to note the majority of the reflections—eons before Jesus was born in a human body—give specific, important attention to the tribes of Judah (1 Chronicles 2:3–4:23) and Levi (1 Chronicles 6:1–81). This hyper-focused concentration is no coincidence. In fact, these are the genealogies of the priestly and the royal bloodlines, given special treatment in history when Israel was seeking the perfect priests and kings to perform the most holy of duties and anointed leadership over the people. As we have shown, Jesus is the flawless, anointed King (Romans 1:3; 2 Timothy 2:8; Revelation 19:16), but He is also our flawless Priest (Hebrews 4:14; 5:5–6; 8:1).

No matter how "perfect" any human can ever be, there is still fault in humanity. Therefore, Israel—and the rest of the Gentile world by extension of God's generous, merciful reach—would always be left waiting and searching for a Spotless One to fulfill our hope.

Hail to the King!

Ezra and Nehemiah

SEVENTY YEARS HAVE PASSED since Israel's demand for a king touched off a series of events that finally spiraled them into captivity during the Babylonian and Assyrian exiles. At this point, most of the Israelites have been born and raised in exile, having never seen the land their forefathers inhabited. For them, returning from exile—an event prophesied in Jeremiah 25:12 and Genesis 12:2 that is about to be fulfilled in the book of Ezra—meant moving to a new place only known from stories handed down from parents and grandparents. As such, some opted to stay in the land they were familiar with.

Ezra picks up the narrative as the Israelites—approximate fifty thousand (Ezra 2) who *did* long for the land of their forefathers—return to Jerusalem and rebuild the Temple that was destroyed by the king of Babylon. Cyrus, the king of Persia, not only conquered Babylon and liberated the Jews from captivity; he was "stirred" by the Lord to provide the Jews with the wealth, goods, and animals they needed to make the trip and restore their homeland (Ezra 1:1–4).

The journey back to the glory days of Zion would not be easy. Relocating would mean traveling over nine hundred miles in challenging conditions for many months. And once they arrived, they would have to reconstruct all ways of life. This wasn't just about buildings, but about the whole culture of holiness; they would need to establish synagogues, work out details surrounding the observance of Jewish feasts and holidays, identify and weed out pagan habits that had cropped up during exile, and reunite a people who had been physically and spiritually fragmented. (Many of these Israelites had very different interpretations of what God expected them to do in some areas of the Law, since they had lived in captivity so long that their initial practices and beliefs would have been influenced by years of living in a pagan land that didn't share their same national, Yahweh-centered history.)

Seven months after their arrival, when everyone was settled enough to come together "as one" to rebuild, they re-erected the altar, resumed the burnt sacrifices, and purchased (or traded for) the cedar and other materials they would need to lay the foundation for the Temple (Ezra 3:1). About seven months later, they began construction and, once the structure was completed, the priests blew the trumpets and all the people celebrated with cymbals, shouts of joy, and song (3:10–11).

Sadly, challenges came early on; they were first caused by the Samaritans, who initially sought to disrupt the Israelites by offering to help build the Temple. The Jews were wise enough to see the ruse for what it was and refuse their offer of assistance. The Samaritans therefore "weakened the hands of the people of Judah" and "troubled them in building" (4:4). By that, to expound on the bribery and frustrations listed in the next verses, they discouraged the Israelite workers during their progress by any means possible. They slandered the Jews, making rulers and leaders of the region (including those who took over Persia after Cyrus) believe they would "not pay toll, tribute, and custom, and so thou shalt endamage the revenue of the kings" (4:13); in other words, the Jews would spend all their money rebuilding "that wicked city" (4:12), refusing to pay taxes and thus deteriorating the royal treasury. It was this kind of rebellion against government, the Samaritans reported, that had destroyed the Jews' so-called horrible, evil, insubordinate homeland in the first place (4:15). The Babylonian leaders commanded that the work stop, and progress remained at an awkward standstill for years, until a new Babylonian creed was issued and they were allowed to continue.

Eventually, about twenty-one years after the arrival of God's people back to their homeland, the Temple was assembled, and the people once again rejoiced, made sacrifices, and celebrated feasts and holidays. But this joy would not be without the heavy burden of warning that they were not impervious to the leadership of the surrounding nations, so they needed a deep-rooted encouragement—an *encourager*—to completely revitalize their nation's pride and confidence. Little did they know they were about to experience a radical revival.

This brings us to chapter 7, which introduces us to Ezra, the book's central character—a faithful scribe who teaches the Hebrews to go back to obedience under God's Law if they want to experience the kinds of legendary blessings they had only until then heard about.

Ezra was from Babylonia; he himself was a child of the exile. While he lived there, because "the hand of God was on him," he was freely able to dedicate himself to the study of the Law, and the Babylonian government gave him anything he asked for in this endeavor (7:6). This verse says "he was a ready scribe in the law of Moses, which the Lord God of Israel had given." The Hebrew word here translated as "ready" is *mahir*, and it doesn't simply mean that he was emotionally, physically, and intellectually capable of doing what he was about to do; the true meaning of this word conveys a deeply developed skill, indicating that he was an "expert" of the Law, so to speak. Unlike some Israelites, who had devoted themselves to the Word of God in captivity as much as they could during the exile and remained faithful despite any foreign threat, Ezra was given the unique opportunity to devote all of his time pouring into the Scripture. He was, at this time in Israel's history, the first and last authority on what God had commanded to His people from the beginning. In the days of kings, he would have been in the position of royal advisor, state secretary, or chancellor—one whose knowledge of the Law is so thorough that the very throne over all the kingdom would have bent an ear in Ezra's direction before making any official decision or decree.[52]

When he left for Jerusalem, Ezra took a great multitude with him, stopping at the River Ahava to fast and pray for safe passage, showing once again that he was at all times humble before the Lord. This bode well for the group, as they were spared from "the hand of the enemy" and many ambushes along the way (Ezra 8:31).

After the masses were settled and Ezra was established as a great authority, Jerusalem officials reported to him that the Israelites had messed up again. Their holy-race bloodline was being contaminated through marriages with those in surrounding pagan territories.

Here we want to emphasize that God was not a racist. He wasn't opposed to interracial marriage in the Old Testament times for the same sociopolitical and cultural reasons this issue has come up in recent history. For God, it is never about skin color or any kind of "imperfect race," as Hitler regarded the Jews. When Israel's men took daughters from foreign lands in the ancient days, it almost always resulted in the intermingling of religion; wives would be allowed by their weak husbands to continue worshipping their false gods, and eventually that practice would bleed into the camps and tribes until Israel, once again, became polytheistic, regarding Yahweh as only one of many gods they were obligated to follow. At any point in history, this corruption of worship would have been a great affront to God, but during some periods it seems to have been expected (such during the times of Judges). They would fall into a cycle of pagan idolatry, "whore" after other gods, face terrible consequences, beg for God's intervention, promise to never do it again, and then do it again almost immediately when their troubles were over, causing the cycle to begin again… Over and over and over, this pattern appears in the Old Testament.

But this point in the story of God's people flies off the page differently. We're not just talking about yet another round of this behavior during a time when such disobedience became common and redundant. These folks had been exiled, punished, because they refused to follow God's Law in this and many other areas. They paid for their crimes against Him in extreme, heavy ways that not only ruined their community for them, but it seeped into their children's culture for seventy years, to the point that the children would never personally know what it was to be blessed as an inheritor of God's most potent blessings. Now, for the first time in ages, the people had been given a second chance to prove to God that if He would only give them back their land and their inheritance, they would never go astray again. God was faithful to return them to the land of promise, where they would be free without persecution—in fact, with the blessing of foreign kings!—to worship God, unite as the community and nation they'd been only dreaming of for generations, and live with the happiness and purity that come from eradicating demonic idols from their midst.

This was their chance! Everything the Jews longed for in the depths of their soul, from the stories their grandparents had told them regarding the days when God had smiled upon them and their people flourished, was culminating into a beautiful return to righteousness and proper relationship with Yahweh. They were about to experience, for the first time in over half a century, the "good life" they had been told about. Fathers and mothers were anticipating the freedom and liberty to raise their children in a community that supported the virtuousness of their forefathers. Sons and daughters were participating in a God-glorifying lifestyle again, preparing to grow and make homes of their own in a society where blushing brides and untainted grooms would once again become the norm, and where marriages would be sanctified, blameless, and free from the heavy burden of guilt. Young children could play in the streets and visit the marketplace without their parents having to fear they would pick up on the defiled, corrupt teachings of locals who bowed to idols of wood and gold. An age of innocence was, for the first time in a lengthy, oppressive era of custody under pagan authorities, coming back to shine upon the Jews with success and prosperity and bless whatever they put their hands to do. Now, in a miraculous turn of events, the Jews had been freed from the chains that bound them for what felt like an eternity. God had granted them that moment to prove they meant all they had prayed about in lamentation during their exile. A remnant of Israel had been spared from the tyranny and domination of ungodly rulers and nations, and it was their chance to make it count. *Everything* they wished for and held dear in their hearts was riding on their willingness to be obedient to the God of blessing.

It was a new Exodus. A *second* Exodus. It was a freeing of God's people out of the hands of immoral captors...

...And yet the people were once again defiling themselves by bringing in from pagan nations wives who would contaminate the spiritual sanctity of the tribes (see Malachi 2:11; Deuteronomy 7:3–4).

No wonder Ezra had such a reaction to this news.

He wrote, "And when I heard this thing, I rent [tore] my garment and my mantle [cloak], and plucked off the hair of my head and of my beard, and sat down astonied [astonished]" (9:3). At that evening's sacrifice (9:4), Ezra was surrounded by those who were trembling at the thought of God's wrath as a result of the returned exiles' intermarital conduct. He appeared before them just as verse 9:3 states, in a state of total mourning with clothes torn and hair missing from his head and beard (9:5). Though the sin was not his to account for, he prayed as if it was, feeling personally ashamed for the sins of his brothers. His prayer (9:6–15) began with the words, "Oh my God, I am ashamed, and blush to lift up my face to thee, my God: for our iniquities are increased over our head, and our trespass is grown up unto the heavens." He went on to acknowledge the desperation of men like himself who mourn the consequence of past error and the opportunity of his lifetime, begging for another chance at purity. The following excerpt is a little lengthier than ones we've included elsewhere, but we're providing it in full so we can reflect upon the potency of his humility and passion:

Since the days of our fathers have we been in a great trespass unto this day; and for our iniquities have we, our kings, and our priests, been delivered into the hand of the kings of the lands, to the sword, to captivity, and to a spoil, and to confusion of face, as it is this day. And now for a little space grace hath been shewed from the Lord our God, to leave us a remnant to escape, and to give us a nail in his holy place, that our God may lighten our eyes, and give us a little reviving in our bondage. For we were bondmen; yet our God hath not forsaken us in our bondage, but hath extended mercy unto us in the sight of the kings of Persia, to give us a reviving, to set up the house of our God, and to repair the desolations thereof, and to give us a wall in Judah and in Jerusalem. And now, O our God, what shall we say after this? for we have forsaken thy commandments, Which thou hast commanded by thy servants the prophets, saying, "The land, unto which ye go to possess it, is an unclean land with the filthiness of the people of the lands, with their abominations, which have filled it from one end to another with their uncleanness." Now therefore give not your daughters unto their sons, neither take their daughters unto your sons, nor seek their peace or their wealth for ever: that ye may be strong, and eat the good of the land, and leave it for an inheritance to your children for ever. And after all that is come upon us for our evil deeds, and for our great trespass, seeing that thou our God hast punished us less than our iniquities deserve, and hast given us such deliverance as this; Should we again break thy commandments, and join in affinity with the people of these abominations? wouldest not thou be angry with us till thou hadst consumed us, so that there should be no remnant nor escaping? O Lord God of

Israel, thou art righteous: for we remain yet escaped, as it is this day: behold, we are before thee in our trespasses: for we cannot stand before thee because of this. (7:15)

Such a meek and unpretentious prayer grabbed the attention of the listeners in Ezra's gathering. Again, though he wasn't personally accountable for the sins that had been committed, he grieved deeply for those who were guilty—those who, despite the warnings, could not personally know the consequences of their choices like their ancestors did. He was not seeking forgiveness and redemption for himself, but for sinful people who couldn't possible know what they were doing.

In essence, he prayed that Yahweh would forgive them, because they knew not the full repercussions of what they were doing.

Sound familiar (Luke 23:34)?

As a result of this powerful and persuasive entreaty before God, Israelites from all over Israel came to join Ezra in a grand, corporate display of bitter weeping and confession. Men, women, and children joined in a mass recognition of their transgressions against God, earnestly pleading that the Lord would forgive them and still honor this chance they had been given to rebuild their nation under God, even though they could never deserve or earn such grace. The immediate response of the Jews after such a grand gesture was the purging of sin from their midst, rededication to God, religious reform, and a massive revival that would far exceed many of the grandest revivals of modern history...

But before we focus on that detail, let's see what happens next.

The story of Nehemiah takes place in the same era as Ezra's—a mere thirteen or so years after Ezra resumed construction of the Temple. Like Ezra, the book of Nehemiah is an account of God's faithfulness to keep His promises despite the unfaithfulness of His people who repeatedly cave to weaknesses. Unlike Ezra, however, Nehemiah is governor of Jerusalem—not a scribe—and his goal is to see the wall around Jerusalem rebuilt. Here's a brief overview of this short book:

When Nehemiah, a former cupbearer to the king of Persia, received word that the gates of Jerusalem had been destroyed, he couldn't shake the sadness. In the presence of the king and queen, his countenance fell, and the king was stirred to help him, granting him all the goods and supplies he would need to rebuild the wall around Jerusalem. When he arrived at the city, he, like Ezra, saw trouble in paradise; once again, as the Jews engaged in construction, the enemies from neighboring territories attempted to sabotage their progress (Nehemiah 1–2). The work ensued, and enemies mocked their efforts, saying even the work of a fox would crumble what they'd built. But the Jews remained steadfast; the wall's height continued to increase as Nehemiah positioned guards to watch over the progress (3–4). Nehemiah's enemies were relentless, sending threats and letters involving a fabricated plan of a Jewish revolt against Israel's neighbors in an attempt to pull him from the wall-building project, but Nehemiah refused to be swayed by their pathetic attempts to distract him, and the wall was completed (6).

Following this, Nehemiah positioned holy men of God as fellow governors over Jerusalem. A registry was established to determine the number of families that had returned from the exiles and give leaders an idea of how the people were to settle within the districts of the city on a more permanent basis (7).

Ezra reentered the story in the beginning of Nehemiah chapter 8. He led all of Jerusalem together, gathered as "one man" (8:1), into worship of Yahweh. Nehemiah declared the day as holy and instructed them all to eat and drink, and then Ezra told them to celebrate the Feast of Booths (a feast that had not been observed since the time of Joshua), and as they did so, there was rejoicing throughout all of Jerusalem (8:13–18). After this, the Levites led Jerusalem held a mass confession in Jerusalem. They retold a shortened version of the

Exodus, revisited the past sin of the people, resealed the Covenant in writing, and detailed for those gathered what offerings were due God (9–10). Chapters 11–12:1–26 include a catalogue of the names of the leaders, priests, and Levites of Israel, as well as the remaining Israelites.

Then we approach the climax of Nehemiah: the dedication of the newly rebuilt wall (12:27–43). Musicians brought instruments and all the singers in Israel joined to form massive choirs that sang out great praises so that the celebration and thanksgiving in Jerusalem could be heard for miles around. The servants of the Temple were also established (44–47). The final reforms of Nehemiah are captured in this book's last chapter, including the separation from pagans (13:1–3).

However, a critical detail comes next: While Nehemiah was away, having returned to the king of Persia to resume his duties as promised (13:6), Eliashib allowed a member of the high priestly family to marry a daughter of one of the primary foreign enemies who had tried to sabotage the Jewish builders, and the result was another mixed marriage. Eliashib even gave Tobiah, the husband of this pagan daughter, one of the sanctified, holy chambers of the Temple to live in (13:4–5). Watch how Nehemiah handles this contamination: "And it grieved me sore: therefore I cast forth all the household stuff to Tobiah out of the chamber. Then I commanded, and they cleansed the chambers: and thither brought I again the vessels of the house of God, with the meat offering and the frankincense" (13:8–9).

Let's look at these same verses in the ESV to see if we can hone in on a parallel here:

And I was very angry, and I threw all the household furniture of Tobiah out of the chamber. Then I gave orders, and they cleansed the chambers, and I brought back there the vessels of the house of God, with the grain offering and the frankincense.

Sound like anyone you know? Compare:

And they come to Jerusalem: and Jesus went into the temple, and began to cast out them that sold and bought in the temple, and overthrew the tables of the moneychangers, and the seats of them that sold doves; And he taught, saying unto them, "Is it not written, My house shall be called of all nations the house of prayer? but ye have made it a den of thieves." (Mark 11:15, 17)

The rest of Nehemiah 13 tells that the discovery that the monies due the Levites for their Temple services was not being distributed, and new treasurers were appointed (10–14); people were profaning the Sabbath by working, so Nehemiah had the gates closed and set up guards to ensure no trade would take place on that day(15–22); children of foreign wives in their midst could not speak Hebrew (they spoke the language surrounding Philistine cities), so Nehemiah chased them all away for defiling the covenant of the priesthood and "cleansed...them from all [pagans], and appointed the wards of the priests and the Levites" (23–30). His last statement in the book is "Remember me, O my God, for good" (31).

Two characters, two types of Christ, two books, *one* story...

In Ezra's *character*, we see a vivid type of Christ: Ezra had done nothing wrong, but interceded for the sake of his brothers' and sisters' chance at new life. Paul wrote that Christ intercedes for us in our transgression (Romans 8:34), and there is none holier to act on our behalf.

In Ezra's *story*, we see God's plan of redemption; we view a future promise of a fresh and permanent Exodus: a way back to purity, an escape from oppression no matter the vices that bind. Only in accepting the gift of Christ's sacrifice are we free—and immediately so—from the sin we heap upon ourselves under the depravities of immoral choice.

And in Ezra's *office*, we see a scribe: a man so dedicated to the Word of Yahweh that he dedicated his entire life to learning to discern whether the Israelites' actions were within our outside of God's will. Ezra knew the Law of God (7:10) and the consequences of disregarding it (9:3). No man knew this like Jesus did (John 17). (Likewise, anyone who knew the Scriptures should recognize that they all point to Jesus [John 5:39].)

Most importantly, Ezra brought reform and revival.

Nowhere else in Scripture—nor in the history of the planet—has anyone shown up to offer up their very life for the cause of God more than Christ, Himself. Since Jesus came, died, resurrected, and ascended to the right hand of the Father, the entire globe has been affected by His sacrifice and dedication in irreversible ways. Though there are occasions to weep for the immorality of our culture, there will always be plenty more occasion to cry for joy because of the Gospel message that prevails over all wickedness among men. Before Christ brought the spiritual "New Exodus" in His time, people were under the Law and ministry of condemnation, despite its glorious nature. But "if the ministry of condemnation *be* glory, much more doth the ministry of righteousness exceed in glory" (2 Corinthians 3:9)! Paul's words remind us that if the *Old Testament* path to salvation was glorious—and it was—how much more exceedingly glorious this "New Exodus" would be under the grace of the cross! Jesus brought not only reform, but a new path to God, unhindered by many of the strict regulations in the Mosaic Law. He went to the cross for *our* benefit and intercedes for us now at the right hand of the Father for *our* benefit!

Like Ezra, Jesus knows the will of the Father because of the endless hours of time He spent in His presence in solitude and prayer (John 17; Matthew 4:1–2; 14:23; 26:36–46; Mark 1:35; 6:46; 14:32–42; Luke 3:21; 5:16; 6:12; 9:18; 22:39–46).

Jesus is our Scribe!

And because He was perfect (Hebrews 4:15; 5:9), He is the supreme interpreter of the will of God. In Him, we have a spiritual pathway away from captors and into the liberty and freedom of the Master!

We are all called to be scribes—to study and rightfully divide the Word of God to show ourselves approved (2 Timothy 2:15). But now, unlike the ancients who floundered in Babylon awaiting a new era when God's promises would be fulfilled, we have the fulfillment of *all* of God's promises within Israel's history in Jesus.

In Nehemiah, the type of Christ is easier to see on an immediate level. Not only did He bring reform (which Christ did, in spades!), he cleansed the Temple!

Prior to the New Covenant in Jesus, the Temple was the only House of God, and Jerusalem was the only City of God. This is why the Jews don't still practice animal sacrifice today. Without a Temple (because it was destroyed again after the days of Ezra and Nehemiah), there is no altar upon which to offer sacrifices. We will visit the idea of the internal "New Temple" (us) at more length in subsequent sections, it's important to understand the weight of Nehemiah's actions in cleansing Jerusalem. He wasn't simply following the rules. Nehemiah knew, as did Ezra, because of the endless cycles of wrath and blessing, that the Lord God of Israel would not bless and sanctify a people who defiled the Temple or His city by disregarding the Law He had put in place through Moses to keep His land holy and separate from foreign religions. In addition to the mountain of Old Testament Scripture that addresses this reality, a couple of New Testament verses, as spoken by Jesus and later as written by Paul, help us understand this today:

And Jesus knew their thoughts, and said unto them, "Every kingdom divided against itself is brought to desolation; and every city or house divided against itself shall not stand." (Matthew 12:25)

Ye cannot drink the cup of the Lord, and the cup of devils: ye cannot be partakers of the Lord's table, and of the table of devils. (1 Corinthians 10:21)

In former books, Donna Howell has discussed the difference between societal pluralism and societal syncretism. Pluralism, as it refers to religion in modern society, is the ideal that says a Jew can live next door to a Buddhist, who can live next door to a Hindu, who can live next door to a Christian, and so on, and no one is forced to worship in the same way as another. Syncretism, on the other hand, represents the blending of two religions into *one*, creating a sort of "hybrid" belief system that is no single religion at all. In essence, it places a theological "they don't even know *what* they believe" stamp on their spiritual life. Jesus is seen as only one of many gods one must follow. In no way can this please God, as the Bible in its entirety makes clear. When these two concepts are kept strictly separate, pluralism does not innately anger God in modern times, because He understands that, via the New Covenant, all people must work out their own salvation with fear and trembling (Philippians 2:12), learning to go to Him on their own, not having to be prompted by a culture established by forefathers. Likewise, we are no longer in the days when the holy bloodline of Israel needed to remain pure from in order to establish the House of God, because the Temple is now internal. However, there is a major push today to mesh the concepts of societal pluralism and syncretism into one, forming the very kind of one-world religion that plays into our eschatology (the study of the end times).

As you can see by the study of Ezra and Nehemiah regarding those who would willingly corrupt the nation of God by marrying into pagan cultures and worshipping both Yahweh *and* foreign gods, this agenda of syncretism has always been present both within the great enemy's plot to contaminate God's people as well as in the temptation of the flesh. Ezra and Nehemiah recognized, well before the words of Christ were spoken, that "a kingdom divided against itself will fall," as the cyclic history of Israel proves.

Nehemiah not only cleansed the Temple in his time, he did it exactly as Christ did: with righteous anger and the overturning of furniture. He knew we "cannot drink from the cup of the Lord at the same time that we partake of the cup of demons." We cannot pollute the precious Commandments stating that we're not to worship false gods or make tribute to them in any way (including the construction of idols; see Exodus 20:3–4). The intense implications behind his cleansing of the Temple was therefore as present in his time as it is today. Israel should have known by then that they were not facing a mere hand-slapping, but a sentence of mass oppression (and possibly exile) for multiple generations if they didn't keep the Law.

Today, adhering to biblical directives can still affect the blessing of God upon our children (who typically follow in the footsteps of those who raise them), but thanks to the sacrifice of our Lord and Christ, salvation and blessing from God has become a matter of personal conviction, no matter what culture or family a believer is a part of. Jesus "reformed" it all by His First Coming. Nevertheless, the pattern in the Old Testament by strict observers of the Law, like Nehemiah, set a standard of behavior for us to keep. If we do, then we demonstrate that we are "of the faith," not "of the world," and we will be recognized for resisting the temptations of syncretism in the final Day of Judgment. We will have partaken in the "New Exodus," following the path that frees us from the captivity of the enemy and propelling us into all liberty in Christ.

There are more parallels that aren't as obvious at first glance:

- Nehemiah was a cupbearer, a position that placed him literally "at the right hand" of the king to perform his duty of tasting the king's drinks (thus "cup") to ensure the king was not being poisoned. Had the king of Persia's drink been poisoned, Nehemiah would have consumed it instead of the king—a job that was quite unsettling and laden with risk. In the Garden of Gethsemane, Jesus noted He would rather not drink the "cup of poison" (His crucifixion) for His King and Father, but He did so, obediently (Matthew 26:39). After this, He ascended to "the right hand of the Father" (Acts 7:55–56). Additionally, as Nehemiah was willing to leave his position beside the king to see to the righteousness and inheritance of his people, Jesus was willing to leave his position at the right hand of the Father to see to the righteousness and inheritance of *all* people when he condescended His divinity and became human.

- Both Nehemiah and Christ wept over the state of Jerusalem (Nehemiah 1:3–4; Luke 19:41–42).
- Nehemiah reestablished the Old Covenant (Nehemiah 8:1–9; 9:13); Jesus established the New Covenant.
- There was a "second coming" of Nehemiah to Israel (Nehemiah 13:9–9); there will be a Second Coming of Jesus (Matthew 24:44; Zechariah 13:1; 14:1–4; and too many other verses to list here, but see our study of Revelation).
- Nehemiah saw to the restoration of the priesthood, the Temple, and the Sabbath (Nehemiah 13:10–11, 22); Jesus, in the New Advent, will see to the restoration of the same list (Ezekiel 40–47; Isaiah 2:1–4, 11:1–10, 66:17–25).

As Nehemiah rebuilt the wall around the City of God to separate the Jews from the evils of the pagan world, Jesus rebuilt the faith, establishing a new order for those of us who would separate ourselves and our families from the same thing.

The Son of God was, is, and always will be the absolute Nehemiah, the Builder of the partition between us and the world—that temporal place we are "in," but should not be "of":

And now I am no more in the world, but these are in the world, and I come to thee. Holy Father, keep through thine own name those whom thou hast given me, that they may be one, as we are… I have given them thy word; and the world hath hated them, because they are not of the world, even as I am not of the world. I pray not that thou shouldest take them out of the world, but that thou shouldest keep them from the evil. (John 17:11, 14–15)

We are called to draw strict lines and boundaries around our lives today, ensuring that we don't, like the Israelites, pollute ourselves, our "temples," and our families with the demonic influences of this world. But praise Jesus that we no longer must, like Nehemiah, draw strict lines around our cities to preserve the sanctity of a holy race. This was done for the sake of a new order, a New Covenant, a contract written and signed in the blood of the Lamb, that frees us from the old order of condemnation (2 Corinthians 3:9)!

What a mighty God we serve, indeed. His mercies *do* endure forever (Psalm 118; 136). His love never ceases, and just as we begin to believe we have done too much sinning to "earn" or "deserve" His grace, we are reminded once again that the God of multiple exoduses renews His love and mercy for us "every morning" (Lamentations 3:22–23)!

Without the love and mercy of God, the Israelites would have perished and the Old Testament would have ended in Genesis. Without the love and mercy of *this same God* and His Son today, we, too, would perish—both physically and spiritually. As we stated at the end of our study on Ruth, we would be left to wander "the damned corners of the earth, belonging to no one other than the prince of the power of the air and awaiting death and judgment." But because of the example set by men like Ezra and Nehemiah who plunged sin from the depths of the ancients—and because of the New Testament type found in Christ—we are given the knowledge of what we must refrain from, as well as the freedom to do so.

It's a pop-culture idea today to see God as angry, faraway, disconnected from His people, and unmerciful to those who struggle with sin. But to the believer of the Bible, there really is *no end to His mercy*!

If that doesn't inspire a hearty "Praise the Lord and Amen!" from God's people, these authors don't know what would.

Esther

THE SETTING FOR THE BOOK OF ESTHER is about a hundred years after the peak of the Babylonian Exile events. As stated at the beginning of our study of Ezra and Nehemiah, not all Jews returned to Jerusalem, as they had lives established elsewhere as a result of numerous generations growing up in captivity. Such is the case for the Jewish community in Susa (pronounced "suza," or Hebrew, *Shushan*), which was the capital of the Persian Empire. Not all the books in most versions of the Bible are arranged in chronological order; if they were, the book of Esther would be situated with or between Ezra and Nehemiah. Because this book's nod to Christ involves understanding the storyline, we'll begin with a summary of its the plot.

The book opens with a description of the reign of King Ahasuerus. (Some translations refer to him as King Xerxes, the Persian equivalent.) Ahasuerus was what we would call today ridiculously wealthy. Esther 1:1–9 describes a ginormous feast the king gave for the duration of 180 days for "all his princes and his servants; the power of Persia and Media, the nobles and princes of the provinces," followed by a second feast that lasted seven days "unto all the people that were present in Susa the palace, both unto great and small, seven days, in the court of the garden of the king's palace." It was quite a spectacle, to be sure; it included the display of grand curtains, marble pillars, couches of silver and gold, all sitting upon a pavement made of marble and precious stones. All of the guests had as much wine as they could drink, and it was served in goblets of gold. On the last day of the second feast, the king called his servants to summon his wife, Queen Vashti, so he could show off her beauty. She refused, prompting one of the king's men to see her insubordination as a bad example that would be followed by all women in the kingdom. Angered, King Ahasuerus wrote a new law "that every man should bear rule in his own house" (1:22). Ahasuerus then decided that Vashti, because of her defiance, would be replaced.

What happens next resembles a sort of Cinderella story, in which all the single women of the land were called to assemble in the citadel where Ahasuerus could choose a new bride and queen. Mordecai, a Jew living nearby who was a few generations removed from the Babylonian Exile, had raised Esther (also called by the Hebrew name "Hadassah"), his orphaned niece. Before Esther went to the palace, Mordecai had instructed her not to tell anyone she was a Jew. (This may have been due, in part, to the slanderous letters sent from surrounding towns and cities by the enemies of Ezra discussed in the last section. Ahasuerus may have been influenced by these reports thus was less inclined to take a Jewish woman.)

So, keeping her nationality a secret, she impressed Ahasuerus, who quickly chose her to become queen. However, outside of the designated times she was escorted to see the king, she wasn't allowed to visit him—unless she was summoned specifically by name. (This is a crucial detail.) Meanwhile, Mordecai chose to spend most of his time at the king's gate in order to keep an eye on Esther.

At this early point of the narrative, Mordecai overheard two of the palace guards discussing a plot to kill the king. Mordecai told Esther what he had heard, and Esther reported it during a personal visit with

Ahasuerus, who launched an investigation and, upon discovering the plot to be true, had the guards hanged (2:21–23). Mordecai was credited for saving the king.

Afterward (and for reasons evidently unrelated to the assassination plot), Haman, the story's villain, was promoted to Ahasuerus' right hand (3:1). The king ordered his servants, and those present at his gate, to bow to Haman and pay him homage. Mordecai repeatedly refused to do this because he was Jewish and therefore would not bow to anyone other than Yahweh. This angered Haman, who told King Ahasuerus that the Jews of the kingdom had their own Law and would not respect the laws passed by Ahasuerus. The Jews, therefore, Haman decided, were of no profit to the king to keep around. Without considering the long-term ramifications of his decision, Ahasuerus agreed to Haman's plan to kill all Jews on the thirteenth day of the month of Adar, a date (about the time of March on our Gregorian calendar) that was decided by the casting of lots (similar to rolling dice). King Ahasuerus and Haman then sat down to drinks in celebration of this plan. The city, however, was understandably thrown into a state of mass confusion and panic at this impulsive decree (3:15).

When Esther discovered her new husband's intent to kill her people, she agreed to plead with the king on their behalf. The law stated she would be put to death if she approached the king without summons, unless he showed her the sign of approval and acceptance by holding out his golden scepter at her approach. So Esther sent word through Mordecai to have all the Jews in Susa fast and pray for three days. One of the most well-known lines in this book is in her message to Mordecai, regarding her own fate should she not receive permission to approach the king: "So will I go in unto the king, which is not according to the law: and if I perish, I perish" (4:16).

After the fasting period, Queen Esther, no doubt nervously anticipating that the king's would a death sentence upon her after seeing his response to Vashti's insolence, arrived at the inner court just as the king was sitting down on his throne. The king surprised her by immediately waving his scepter toward her; she responded by touching its tip (5:1–2). Ahasuerus was so taken with her that, even before she spoke, he promised he would give her anything she wanted—up to half his kingdom. All she asked was for the privilege of the king and Haman's company for dinner. They attended as she requested, and the king again offered to give her whatever she wished up to half the kingdom (5:3–6). She requested that Ahasuerus and Haman join her for yet another dinner, after which, she said, she would present the king with her humble request (5:7–8).

Between the two meals with Esther, Haman made another one of his trips to the king's gate, expecting all to bow to him. When Mordecai again refused, Haman left in fury and told his wife and friends about the offense, bragging about his position in the kingdom and noting that he was so powerful that he was the only official invited to the queen's dinner besides Ahasuerus. Yet none of this meant anything to him as long as he had to continue putting up with Mordecai's refusal to bow. The idea to hang Mordecai was presented to Haman, and he agreed, placing the orders for Mordecai's gallows to be erected (5:9–14; 6:9).

That night, King Ahasuerus couldn't sleep. He ordered the records of his kingdom to be brought and read to him, which, among other things, recalled the event when Mordecai had saved his life by exposing the assassination plot of the palace guards. Ahasuerus asked if any official gesture of gratitude had been bestowed on Mordecai to thank him for his timely intervention, and upon discovering his deed had been overlooked, the king called for Haman and asked what should be done for the man "in whom the king delights" (6:1–6). Haman, believing Ahasuerus was referring to himself with this query, said the man should be dressed in the king's clothing, placed on the king's horse, adorned with a royal crown, and paraded throughout the streets of the city while an entourage proclaimed, "Thus shall it be done to the man whom the king delighteth to honour" (6:7–9).

Ahasuerus agreed to the plan and, to Haman's chagrin, instructed Haman to do all he had suggested for the other man: Mordecai, the

Jew who sat at the king's gate. Haman did as he was ordered, but quickly thereafter went home to mourn the event, whining about the ordeal to his friends and wife. Instead of coming up with another plan for murdering Mordecai, Haman's associates acknowledged that Mordecai was the beginning of Haman's downfall. Before they were finished speaking, Haman was invited to attend Esther's second dinner, to which he hurried to attend (6:11–13).

Once again, for yet a third time now, Ahasuerus promised Esther she could have anything her heart desired, up to half the kingdom. Without initially offering details, she told her husband of one man's plan to annihilate both her and her people. Her request, then, had nothing to do with the royal property, riches, cosmetics, or any personal gain. Her heart's desire was for nothing than to see her own life spared. The king, enraged, asked who would be audacious enough to strategize such an evil against the queen of Persia. "And Esther said, 'The adversary and enemy is this wicked Haman'" (7:1–6).

In an act of unmatched irony, King Ahasuerus had Haman hung on the gallows that had been prepared for Mordecai; only then did his wrath subside (7:9–10). The king gave Haman's house and the king's own signet ring to Mordecai. However, a law in Persia, once decreed by the king and sealed with his ring, cannot be revoked by anyone, royal or otherwise, so the king could not go back on his earlier order to put the Jews to death.

Mordecai wisely thought of a plan, and sent out an edict—sealed with the signet—that the Jews would be allowed to defend themselves by any means necessary on the day of their attack. All the Jews in the kingdom prepared for an extensive battle. When the attack was launched, Mordecai's fame had spread. The confidence of the Jews had increased while the confidence of the royal army had dwindled. So, on the thirteenth day of Adar, "the officials of the provinces and the satraps and the governors and the royal agents also helped the Jews" in the fight (9:3). The people of God were victorious in their mass self-defense (8:1–9:18).

The following day, the fourteenth of Adar, became the day of a great feast and gift-exchanging for the Jews in the kingdom of Ahasuerus (9:19). This is the story of how the Feast of Purim got its start. (The term *pur* means "dice" and refers to the casting of lots—the method by which Haman first settled on the thirteenth of Adar as the day all Jews would die.)

Esther...what a brave soul! A Jewish girl, robbed of her parents through death and raised by another, desperate to simply survive surrounded by people who didn't know her God or her ways of life, was suddenly whisked into an opulent palace and made part of the royal family. And, once she was placed in a position in which she should have been second in command over the whole kingdom, her life was threatened by cronies of the court. In the end, a mere orphan saved a nation otherwise doomed to genocide. If Haman's wicked plan had been carried out to the fullest, the political link between Persia and the Jews rebuilding in Jerusalem would have likely fallen as well, leading to an eventual Hitler-like holocaust for Jews who had returned from exile. At that time, such an act of wickedness could have prevented the eventual birth of the Messiah.

Yet, while this was happening in the city of Susa, God was not only watching over and guiding the sweet queen and defender of the Jews, He was hatching a longer-term plan of His own that He would carry out through the bloodline of those He already knew would remain...

It's not difficult to see Jesus in this story. Esther was more than willing to die for the sake of her peoples' salvation. In choosing to be bold and enter the throne room of the king, Esther not only delivered her people by acting as a mediator, she also inspired confidence and faith in the Jews. All of the Old Testament points to a day when another Jew, a Man from Galilee who has access to the throne room of the Father King (Hebrews 1:3, 12:2; 1 Peter 3:22; Acts 7:55-56), would become the savior, mediator, and deliverer of God's people (Luke 24:27, 44; John 5:39, 46). He would offer Himself as well, submitting His very life to the cup of poison that would be the crucifixion, saying to the Father, "not my will but yours be done," echoing the striking dedication of Esther toward God and her people: "If I perish, I perish." Esther is a type of Christ for many reasons:

- Her willingness to be put to the sword and die for the cause, the very queen of the land, as Christ is King.
- Her life was one of humble origins and she was later crowned royalty; this brings to mind our Lord and Savior, who had a humble upbringing, but who would someday be viewed as the King of all kings.
- Esther was the advocate for the Jews, and Jesus is the advocate for sinners everywhere (1 John 2:1).
- Esther was called "for such a time as this," the precise time in the history of the Jews' powerless life in Persia to reap the greatest harvest in their salvation (Esther 4:14); Jesus came at the precise time in Israel's history to reap the greatest harvest in the salvation of both powerless Jews and Gentiles (Romans 5:6; Galatians 4:4).
- While Esther knew it would be impossible to go against her enemies without fasting and prayer (4:16), Jesus relied on His oneness with the Father (John 17), fasting and praying for success in His ministry against the enemy (Matthew 4:1–11; Luke 4:2).
- Esther's miracle came in three days; Jesus' resurrection came in three days.
- Esther kept her true *Jewish* identity a secret until the timing was right for her grand plan; Jesus kept His true *messianic* identity a secret until the timing was right for His plan, at the start of His ministry (John 4:3–42).
- When folks followed Esther's words, it resulted in a feast; when folks follow Jesus' words, it results in a feast (Revelation 19:6–9).

Mordecai is a type of Christ in some ways, also. He saw an orphan girl without a family and took her in, providing her a father. Jesus, too, as the Way, the Truth, and the Life, will take in any wandering soul; in Him a Father is provided to the fatherless (John 14:6). Other ways Mordecai's life is a type of Christ include:

- Mordecai was Esther's kinsman redeemer, and, as discussed in our study of Ruth, Jesus is ours (Revelation 5:5–10).
- Mordecai took care of Esther's debts and cared for her; Jesus took us into the family of God, caring for us spiritual orphans in the same way (Ephesians 1:7).
- Mordecai was hated by worldly authorities whom he wasn't afraid to oppose; Jesus was hated for the same reason (John 15:18).
- Mordecai rode through town triumphantly as the king's prized servant; Jesus rode into Jerusalem in His Triumphal Entry as the Father King's prized Servant (John 12:1, 12).
- Because of his choice to commit to the will of the king, all power and authority of Persia was given to Mordecai, who received the signet seal of the king and could therefore speak on the king's behalf; because of His choice to commit Himself to the will of the Father King, all power and authority over heaven and earth was given to Jesus, who can speak on the Father's behalf (Matthew 28:18).
- As Mordecai sent messengers with the good news that the people could be saved through self-defense and faith in God (Esther 9:20–32), Jesus sends messengers with the Good News that people can be saved through faith (Matthew 28:19–20).

The list of parallels between Esther and Mordecai with Christ is long, but we'll stop here, and wrap up with these words:

Jesus is "seen" throughout the Old Testament in the obedient characters of God. Unlike so many who have sinned against God and failed in their calling, Jesus is the absolute example of obedience to the Father, in whose Kingdom believers are welcome, regardless of failure. The grace of God and His interest in His people—*us*—just

never, never, *never* stops. Scripture makes it clear: From the beginning, we've always had a Redeemer—timelessly so, though our linear
perceptions often place Christ in the "waiting room," "stuck" in the
Old Covenant of Israel's history.

This brings us to a final thought: The book of Esther is the last of
the history books. From the beginning of this study until now, we've
been reflecting on the narrative of how God's covenant people were
developed, the mistakes they made, the miracles they witnessed, and
the typology of Jesus in their passages. Now we'll turn in another
direction to see where we can find Christ in what scholars refer to as
the Wisdom literature of Scripture.

Wisdom Literature

THE BOOKS INCLUDED in the "Wisdom" section of Scripture are Job, Psalms, Proverbs, Ecclesiastes, and Song of Solomon. They're in a category of literature that's shared with a few extrabiblical/apocryphal books (such as Sirach and Wisdom of Solomon), grouped as material ancient Israel looked to for answers to the questions of daily life. They don't fit into the categories of the Law, history, the prophets (major or minor), or any other Old Testament theme. Nor do they overemphasize the transcendent, spiritual, and theological principles of God like the didactic— or "teaching"—books (Epistles) of the New Testament...at least not intentionally. Because their central purpose is to explore the interaction between God and man in light of human emotions, decision-making, and the pursuit of a good life, they sometimes resemble the Epistles, though they differ in their approach by not specifically addressing the arrival of the long-awaited Messiah (who became "the" answer to every question thereafter). Nor do they focus on a main character at any point (with the exception of Job, discussed first in the following pages), so their typology depends on a different, higher perspective. Additionally, they tend to mesh many of their conclusions together, as well as provide accounts of the unique journey each writer took to make those conclusions. So, because every Wisdom book tends to sharply contrast books in the rest of Scripture, they belong together in one study.

Remember as you read along that the historical context of the word "sage" refers to the wise men throughout Israel's history that deeply studied the texts of the Hebrew Scriptures (the Old Testament before it was canonized with the New Testament). Jesus, Himself, was the greatest Sage, having become the Rabbi He was as a result of His studies of these Wisdom writings while He walked the earth. While He lived in human form, He was opposed by men who believed themselves to be Jewish sages (like the Pharisees). These "wise men" challenged Christ repeatedly in the attempt to stump Him or put Him down in front of a crowd, yet His answers were always unbeatable, putting His agitators back in their place and reasserting Himself as the all-knowing Son of God. So, as modern readers take in the words of the ancients, we need remember that Jesus was familiar with these books, too, and He knew very well not only what they *said*, but their *intent* as well—in context of their culture, background, original audience, and the rest of Scripture. That said, Jesus would have known when one of the Wisdom writers was speaking of the Messiah in the original texts. Some of these references are astonishing, especially one made by a man in what is widely considered the oldest book of the Bible.

Job

As noted, the book of Job (pronounced "jobe") is unlike the other Wisdom books in that it provides a bit of a storyline and a main character who, in many aspects, belongs in a category all his own. Yet, because he ultimately visits questions exactly like, or strikingly similar to, those of his Wisdom-literature-writing counterparts, his book accomplishes the same goal. Let's dig a little deeper to explain what we mean.

Most people know about Job. He was the guy who had it rough; he was tested by God, lost everything, and only gained it back through what must have felt like nearly endless faith in the face of disastrous solitude and trials. From time immemorial, those experiencing their own seasons of loss have dropped his name as the one who had it worse. And that's not an irresponsible conclusion. Job faced misery most of us will never know in our lifetimes (and hopefully will never know in the next).

After reading that Job is a godly man who loved and cared for his family (Job 1:1–5), we read about a bizarre scene that takes place in heaven, wherein God is approached by Satan.

Many questions arise as to whether this is the same Satan who appears in the New Testament, the one who has unequivocally been God's enemy since the time of his fall from heaven. Until we can stand at the throne of God and ask that question, we may never know for certain, as even the brightest scholars in the world do not agree. There is good reason for this. Apart from being a name, the Hebrew word *satan* also means generically "adversary." But not every "adversary" in the Hebrew Bible was a bad guy. For instance, when studying Old Testament Christophanies, Numbers 22:22 (in the account of Balaam's donkey) comes into the picture quite regularly. The text, in English, states: "And God's anger was kindled because he went: and the angel of the Lord stood in the way for an adversary against him." This "Angel of the Lord" is, many scholars teach (as we noted near the beginning of this book), Jesus, Himself, in His eternal nature prior to the Incarnation. In close proximity, even the English makes it clear this angel is sent by the Father to intervene in an act of evil. Therefore, this character cannot be the same "Satan" that appears as the enemy of God in the New Testament. However, the "adversary" in Numbers 22:22 is, in fact, the Hebrew word *satan*. This angel (or Angel) may have been an "enemy" or "adversary" in his opposition to Balaam or his donkey, but his purpose was to accomplish a righteous task for God, negating the idea that every time *satan* appears in Hebrew, it's

one of the "bad guys." (Many other examples of this same transla-
tional code appear when bringing the Hebrew language into words
we can understand.)

So, back to our question: Is this being in Job the enemy of God
or a mere messenger? Many believe he is *not* the enemy of God, but
rather just another angel. Their reasoning is, briefly, that personal
names in Hebrew usually don't involve the definite article *ha* (Hebrew,
"the") before them. In the Old Testament, this almost always suggests
a title—even a temporary or circumstantial one, just as the "angel" in
Numbers opposed wickedness, not God, and wouldn't otherwise have
been referred to as an "adversary" in every case. There is also no lingual
or theological connection between Job's *ha satan* and God's enemy
elsewhere in Scripture (such as the serpent in Genesis 3). Lastly, they
support their case by stating that *ha satan* of Job is provoking a test of
Job's faith, not necessarily performing an act of outright malice (that
would have resulted in God's rebuke anyway).

Yet, many others view the character in the book of Job as the
being the same Satan, the enemy of God. Their arguments are also
logical, though we won't discuss them here. We'll simply leave it to
readers to decide and simply refer to this entity in Job as "the accuser."

The accuser stood before God in heaven, presenting himself as a
servant alongside the other angels and stating that he had been walking about the earth. At this, God brought up His faithful servant,
Job, by asking the accuser if he had yet "considered" him. The accuser
answered that, yes, he had, and he followed up by asking whether
Job's faithfulness to God was born from the correct motive: Did Job
fear God for the right reasons? (Job 1:9). He went on to describe
Job's current blessings: "Hast not thou made an hedge about him,
and about his house, and about all that he hath on every side? thou
hast blessed the work of his hands, and his substance is increased in
the land" (1:10). The question was essentially this: If Job was merely
a pampered follower of God, how could it be known whether his
faith was real, and not just a religious lifestyle based on convenience?

Would Job turn his back on God if he didn't have so much going for him in his life?

From this moment, a barrage of horror befell Job: He lost his servants, livestock, camels, and children. He then rose, tore his robe (an expression of grief), fell back to the ground, and worshipped God, saying: "Naked came I out of my mother's womb, and naked shall I return thither: the Lord gave, and the Lord hath taken away; blessed be the name of the Lord" (1:21).

After this, the scene in heaven occurred again, but this time the accuser wondered if the reason Job remained faithful was because he still had his health. So, God allowed the accuser to put Job to the test again; the next portion of the account describes Job sitting in ashes scratching festering, painful sores with broken bits of pottery. His wife then uttered one of the most often-quoted lines in all of Scripture: "Curse God, and die" (2:9). We love what one commentator has to say about the truth behind this: "Nothing makes the ungodly so angry as to see the godly under trial not angry."[53] But Job dismissed the "advice" of his wife to curse God and die, choosing instead to show he had layers of spiritual depth and maturity in his faithful relationship with Yahweh beyond the disappointment of his expectations and circumstances, saying, "What? shall we receive good at the hand of God, and shall we not receive evil?" (2:10).

This is the point where the gears shift and the trial of Job vs. God begins. Job's friends—Eliphaz, Bildad, and Zophar—sat with him in mourning for seven days before beginning their own investigation into why all of this was happening. Over and over throughout much of the rest of the book, they continued to poke and prod at the idea that Job had done something to deserve all of these troubles.

A central reason this book is considered part of the Wisdom literature and not a narrative or history book is because of its form and content, with its themes of justice and legal terminology. We not only encounter the "trial" theme as it applies to the hardship and tribulation God allows to happen to Job, but we also see "courtroom" imagery as the almost literal framework throughout the whole work. Legal phrasing and terms of justice (introduced in 8:3) either directly mentioned or implied include: Job was put on "trial" by God, so to speak, and was "released" in the end as an "innocent" man. Meanwhile, the debate that raged between Job and his religious-spirited friends strongly resembles the relationship between a defendant and his prosecutor. Job's "crime"—his character—remained in question until he was proven "not guilty" and allowed to resume and rebuild his life.

In these conversations between Job, God, the accuser, and the friends (which could be interchangeably referred to as either "persecutors" or "prosecutors," depending on one's interpretation of the "courtroom framework" here), the emphasis is not on the history of God's covenant promises for Israel, the exile, prophecy, kings and queens, priestly duties, judges, or Law, but upon an individual's account of loss and gain and the wisdom of his faith during the worst of this earthly life. Thus, Job is a Wisdom book instead of a mere narrative, because it offers wisdom to the reader who may feel like Job. One overall, crucially important question that underlines the entire book is this: Does God *really* allow bad things to happen to good, obedient people?

This question is irrefutably the crux of a theological principle called "retributional justice." It draws its root from Deuteronomy 28–29, wherein the Law of God explains that the righteous will be blessed and the wicked will be cursed or punished (cf., Deuteronomy 28:3–4; 28:16–17). This blessing or punishment can come either through a direct act of God's hand, or through a more natural order of the operating world. One theologian refers to this as the "hot" and "cold" system of retribution: In the "hot" system, God is an active agent, seeing to justice personally; in the "cold" system, the righteous or wicked face natural outcomes from good or bad decisions in relationships, business dealings, etc.—a kind of "you reap what you sow" effect.[54] However it comes about, though, this lingering question is one that *all* the Wisdom books address, thus reinforcing the case for

Job's proper placement among the Wisdom literature (despite some storyline).

In the beginning, Job is pronounced blameless and upright (1:1, 8). This is not to suggest he is sinless or perfect like Jesus, but that he has lived his life in accordance to God's will as best as an imperfect human can. In this sense, Job can be viewed already as a type of Christ. Jesus never sinned, even though He faced unfathomable punishment. Using the Christ as our example here, we immediately have at least one answer to Job's question: Yes, God *does* allow the righteous to suffer, often for the sake of their own sacrifice being a blessing or a lesson to God's people from that day forward. In Jesus, we have both the blessing *and* the lesson: 1) His sacrifice brought salvation; 2) His behavior throughout trial set the highest example of faithfulness to the Father during seasons of strife. No matter what Job faces, he, like Jesus, endures.

Many see Job as the prime example of "the patient sufferer." But this popular moniker misses something essential. In order to see him as always being patient, we have to ignore most of what he says in his defense, which frequently includes words of anger, frustration, and even doubt. It's not hard to see that Job's expectation aligned with some in ancient Israel who saw the principle of retributional justice, believing that through his righteousness and obedience he would experience blessings, generally. The argument of his innocence is heavily maintained throughout the work, and not one accusation against him by the accuser or his friends about hidden sin or any other possible cause for suffering is justified or acknowledged by God. In fact, God's comment to Job's friends, who sought to find some blame in Job, was, "My wrath is kindled against thee…for ye have not spoken of me the thing that is right, as my servant Job hath" (42:7). Nevertheless, Job was human, and therefore, he spoke like one who faces the same human emotions anybody in his position would. In the end, though Job is *not* always patient, he *does* always persevere, and that is something we can all learn from him as he is vindicated in the end of the book (something we all hope for during heartache).

Ultimately, then, the conclusion of Job that convicts the reader is not a question of whether God allows bad things to happen to good people, as we know He does, but whether God is sovereign in His decision to allow it. Without the suffering of Christ, we would not have salvation, yet He was the supreme example of "a good person." Without Job in the canon, we may not ever fully comprehend just how intense our responsibility is to acknowledge the sovereignty of God in this area. But because of its inclusion, countless believers now have the most extreme example of the theological exceptions to the principle of retributional justice, and the "happy ending" of his story will never stop inspiring people to keep persevering in the midst of anguish.

But, viewing the Jesus of Job doesn't solely rely on the blameless-ness of the book's central character or on how his undeserved suffering would influence the world. Many interesting parallels illustrate Job as a type of Christ:

- Despite everything, Job never stopped obeying God and trust-ing in His sovereignty and will (13:15), even going as far as to challenge his greatest skeptic with the question, "Shall we receive good at the hand of God, and shall we not receive evil?" (2:10); Christ never stopped obeying God and trusting in His sover-eignty and will (Luke 22:42), even going as far as to challenge the skeptical Peter with the question, "The cup which my Father hath given me, shall I not drink it?" (John 18:11).
- Job treasured the words of God more than his portion of food (23:12); Jesus said that *His* portion of food was to listen to the words of the Father, "to do the will of him that sent me, and to finish his work" (John 4:34).
- Job's friends goaded him to cry out to God for help in his afflic-tion, if he was so pure (5:1); at His death, Jesus was taunted in the same attitude (Matthew 27:43). Both resisted lashing back.

- Job's friends repeatedly failed him; Jesus' disciples abandoned Him to die alone, and His closest apostle denied Him (Matthew 26:69–75).
- Job's suffering was referred to as "labor" (9:29); Jesus' suffering was prophesied to be "labor" (Isaiah 53:11).
- Both Job and Jesus were fully restored (Job 42:10–17; Luke 24; Philippians 2:9–10).

It's a beautiful picture that, if it ended here, would be glorious enough to call for devoting an entire book just to the similarities between the faithful Job and Christ.

However, there is a crucial moment in the tale we can't miss…and it happens to be one that leads straight into the Psalms: In the middle of the "trial," Job longs for his own legal representation—a defense attorney, for lack of a better term—whom Job refers to as an "arbiter" in the ESV translation of 9:33. This is the Hebrew word *mokih*: "For he is not a man, as I am, that I might answer him, that we should come to trial together. There is no arbiter [*mokih*] between us, who might lay his hand on us both."

Francis Anderson of *Job: An Introduction and Commentary* acknowledges that "the Hebrew word *mokih* does not mean a judge, who merely decides who is in the right; he is a mediator who settles the quarrel by reconciliation, a negotiator who brings both parties together, by laying *his hand upon us both* as a common friend."[55] Richard Clifford, scholar and author of *The Wisdom Literature: Interpreting Biblical Texts*, states: "In the ancient world, law was important and a common source of metaphors for describing the relation between the gods and the human world…. To combat his friends and to confront God, Job must use legal language. One aspect of the legal metaphor drives the plot forward…. The mediator someday will appear in court to vindicate him."[56]

This verse is not the only time we read of Job longing for this mediator (cf. 16:19–21; 31:35). Then, in 19:25, Job says something odd, almost prophetic: "For I know that my redeemer liveth, and that he shall stand at the latter day upon the earth."

Wait, what? Surely he couldn't mean…

Actually, he very likely *is* referring to Jesus. The authors of the classic commentary, *Jamieson, Fausset, & Brown*, are among many to make the connection that Job is here referring to the Someday Messiah: "The idea in 'redeemer' with Job is Vindicator…the idea of the predicted Bruiser of the serpent's head. Tradition would inform him of the prediction"—meaning Job would have heard about the Redeemer through Israel's traditional messianic teachings and referenced Him here—"Job's sacrifices imply sense of sin and need of atonement [which comes from] Jesus Christ his Vindicator, the Living One who giveth life."[57] Another classic, *Matthew Henry's*, treats the concept of Job's familiarity with the Someday Messiah as common knowledge, saying, "Here is much of Christ and heaven.… Job was taught of God to believe in a living Redeemer; to look for the resurrection of the dead, and the life of the world to come; he comforted himself with the expectation of these…and expected salvation through him."[58]

Albert Barnes, in his *Barnes' Notes*, was thrilled when he finished his Hebrew study on this Scripture! He shared his enthusiasm in strong words: "**For I know that my Redeemer liveth**—There are few passages in the Bible which have excited more attention than this… [I]t is one of the most valuable of all the testimonials now remaining of the early faith on that subject."[59] Zondervan Press superstar, D. A. Garrett, in the "Poetic and Wisdom Books" section of *Holman Concise Bible Commentary*, notes that "it is pointless to deny that Job looked for a resurrection and a Redeemer. The book, through the sufferings of its hero, points to the two universal human needs: the need for a Deliverer and the need for release from mortality.… These needs, poignantly portrayed in Job, are dramatically fulfilled in the New Testament [in Christ]."[60]

And in case you may be wondering, yes, the Hebrew word for redeemer here *is* the same as the *go'el* of Ruth.

How can we know that Job was referring to the Redeemer, Christ, and not just a redeemer, like a court official?

Countless scholars unite Job's words in 19:25 with 16:19 as a reference to the same entity: "Also now, behold, my witness is in heaven, and my record is on high." What "witness" would be "in heaven" if the redeemer were a mere mortal? *Benson Commentary* asks, and then answers, this question:

> But what Redeemer, and what deliverance, does Job speak of in this and the two following verses? **Answer:** Some late interpreters understand this passage metaphorically [as the present Yahweh, the Father, restoring his life]... But most interpreters, both ancient and modern, understand it of Christ, and of his resurrection, and of Job's resurrection to life by his power and goodness. And this seems most probable, for many reasons: 1st, Because a proper and literal interpretation of any passage of Scripture is always to be preferred before the metaphorical, where it suits with the text and with other passages. 2d, Because the Hebrew word, *go'el,* here used, although sometimes used of God, absolutely or essentially considered, yet most properly agrees to Jesus Christ: for this word is primarily spoken of the next kinsman, whose office it was to redeem, by a price paid, the sold or mortgaged estate of his deceased kinsman... All which most fitly agrees to Christ, who is our nearest kinsman and brother, as having taken our nature upon him, Hebrews 2:11; who hath redeemed that everlasting inheritance which our first parents had utterly lost, by the price of his own blood... [We will skip the highly theological and extensive points 3 and 4 for the sake of space.] 5th, Because this well agrees with several other passages in this book; wherein Job declares that, although he had no hope as to this life, and the comforts thereof, yet he had a hope beyond death, which made him profess, **Though he slay me, yet will I trust in him,** Job 13:15. **Trust in him** for what?

Surely, for comfort and happiness. Where? Not in this life, for that he supposes to be lost; therefore it must have been in the next life [the following verse in sequence, Job 19:26, refers to Job's death. The commentary goes on to list a lengthy argument for how Job, "in those ancient times, and in that dark state of the church, should know these great mysteries of Christ's incarnation," using a compelling scriptural comparison of the teaching of the patriarchs. Then, it says:] therefore, it cannot seem strange that Job professes his faith and hope in these things....

And that he shall stand in the latter day—In the days of the Messiah, or of the gospel, which are often called the latter or last days.[61]

It's nearly unbelievable to think that Job, in such an early era of human history, would come to expect or yearn for a future promise like that which Jesus would provide in the New Testament. Yet that's the interpretation many theologians allow. But even if the writer of Job didn't intend a messianic reference here, it is still prophetic in its hope. How can we say this? Because God wouldn't position Jesus to be the fulfilment of something casual someone said in the Old Testament just to make it link up with something or Someone in the New Testament, especially since a human courtroom "arbiter," "mediator," or "redeemer" could have easily been viewed as the intended meaning here.

It was in God's plan from the beginning, and whether Job (or the writer of Job) knew it or not, the New Testament would make it clear that "there is one God, and one mediator between God and men, the man Christ Jesus" (1 Timothy 2:5).

For Job, this Man was the answer to all of his trials. With all the evidence we've discussed, we can responsibly say Job was able to glimpse the future promise of our Redeemer. He knew he could never adequately defend and free himself without a Deliverer, to whom he looked toward for final rest beyond the grave. He knew that, because this Redeemer lived (Job 19:25), he would one day see God in the flesh (19:26). It was a trust in life beyond death that nobody in Job's time could have imagined unless he was so in tune with the Creator that he was able to perceive—even if not intellectually—eternal salvation through a grand Intercessor and Mediator. Obtaining one who would negotiate on his behalf during this biblical courtroom drama was *everything* to him when his life was in upheaval!

Do you see it? Job "got it," even before there was something to "get," and he believed so wholeheartedly in this hope of the Resurrected Redeemer that when everything else in his trial failed, there was a Protection Service that would whisk him away from his enemies and into the safety and presence of the Holy Father!

In the end, in His majestic and long-awaited response to Job, God asked who laid the foundational cornerstone of the world (38:6). In biblical context, a cornerstone is the rock upon which the entire foundation of a structure rests. Job admitted he had no answer to this, and conceded to put his hand over his mouth in defeat (40:4). But, in the New Testament, we discover that the cornerstone is Jesus, Himself (Ephesians 2:19–22).

Though Job wasn't aware of this detail then, he is no doubt aware of it now. Isn't it going to be glorious when we can sit and break bread with him to ask for ourselves what was going on in his mind during these trials? No doubt his faith has earned him quite the spectacles in heaven. We can't wait to see it all!

Psalms

Job wasn't the only one besides Ruth to champion the *go'el* as such a spiritual character who would one day be called "Redeemer." The Jewish sages knew this also.

The book of Psalms is incredibly lengthy. In regard to its form, it doesn't follow the same patterns as Job, Proverbs, Ecclesiastes, or

Song of Solomon. In fact, it is a collection of 150 songs (or poems) of the nation of Israel. This is why, in at church gatherings, it's not uncommon to hear the Psalms referred to as an ancient hymnal for the Jews. Its form does, however, fit the criteria for a Wisdom book, as its smaller-sectioned and disjointed staccato style resembles proverbial wisdom writings of the era (though that isn't the only reason). As for content, not all of the Psalms are "Wisdom Psalms." Nine of them, in particular (Psalms 1, 14, 19, 37, 73, 91, 112, 119, and 128), teach what needs to be known for a long, healthy, and blessed life under God's rule. The principle of retributional justice is overwhelmingly present in these, though the "hot" and "cold" retributional system (God's direct intervention of justice versus the natural outcomes of decisions) fluctuates. Nevertheless, the entire book is rich with ruminations of wise choices that lead to happiness and contentment, well beyond just those labeled "Wisdom Psalms," and as this study is on Christ as He "appears" in all of Scripture, more than just these nine songs will be mentioned in our reflection.

As a quick review: God was certainly called "Redeemer" (and other terms that would one day be viewed in light of the Messiah) in some verses of the Old Testament, as some of the researchers of the subject of Job acknowledge. Additionally, as shown in the study of Ruth, "redeemer" is a term relating to one who can purchase something (usually land) and return it to one who had lost it (usually because of hard times). Therefore, not every Old-Testament reference to a "Redeemer" (or, again, other messianic terms) should be viewed as a statement about Christ.

However, the Sage known as Jesus, the Christ, somewhat dismissed this argument, having made the connection to references regarding Him before many other wise men when He said, "all things must be fulfilled, which were written in the law of Moses, and in the prophets, and in the *psalms*, concerning me" (Luke 24:44; emphasis added). (The intervention of a *go'el* appears in quite a number of Psalms: 19:14; 69:18; 72:14; 74:2; 77:15; 78:35.)

At other moments in His ministry, Jesus quoted from the Psalms, taking the link to a whole new level. For instance, when Jesus was dying on the cross, He said, "My God, my God, why has thou forsaken me?" (Matthew 27:46). Understandably, as Jesus was God, this question has stirred discomfort in those who view these words as a lack of faith on behalf of our Savior to His Father in His final hour when His faith counted most. If Jesus was one with God, as we know He was, then why would He accuse the Father of abandoning Him at death when He would have certainly known the character and nature of the Father is opposed to such desertion of His own?

One argument—and it's a *great* one, we will give it that—is that this question was asked during the precise moment when something in the spiritual realm shifted and the Savior took on the sin nature of the world. Thus, He was covered in sin and speaking out of the doubt and desperation the sinful nature promotes and identifies with: Only when the Savior became covered in sin would He say something like that, the argument claims: "Jesus sensed a separation from the Father He had never known, for in becoming sin the Father had to turn judicially from His Son," one commentary states.[62] Others collectively describe that the Godhead—made up of Father, Son, and Spirit— were at this moment divided, and would remain so for the duration of Jesus' time in the grave until He rose again, resuming back into His function and role within the Trinity.

But however true certain aspects of this spiritual-shift theory may be, this is an unnecessary step. Jesus would never have had to be covered in sin to utter these words because, as the Jewish sages of the time knew, they were a word-for-word quote from Psalm 22:1, which had been written by David (and considered to be one of the most messianic of the Psalms in nature). This proves Jesus' familiarity with the Wisdom literature of His Israelite forefathers who were led by the Spirit of God to write what they did (2 Timothy 3:16; 2 Peter 1:21). But it also shows that He, in His death event, spent one of His last breaths making it clear to the Jewish wise men in the crowd that

He *was* the Messiah prophesied in the Psalms—whom many had still refused to acknowledge.

When we look closer at the outline of Psalm 22, we see it begins with the question of why God has abandoned the psalmist (22:1); goes on to describe the detailed areas of just how deliverance is needed during a season of anguish (22:2–18); calls to God to come nearer to the psalmist and strengthen, deliver, and save him (22:19–21); and turns into a promise by the psalmist that God will be praised no matter the circumstances (22:22–29); ending (22:30–31) with an oft-misunderstood statement: "A seed shall serve him; it shall be accounted to the Lord for a generation. They shall come, and shall declare his righteousness unto a people that shall be born, that he hath done this."

Overwhelmingly, the "seed" of verse 30 and continuing into verse 31 has been linked to Gentiles. David is here saying that every generation will and should tell the next generation how the Lord will someday provide a Savior and Deliverer from trouble, and that this lineage will at some point in the future involve the "seed" of another people other than the Israelites. In short, it's a prophecy recognizing that the Jews will not be the only ones "delivered" in the last days, and that "seed [Gentiles] shall serve him [the Messiah]…and shall declare [Jesus'] righteousness unto a [new generation of] a people that shall be born, that [Jesus has died for them]." In the middle of this song, however, there exist some graphic and colorful words that, though written *well* before the crucifixion scene, describe what the Someday Messiah would face. Take specific note of the Scripture references in this comparison that show the prophecy in the Old Testament and its fulfillment in the New Testament: "They pierced my hands and my feet" (22:16; Luke 24:40); "They part my garments among them, and cast lots upon my vesture" (22:18; Matthew 27:35). In no uncertain terms, David—whether he meant to or not—was prophetically confessing that the Messiah would deliver Israel *and* everyone else, precisely describing details of His death along the way, and ending with a statement that all people from that day forward would continue to tell His story of sacrifice for the purposes of salvation for all.

It's also important to remember that the mistake of isolating one verse out of its context is not one Jesus chose to address from the cross. In other words, He did *not* spend His last breath telling the crowd, "Make sure that when you compare My words about the Father 'forsaking' Me just now that you read to the end of the Psalm for proper context!" Psalm 22, *when taken as a whole*, begins with the heaviness of feeling "forsaken" and concludes with the triumph of the cross and its reach to Gentiles. As such, Jesus, when He was at the very peak of His pain and torment, reflected on the feelings of David, identifying with the sourer portion of the Psalm. That is, He was classifying the moment on the cross as the one that connected to the *beginning* of the work of salvation, knowing that the *end* of the work of the cross was nothing but Good News. As an imaginative way of peeking into this moment of death, we can see a silent message following His words of being "forsaken": "Crowd, listen to Me. This is the beginning of that which you have heard about in Psalm 22. Yet, just as David saw the beautiful end, I will now submit myself unto death, though I will rise again in three days, fulfilling that which you have heard in the *end* of Psalm 22: that a generation of Gentiles will serve Me—they shall come, and shall declare My righteousness unto a people that shall be born, that he hath done this for *them*."

We need never feel the need to be "uncomfortable" with anything Jesus said. If it looks or feels weird or "off" in the text, it's likely a picture of the Messiah showing His true identity through the lives or writings of those who have gone before Him. Jesus declaring the Father had forsaken Him on the cross was, oddly enough, His recognition that the ancient promises of the Father were only Good News forever, and that they were being fulfilled in that moment! He proved this by dying, rising, and then telling His disciples to *spread* that Good News throughout the world (Matthew 28:16–20)!

Commentators are not oblivious to this irony. They see Psalm 22 as "a psalm which moves from despairing appeal to triumphant faith, and the Christian reader can, with hindsight, see the appropriateness of this total message."[63] After spending pages discussing the "spiritual shift" theory related earlier (that Jesus would only claim to be forsaken by the Father after He had taken upon Himself the sin of the world), classic Bible theologian Joseph S. Exell explains in his *Biblical Illustrator* "the true sense of this cry," stating: "[There are] two reasons why Christ chose to express Himself on this occasion in the language of David. 1. That the Jews might call to mind the great resemblance between His case and that of this illustrious king and prophet. 2. This psalm was allowed to belong to the Messiah, and to have its ultimate completion in Him."[64]

This was merely *one* example among many that we could, with proper space that we don't have, spend the next five hundred pages reflecting upon…easily.

In Matthew 21:16, during the cleansing of the Temple, Jesus quoted from Psalm 8:2 in regard to the praises of those who had shouted "Hosanna!" at His Triumphal Entry into Jerusalem; in Matthew 21:42, 44, while He taught the parable of the tenants, He quoted from Psalm 118:22, 23 regarding the cornerstone; in Mark 12:36, while teaching in the Temple, He quoted from Psalm 110:1 regarding how He could have been interpreted to be the Son of David; in John 15:25, while He addressed the hatred of the world toward believers, He quoted from Psalm 35:19; 69:4, explaining why the world could hate followers of God "without a cause"; in Luke 23:46, Jesus said, "Father, into your hands I commit my spirit!" which was another word-for-word quote from Psalm 31:5.

In the eyes of the Savior, the Psalms consistently mentioned Him, and His teachings consistently mirrored them. Thus, to read the Psalms without that understanding would be to discredit the very methodology of reflection and study used by history's greatest Sage; we would be failing to study the Word the way Jesus directed His disciples in Luke 24:44.

We know, too, the Israelites spoke and wrote within the limitations of human language, and their words about God or His Son frequently did reflect terminology they used daily. Also, Christ is not only paralleled in characteristics of Israel's heroes throughout this larger portion of the Word, but He is also spoken of directly through the mouths of God's prophets (a topic we have yet to discuss). That being true, *many* references to "Redeemer" and equivalent messianic terms in the Old Testament can (and should) be viewed as representing the Someday Messiah. This is true in both a direct and indirect way: It's not only about the *words* (such as "redeemer" or *go'el*), but of the description of the function of a future Man who would answer some of the problems of deliverance faced in the Psalms.

Let's look at a handful of examples: Early on in the book, Psalm 2 predicts the day when the prophesied Messiah, or the Lord's "anointed" (2:2), will arrive to reign over the unruly nations. Verses 6–7 and 12 are as clear as the sky on a sunny day in their regard to King Jesus: "Yet have I set my king upon my holy hill of Zion. I will declare the decree: the Lord hath said unto me, Thou art my Son; this day have I begotten thee [John 3:16].… Kiss the Son.… Blessed are all they that put their trust in him."

Other passages, such as Psalm 45 (especially verse 6), show the formerly addressed fulfillment of Christ as the sovereign Davidic King. The Davidic Psalm 72, verse 14—"He shall redeem their soul from deceit and violence"—is viewed by the translators behind the New English Translation (NET) as messianic in function: The psalmist depicts the reign of prosperity and peace, and "the ideal it expresses will only be fully realized during the Messiah's earthly reign."[65] In fact, the New King James Version (NKJV) has as its header for this psalm: "Glory and Universality of the Messiah's Reign."[66] Psalm 110 is also considered in the NKJV to be the "Announcement of the Messiah's Reign."[67] The Messiah's connection to the Davidic line of kings is also linked with Psalms 65, 74, 89, and 120–134.[68]

The apocryphal *Psalms of Solomon* (especially 17:28–33) "give the Messiah a significant role in relation to the eschatological temple."[69]

Along with 2, 22, and 110, Davidic Psalm 118 "portrayed the suffering and death of the Messiah."[70]

As you can see, this comparison could go on and on. But other than to pick and choose bits and pieces that some would see as messianic, the overarching sentiment that summarizes all the songs together as one requires us to reflect on the book *as a whole*. This collection of verses is, in the end, one enormous gathering of the heartbeat of Israel who looks toward the Someday Messiah as the answer to everything, including their grief. They cry out for forgiveness (32; 51; 130); in lamentation (12; 13); with confidence in God's presence even during their walk through valleys of death (23); with praise and thanksgiving (8; 93; 145; 9; 106; 138); remembering the glory of, and blessings that come from, obedience to the Law (19; 119); and in remembrance of God's mercy throughout history (78; 107). In addition, they offer countless other expressions of relationship between God and Israel *before* the coming of the One who would be the fulfillment of all of these cries and more (Luke 24:44; also see: Matthew 1:22; 2:15, 23; 4:14; 8:17; 12:17; 13:35; 21:4; 26:56; Luke 21:22; John 12:38; 15:25; 17:12; Acts 3:18). Jesus forgives; He lamented; He brings confidence; He is worthy of our praise and thanksgiving; He fulfilled the Law; He is merciful; and He brings the Old Testament to a close with a promise that was satisfied in His death and Resurrection. He is *everything* the Psalms stood for!

In every Psalm—*not just those identified by scholars as "messianic"*—there is an old hope accomplished in the Christ.

In this way, we can enthusiastically declare that *all* the Psalms are about Christ, and the silent voice that echoes from the pages of these ancient songs draw their conclusion in Him.

The whole of Scripture, together as one, points to this Man. Nothing reminds us more of this fact than the Psalms.

The book of Proverbs, however, is not at all silent on the Christ.

Proverbs

Proverbs begins and ends with a longer contemplation. The middle portion, however, is a lengthier collection of short, proverbial teachings—hence the book's name. Traditionally, King Solomon, son of King David, is believed to have written this book (as well as the next two, Ecclesiastes and Song of Solomon).

A quick note about Solomon, since he has amassed great wealth; drafted the sons of Israel into his service; wrestled with God (as we read in Ecclesiastes) to the point that some believers are, like they are with Jesus' "forsaken" cry at the cross, uncomfortable with some of the bolder things he said; and accumulated so many wives (seven hundred) and concubines (three hundred; 1 Kings 11:3), we may find it hard to believe he did anything besides visit women for pleasure all day. It's easy to assume that this literal son of David had no integrity when his actions clearly demonstrated otherwise; for example, some of his wives/concubines were foreign and brought pagan worship back into Israel's kingdom. We read in 1 Kings 11:4 that "his wives turned away his heart after other gods: and his heart was not perfect with the Lord his God, as was the heart of David his father."

However, the Word is clear that Solomon began as one who "loved the Lord, walking in the statutes of David his father" (1 Kings 3:3). A couple of verses later, when Solomon was visited by the Lord in a dream and invited to ask for literally anything he wanted, he asked for discernment and wisdom, so God gifted him with "a wise and an understanding heart; so that there was none like thee before [him], neither after [him] shall any arise like unto [him]" (1 Kings 3:5–14). (It should be pointed out that the Lord never guaranteed he would get what he asked for. Had he asked for a plasma TV and an Xbox with unlimited video games, God probably would have said no because those requests wouldn't have been in line with the Lord's will for Solomon's life. He did receive what he asked for because his request for wisdom pleased God.) God predicted truthfully; no other man in Israel's history ever ruled like Solomon. He would never be perfect, because he inherited the sin nature of a fallen world as much as anyone after Adam and Eve—and we can discuss his mistakes all day, but it will not change the fact that he was likely the greatest wise man in human history (apart from Christ, that is). It's therefore not surprising that he would be credited with the writings of three of the greatest Wisdom books. We learn in 1 Kings 4:29–34 that, because of his request to God, King "Solomon's wisdom excelled the wisdom of all the children of the east country, and all the wisdom of Egypt," that "he spake three thousand proverbs: and his songs were a thousand and five," and "there came of all people to hear the wisdom of Solomon, from all kings of the earth, which had heard of his wisdom." Goodness! Three thousand proverbs! One thousand five songs! This guy doesn't do anything halfway, does he? In Proverbs 9:10, we read of his belief that the beginning of *all* wisdom is righteous fear of the Lord.

See, this is actually more important than many realize, because Israel wasn't the only nation to produce wisdom writings extremely similar to those in the biblical canon. For instance, "The Instruction of Kagemni" was only one of the many "Egyptian Wisdoms" written by Israel's neighbors in Egypt between 2500 and 2100 BC that read in a style that's nearly identical style to Proverbs. Such writings— biblical or otherwise—draw their roots from the royal courts in the ancient Eastern world. A king needed to establish the stability of his kingdom—politically, socially, and economically—by example of his own behavior and leadership, if he wanted to remain on the throne and experience (along with his subjects) prosperity and success. One of the ways he established this kind of authority was by using the scribes of the royal courts to write, then circulate, texts that promoted wisdom. These texts were sort of manuals of life that were stacked atop the kings' laws of the land. These traditions were practiced in Mesopotamia (especially the Sumerian, Babylonian, and Assyrian kingdoms), Egypt (as we said), and Canaan around the same time as Proverbs. Wisdom literature expert Richard Clifford states: "The most important institution for the production of literature was the royal court, for the temple had yielded its economic and political importance to the palace. The king sponsored scribes and paid for their literary production, accepting it as part of his responsibility to maintain political and economic order and stability."[71] So, by the time King Solomon reigned over Israel, the Wisdom literature in circulation throughout the land was the sign that a king was a good leader... and nobody before or after Solomon in the·ancient world would produce wisdom-laden writings like him.

Some question the authorship of his three works, and although attribution is important and the reasons for doubt are valid, there are mountains of convincing evidence supporting the belief that Proverbs, Ecclesiastes, and Song of Solomon were either the work of Solomon's own hand or were written in dedication to the kind of wisdom he conveyed in his lifetime. Proverbs, itself, also attributes him as author (1:1; 10:1; 25:1).

Before we dive into how Jesus appears in the book of Proverbs, let's consider how a biblical proverb should be read, as it is terribly abused in Western society today (and a short clarification here may prove important enough to rescue a few people from a faith crisis).

A proverb is a short, pithy saying that gets straight-as-a-razor to the point. Its purpose is to tell one how to live and, frequently, it includes a comparison between two contrasting truths to accomplish this. In fact, the literal meaning of the Hebrew word for "proverb," *mashal*, means "to compare." For instance, using a familiar quote, US President John F. Kennedy stated, "Ask not what your country can do for you; ask what you can do for your country." Though this was originally spoken in a slightly rearranged manner by Oliver Wendell Holmes, Sr., once it was spoken by a powerful Western president, the phrase was inaugurated into the "Proverbs Hall of Fame" due to its frequent use in society. The value of a proverb is that it inspires deep conviction in few words and places responsibility of its hearer/reader to act in some way that will improve one's life or community. The downside of a proverb is its tendency to oversimplify: A person can hear the words of Kennedy and feel inspired to do something for his or her country, but the action he or she should take to accomplish that endeavor is ambiguous and impersonal. Instructional proverbs that *do* tell one precisely what to do are often misinterpreted as promising a specific outcome when they should be interpreted as a guideline. As one popular example from Proverbs 22:6 states, "Train up a child in the way he should go: and when he is old, he will not depart from it." It may seem disappointing, but we take this as a promise—a guaranteed outcome for every child whose parents follow this advice—then God owes an apology to a lot of folks who "trained up their child" correctly yet whose children still fell away—and remained away—from the faith as an adult. At the end of the day, this Proverb, though true in its general advice, cannot cancel out the gift of free will God has given to humanity. So, if children are raised in the ways they should go, and then they depart from it and do not return before an untimely death, the issue is not that a *proverb* (general guideline) was wrong, as much as it is the acknowledgment of the exception. As much of a bummer as it is to admit that proverbs are "guidelines" and not "promises," thinking they're more than what they are ultimately leads to disappointment when life doesn't go the way we expect, which can lead to doubting God's Word. Therefore, it's important, while reading through the writings of King Solomon, to keep this in mind.

As an additional warning, to avoid reviving old heresies about Christ that were silenced during the early Church councils, we must take a moment to address Lady Sophia, the personification of wisdom, and her influence upon culture during and following the Hellenistic period.

When Alexander the Great succeeded in his many conquests over large areas of the ancient world, an early sort of single world order was established. This is not the same one world order as that which fits the Antichrist's agenda explained in the book of Revelation, but aspects are similar enough that the term is useful in conveying the immensity of its political and societal impact in its day: It shifted the world from the Classical Greek period to the Roman Greek period; achieved geographical expansion unlike anything the planet has seen before or since; and launched Rome into the ancient world's top influence and authority, uniting all peoples of surrounding regions in language, artistic expression, stage drama, scientific discovery, music, literature, and every fathomable branch of academic education. (This is the era known as the Hellenistic Period.) Prior to this, the Wisdom literature—Proverbs, as well as the apocryphal Sirach, Baruch, and Wisdom of Solomon—personified wisdom as a woman.

In Israel's history, this woman was never seen as a goddess or an equal to the Creator. Much to the contrary, "she" was kept in her rightful place simply as a literary motif: In Proverbs 1–9, she is depicted as "the soul's true bride, true counselor, true hostess, and as the very offspring of the Creator."[72] She manifests in varying ways: proclaiming loudly in public like a preacher (1:20–33); waiting to be pursued (8:34); a sister, friend, or wife (7:4; 4:6–8); or the giver of generous gifts (3:15–18; 8:18–21). She demonstrates the importance of wisdom principles over foolishness, or "Folly" (another personification in Proverbs; the lady of foolishness who stands as the opposite of everything wise). The purpose of portraying wisdom as a woman was as a tool to enhance understanding: a way to conceptualize the epitome of wisdom's function. For instance: The pursuit and application of wisdom in life results in blessings, prosperity, order, stability, success, and happiness—all wonderful "gifts" given to the one who therefore "knows wisdom," as if it were "a generous friend." So far, so good. Nothing is innately wrong with this picture as it was portrayed in its first light.

However, somewhere around the time of the Hellenistic period, apocryphal and secular writings extended the concept in a way that this woman became more than just a theme. The author of the apocryphal writing, Wisdom of Solomon (originating around Christ's birth), associated her with the Spirit or breath of God (verses 1:6, 7:25; 8:3–4 in that text), as well as with encompassing characteristics of Christ.[73] The book Sirach adds to Proverbs that she is connected to the Torah (24:23) and Jerusalem is her home (24:8, 10). Though none of the traditional Wisdom books went as far as to definitively teach that the personification was literal, due to the unity of expression in society and the influence of the polytheistic Greco-Roman pantheon in culture, language continued to "wrap" her into terminology that edged closer and closer to the image of a goddess. Proverbs is clear that she was present at Creation and was the Creator's first brainchild (Proverbs 8:22–31), but it nowhere claims that she participated in the origins of the earth in any way other than to be an observer. Importantly, "she" was merely the wisdom of God.

The Koine Greek word for wisdom is *sophia*, so when Greek became the dominant language, "Lady Wisdom" was given a new name, "Sophia," as well as an unfortunate new identity. It's more complicated than stating she was seen as being equal to God, because that wasn't frequently declared in literature circulating in the general population. It was, however, heavily implied by some writers, which led to heresy in the Church. The secular and philosophical minds of the day saw Sophia's existence at Creation and flirted with the idea that she was in "hypostatic union" with God. The theological term "hypostatic union" describes the convergence of the divine and human natures into one. We see this in the person of Christ...and that is precisely where this all went terribly wrong...

The link can also be traced to some New Testament Scriptures, but only when recklessly interpreted. As one example, Paul stated that Jesus was the Rock in the wilderness (1 Corinthians 10:1–4). The writer of the apocryphal Wisdom of Solomon, in verse 10:17, wrote that Sophia accompanied Him there.

The Greek word *logos* ("word") is used in John's Gospel to refer to Jesus as "the Word" of God who was there in the beginning at Creation. Follow this trail: 1) wisdom was *also* present at Creation; 2) she is personified as a woman; 3) "the Word was with God, and the Word *was* God" (John 1:1; emphasis added); 4) "words" were used *by* God to create the world; thus, 5) philosophically (but not responsibly, in the theological sense) Christ and Sophia are one and the same entity who assisted in the formation of the universe. Wisdom of Solomon, in verses 7:22–27, teach that Sophia was actively involved in Creation and "in sustaining it once it is made."[74] Therefore, some scholars note that her character is a precursor to New Testament Christology.[75]

Other scholars appropriately teach that this is dangerous feminist ideology, as it leads to a heretical, hybrid "Jesus-Sophia," the personified Lady Wisdom being "the same as the Logos of John 1:1."[76]

We couldn't agree more.

Why? Because it's wrong to associate Jesus with a feminine concept?

Not quite…

Remember that Jesus was and is eternal (John 1:1–4). Lady Wisdom was, according to Proverbs, God's first *creation*. So if Jesus is viewed as Sophia, then He becomes a created being, unequal to the eternal Father.[77]

While writing this book, we dug through what the rest of the Church thinks of Jesus-Sophia. Whereas most sources don't refer to Him as that name specifically and outright, it is absolutely *shocking* how many people—albeit sincere and well-meaning people—build an entire theology around the idea that Jesus is the same being as Lady Wisdom…yet they miss the fact that this constructs an elaborate "created being" heresy! We cannot count the number of books, articles, and blogs that take Proverbs 8 (Lady Wisdom's main chapter) and show that Jesus is, in some way or other, the personification of Sophia. These sources get all the way to the point that we think they've spotted the "creation" error, expecting that their next statements will be an attempt at a theological defense for it, and then they just…stop talking about it altogether.

This is something we refuse to do. We realize that places us somewhat in the minority for those who want to accomplish our same goal (illustrating how Jesus is reflected in every book of the Word), but we refuse to allow for any interpretation that places a limit on the Son's eternality as equal to the Father.

Nevertheless, it is *not* wrong to see Jesus as the *literal* personification of wisdom, or its association to Creation apart from the created Sophia. In fact, 1 Corinthians 1:24 says that is precisely what He is: "But unto them which are called, both Jews and Greeks, Christ the power of God, and the wisdom of God." This is why the background on Sophia needed to be addressed before we continued. As long as we remember the lines drawn between Jesus and "Lady Wisdom" (or Sophia) are stiff and solid, and must remain that way always, we can visit Jesus *as* Wisdom without making the same mistakes as some in the early Church who were rebuked during the councils. This brings us to perhaps the most important typological relationship between Jesus and the book of Proverbs.

Christ has a type in Solomon, at least as it pertains to the pursuit and attainment of wisdom. But there are other comparisons:

- Solomon was a king over the grandest, most opulent, peaceful, and successful kingdom in Israel's history (1 Kings 10:14–27); Jesus was, is, and always will be the King over all kings, reigning over the grandest, most opulent, peaceful, and successful kingdom in Israel's—and the rest of the world's—history.
- Solomon was rich, and compared to other kings, he owned everything one could imagine (1 Kings 10:14); Jesus literally does own everything one could imagine: "Wherefore God also hath highly exalted him, and given him a name which is above every name: That at the name of Jesus every knee should bow, of things in heaven, and things in earth, and things under the earth; And that every tongue should confess that Jesus Christ is Lord, to the glory of God the Father" (Philippians 2:9–11; also see Revelation 21; Isaiah 66:1–3; Haggai 2:8).

- Solomon's servants were happy to attend to him, and his judgments were fair and righteous (1 Kings 10:8–9); this is especially true of Christ (Revelation 22:3–4; Colossians 3:23–24; 1 Corinthians 15:58; 1 Peter 2:9; Luke 6:38; Matthew 6:33; 25:21; Proverbs 19:17; Galatians 6:9; and so many other verses it's uncanny).

- Solomon's people were astonished by his logic and administration of justice (1 Kings 3:23); the crowds were astonished by Jesus' logic (Matthew 7:28–29).

- Solomon supervised the building of the grandest palace (1 Kings 7) and holiest place (the Temple: 1 Kings 6); Jesus is building the grandest and holiest place right now for His followers (John 14:2–3).

- God personally came to dwell on earth in the place Solomon built (1 Kings 8:10–11); God personally came to dwell on earth in flesh of the Son (John 1:14).

- And, as we've already covered, Jesus is the Son who was prophesied to be of the line of King David, who was Solomon's father.

Christ was the absolute gift of wisdom to man, both in prophecy (Isaiah 11:2) and fulfillment (1 Corinthians 1:30). Matthew 12:42 mentions how the queen of Sheba came from "the uttermost parts of the earth" to seek Solomon's great wisdom in person. The verse ends with a bold and exciting announcement in reference to Jesus: "behold, a greater than Solomon is here!" In the next chapter, verse 13:54, this proclamation plays out in real time: "when [Jesus] was come into his own country, he taught them in their synagogue, insomuch that they were astonished, and said, 'Whence hath this man this wisdom, and these mighty works?'" As a separate entity from Sophia, Christ personified wisdom—like a walking, talking book of Solomon's Proverbs—and the early Church (as well as ancient Israel), for reasons just discussed, was more than familiar with, and embraced, the idea that a Person could *be* Wisdom. After Jesus left His indelible mark upon the world, climaxing in His grand ascension to rejoin His Father, His followers saw Him as the definitive, perfected Solomon: King Solomon's greatest moments and reflections made flawless and fully realized in Christ.

And it started in His youth. At only twelve, Jesus entered the Temple and astounded the wisest scholars of His day (Luke 2:41–50). Don't miss this: This account is the first time in the Bible we see how Jesus would interact with other human beings. Twelve-year-olds are typically found making mudpies outside and bonking other kids on the head in the playground for stealing their seats on the teeter-totter. Their greatest concern should be whether they are first in line to get the elusive blue raspberry popsicle in a variety pack from his or her grandmother's freezer. (Allie Anderson remembers an occasion like this endearingly... The blue popsicle was rare in the 1980s, but Grandma "Goodie" [her nickname, as bestowed upon her when it was discovered there was no treat impossible for her to get her hands on] always had a blue popsicle for Allie around this age.)

Many children, at twelve, can't even define the word "wisdom," let alone practice it. But there was Jesus, as a little boy, challenging the thoughts of the teachers of the Law who had spent their adult lives studying complicated Scriptures they would never be able to understand as well as Jesus did before He was even old enough for a bar mitzvah (by standards outlined in the Mishnah, Pirkei Avot 5:21). Luke 2:52, a verse immediately following this narrative, says that Jesus, *after* having wowed the scholars, actually went on to "grow in wisdom"! It wasn't enough that precious Yeshua was already the definitive Sage at twelve. Our Lord and Savior *increased* in wisdom even after that! It's not surprising, then, that when He began His ministry, He told His disciples, "For I will give you a mouth and wisdom, which all your adversaries shall not be able to gainsay nor resist" (Luke 21:15).

Not only did Jesus read the Hebrew Bible (few Jews of His day could read Hebrew) and become well-versed in its teachings, He also devised proverbs such as "For where your treasure is, there will your heart be also" (Matthew 6:21) and "For all they that take the sword shall perish with the sword" (26:52). Parables were a highly concentrated form of wisdom-training championed for the way they reduced complicated concepts into simple terms, yet Jesus, who had the right and the authority to "talk over someone's head" chose to use them habitually so His students could understand Him.

Not all of His instructions are easy on the ears of unbelievers, however, as the wisdom of Jesus and the wisdom of this world don't often play well together. In fact, people who believe themselves to be wise in every age will view the wisdom of God and His Son as "foolishness" (1 Corinthians 1:19–25). But those who have followed the Son of God and sought to consistently apply what He taught to their lives have discovered His words bring longevity, inspiration, purpose, and unrivaled sustenance to the temporary human condition called "life." Proverbs 2:10–11 says, "When wisdom entereth into thine heart, and knowledge is pleasant unto thy soul: Discretion shall preserve thee, [and] understanding shall keep thee."

Like His presence in the Psalms, the embodiment of Jesus in the book of Proverbs does not rely on one verse above the others. We couldn't possibly show how Jesus "appears" in Proverbs on a verse-by-verse basis, as He is the fundamental beginning and end of all wisdom. To better understand what we mean, consider these models: In Proverbs 18:24, a good friend "sticks closer than a brother." Jesus calls His followers "friends" instead of "servants" (John 15:14–15), and He is always by our side, even to the end of the earth (Matthew 28:20). In Proverbs 8:10–11, instruction is worth more than silver, knowledge is better than gold, and wisdom far surpasses the value of rubies. All "riches" and "treasures of wisdom and knowledge" are hidden in Christ (Colossians 2:2–3). The entire chapter of Proverbs 12 describes who Jesus was while He lived as a human. Many verses in Proverbs are from the perspective of a father directing his son to grow in wisdom. Jesus was and is the Son hearing His Father's instructions— exemplifying the entire purpose of the book as He grew in wisdom.

Once we realize the heretical, hybridized "Jesus-Sophia" should be set aside, the book of Proverbs as a single unit comes clearer into focus. Israel needed wisdom, and Proverbs provided it. Humanity needs a source of instruction on right living, and Proverbs is that source. We will always face the necessity to identify foolish behaviors and avoid irresponsibility and recklessness brought on by ill-advised decisions. We must be shown what ignorance is in order to recognize and avoid it. As long as we remain fallen—and we always will (until the very end)—people of all ages, all cultures, and every era will never stop requiring lessons on how to think, behave, and make good decisions…and Proverbs delivers. Viewing the outline of the entire book, we see Proverbs addressing every possible topic, from good and evil in general, to happiness, comfort, liberality, chastity, temperance, mischief, idleness, industry, obedience, family, spouses, household care, fame, excellence, achievement, power, riches, discipline, foolishness, moral virtues, royalty, government, politics, privacy, anger, pride, thievery, cowardice, corruption, faith, prayer, quarrels, love, self-love, wrath, integrity, busybodies and gossips, minding one's own business, what pleases God, and what doesn't please God…just to name a few.

In the *Old Testament*, the answer to the deeply seeded issue of poor judgment inherent in the sin nature is found in Proverbs, but in the *New Testament*, it is found in Wisdom personified: Jesus the Christ.

What a Sage we serve! He is sincerely and faithfully wonderful, isn't He?

We think so, too. We mean it when we say that following the advice of the Savior leads to the best possible life. Jesus is Wisdom. He *is* Proverbs!

And one day, we will meet with Him in paradise. We will not have to wait in line to see what He thinks of a particular subject or what advice He would give in any area. We will have forever—literally all of eternity!—to bask in His never-ending teaching.

Right now, in this life, many of us have occasional moments when someone we know—whether it's a professional in the world of earthly wisdom (like a counsellor or psychologist) or a life-sage who just happens to have magnified understanding of our existence through experience—tells us something we'll never forget. We may be puzzled by some issue, and the simplest words hit us in a way that we just *know* that's the best answer. We have an epiphany, and we embrace it, applying those great words of wisdom with gusto, observing later on that it was the best, or the *only*, advice that could have solved that puzzle. If you've experienced this, imagine that person being there with you always, with his or her attention never distracted from you by work, family matters, or anything else. Can you even imagine having that kind of access to a sage?

This is exactly how Jesus will be for us, with one exception: His words of wisdom will be *perfect!* There will never be any greater wisdom than what is shared through the mouth of Christ, and believers will have eternity to experience this over and over. Jesus, our Wisdom Sage, will never run out of truths to share with His people, and He will *never* be unavailable!

We have access to Him now through prayer, but one day, that access will be in person, and when it is, there will be no room for misinterpretation of His glorious response. Hallelujah to the King of every Proverb!

Okay…time for a deep breath. Go ahead. Take in a big one.

Hold it…

Keep holding it…

Keep holding it…

Count to a million…

Now let it out and brace yourself. Are you ready for a startling halt to all this glory for a few minutes?

Don't say we didn't warn you: Ecclesiastes can be rough, and yes, we're going there. But we think you'll ultimately like exactly *where* we are going with it. As of yet, we've never seen another Bible study like this one.

Oh, and be prepared to immediately dismiss everything you *thought* you knew about the book.

Ecclesiastes

Shifting our attention to Ecclesiastes—especially after being immersed in the instructional tone of Proverbs—is a sharp, almost painful transition. Up to this point, our book has been positive, focusing on the beautiful picture of our Savior and how He is the magnificent, majestic answer to everything.

If you must, put your hands over your ears and imagine you don't hear the deafening noise of the squealing breaks as our book screeches to a halt on the highway of happiness, but whatever you do, *don't stop reading*. Ecclesiastes is not only necessary for believers *despite* its seemingly endless negativity, it's crucial *because of* its negativity. Without looking deeper, the entire book feels like a long rant about how everything in the world is "meaningless" and every pursuit in this life is "vanity." (Seriously. Have you read it?!) Those who believe Jesus' "forsaken" inquiry at the cross was the most uncomfortable moment in the Word probably haven't yet read Ecclesiastes...

The outline of all twelve chapters (without repeats) of Ecclesiastes spells a message about like this: human efforts in every area are vain; self-indulgence doesn't satisfy; hard work is merely chasing after the wind; mankind has no advantage over animals (or beasts) because, in the end, they both die; there is much evil and oppression in the world; wealth and honor don't amount to much; having everything the heart desires doesn't make one content; the wicked *can* live long lives and prosper; both the wise and the foolish end up dead in the ground; nobody is truly righteous; humanity will never fully understand the mysteries of God; no one will ever find gratification in the pursuit of wisdom; everybody's gonna die; and everyone faces judgment...but we should still follow God's rules. (We're not kidding. That's how the book ends. The number of times Solomon declares something is "meaningless" can be a bit overwhelming—especially for readers who are who new to the book. See Ecclesiasties 1:14; 2:1, 11, 15, 17, 19, 21, 23, 26; 3:19; 4:4, 7, 8, 16; 5:7, 10; 6:2, 4, 9, 11, 12; 7:6, 15; 8:10, 14; 9:9; 11:8, 10.)

In short, nothing really matters and life has no meaning.

Good grief!

Just remember, *we* didn't write it.

But before we assume Ecclesiastes has no merit other than to depress people, it's important to understand that we can find out *one of the most important fulfillments of Christ* by studying this book! Also, the book's not only about pessimism, as we're about to address. The "good news" of Ecclesiastes comes with understanding that the shockwave caused by the book's "meaninglessness of the whole universe" claims were *intentional.*

The writer knew very well what he was doing and how to get people's attention…with a form of literature that is now extinct across the globe.

Whoa, wait just a second, you guys. Are you saying there's something about Ecclesiastes that Christians typically don't know? Are you suggesting there's some mystery behind the book that has yet to be unlocked, and you authors know about it?

As a matter of cold, hard fact, that is precisely what we're saying… and it's a doozy of a secret! However, we don't want to keep this secret locked. We hope the true purpose behind Ecclesiastes—a purpose inadvertently hidden throughout centuries of the Church's historical emphasis on only reading the canonical books—will be brought out into the open by folks just like you. Let's dig in, and you'll see what we mean.

As stated, Solomon is considered the author of Ecclesiastes, according to tradition. As a man of excessive wealth and one who appeared to have full access to every material luxury available, it's incredibly significant that he couldn't find gratification in any single thing. But, unlike a lot of folks since the time of Adam who fake piety and pretend to be happy with life because they think it sounds sanctimonious and pleasing to God, Solomon didn't attempt to censor how he really felt about life and the world, and he certainly didn't worry about who he might offend with his directness.

In that sense, Ecclesiastes forces believers to be honest. How often do we hear, "Hey, how you doin'?" In many cases, that universal form of greeting produces an outright lie: "Good! You?" We say it, though, because it's polite and expected, but it isn't always true. Solomon, considering his mindset at the time he was writing Ecclesiastes, would likely have said, "What does it matter how I'm doing? Every activity and endeavor of life is irrelevant, trivial, tedious, and hollow, and in the end, we die. You?"

We can see the smile fading from the other person's face as their countenance falls and they walk away. (These authors understand this greeting is as common as "hello," and we understand that the one asking isn't usually genuinely soliciting a long and literal answer, so we're not suggesting that our readers need to feel guilt for participating in this jovial exchange in this way. We're merely using this illustration to magnify the brutal honesty of Solomon's writing.)

In another sense, however, once we've decided to be as crudely honest as Solomon was in this work, Ecclesiastes addresses the symptom of the human condition that we all face. Although there are, without doubt, happy moments in life—Christmas morning, theme-park vacations, fancy dinners, marriage proposals, puppies and kittens, ice cream, frolicking at the beach, or that one time you (insert your "cheery memory" here)—life's disappointments can come hard and fast, reminding us all too soon that the contentment we find on this planet is fleeting. Nothing—absolutely *nothing*—can fill us with gladness on a permanent basis if it originates from this world. Most of us don't like admitting this, but that doesn't make it any less true.

But what if Ecclesiastes isn't what people think it is? What if there is another explanation for its murky, dreary words?

A fact many don't know (because unfortunately, it's never taught anymore) is that Solomon was following a writing style customary in the ancient Near East, literally termed "pessimism literature" (alternatively, "pessimistic philosophy"). Today, some readers take in the words of Ecclesiastes and think, *Man, what is this guy's problem?* But the tradition of pessimism literature traces back to at least 2000 BC, as antique Egyptian and Mesopotamian texts show.[78] (Related works include the Egyptian *The Good Fortune of the Dead*, *A Dispute Over Suicide*, and *The Satire on the Trades*.) Specific to Egypt, rulers would explore the unanswered questions of life, blame their many gods for being unfair, characterize the heroes of their religion as being distant and aloof to the problems of the world, and finally, through the process, attempt to find answers to the social and political problems they confronted in daily life. Thus, the purpose of pessimism literature was ultimately to explore difficulties and then show transparency to the people while the government worked out a fix for them (although it could be debated whether the "answers" led to any real solutions, and some of these texts never arrived at remedy at all). It's irony at its finest, but the result of these writings was optimistic: *Negativity, doubt, and cynicism were the framework upon which a positive message could be constructed.* More simply: You can't *fix* a dilemma until you admit that you *have* a dilemma. Beginning in or around ancient Egypt, kings would use pessimism literature to address these problems, make sure everyone knew it was "the gods' fault," and then produce an optimistic response, kind of like a "State of the Union Address" would for Western politicians today.

The writer of Ecclesiastes, however, doesn't blame God for the predicament of this mortal plane. In fact, the very end of the book reveals great hope (note that references to "the preacher" are believed to be King Solomon):

And moreover, because the preacher was wise, he still taught the people knowledge; yea, he...set in order many proverbs. The preacher sought to find out acceptable words: and that which was written was upright, even words of truth. The words of the wise are as goads [sticks that the ancients poked animals with to make them move; the word-picture here is that the words of the wise provoke people to action], and as nails fastened by the masters of assemblies, which are given from one shepherd. And further, by these, my son, be admonished: of making many books there is no end; and much study is a weariness of the flesh. Let us hear the conclusion of the whole matter: Fear God, and keep his commandments: for this is the whole duty of man. For God shall bring every work into judgment, with every secret thing, whether it be good, or whether it be evil. (Ecclesiastes 12:8–14)

In the end, God knows who is up to no good, and that activity will be revealed in eternity. Fearing the Lord and obeying what He asks of us is, Solomon says, "the whole duty of man" in this beautiful arrangement.

The whole duty of man.

We don't have to do anything else. We have the easy part, while God took on the hard part. Our sole requirement while we occupy bodies of flesh is to trust God and let Him do what He's perfect at. Again, it's ironic, but the point is: Life can be as easy and as enjoyable as that! It's a pleasure to serve God, so if we live to accomplish that, then life is pleasurable!

Solomon's whole goal, in following the tradition of the "pessimism literature" of his day, was to produce a holy counterpart to Israel's secular, pagan neighbors! Its work is "a reply to the unrelieved pessimism of much ancient thought."[79] Though the "tone" and "attitude" of Ecclesiastes rubs us wrong in the contemporary Western world, that is most certainly *not* how it would have landed with original readers who were familiar with that type of literature. Solomon's bookworms would have seen Ecclesiastes as an exploration of humanity similar in tone to other literature of the day, and they would have recognized its God-fearing tone and inflexible insistence on serving Yahweh as the answer to all of life's hardships. Ecclesiastes serves the purpose of exalting our One and Only God above all others.

Earlier in this work, we talked about God leading Abraham all the way up the mountain to sacrifice his son, Isaac, to illustrate His *rebuke* of such a practice. It was an Almighty "smackdown" of what the pagans of Ur (Abraham's former culture) were up to. God wasn't endorsing, or even entertaining the idea of, human sacrifice. He used the journey up the mountain to make His replacement sacrificial system stick with Abraham in a way he could never forget. Here, Solomon leads readers all the way up a mountain of pessimism well known to his readers and the pagans of his day to find answers to human problems to *rebuke* the negative attitude brought on by relying on one's self to find answers! It's an Almighty "smackdown" of the way kings in Solomon's day and age would handle the problems of the people. Solomon wasn't endorsing, or even entertaining the idea of, the pursuit of happiness through "gods" or human means. He used the journey of his book to make his optimistic teaching stick with his readers in a way they can never forget!

And, in the end, God is always the answer.

Ha! Who knew Ecclesiastes was written to dispute and defy the hopelessness of those who adhered to the pagan religions? (If you're a pastor, *please* preach this!)

To be fair, this is not all to say the rest of the book that reads in a melancholy way wasn't honestly felt and personally experienced by the author. The darkness is so expertly articulated it could only come from one who had gone through tremendous dissatisfaction. And from what we know of Solomon, he really *did* have it all, so for him to say that nothing on earth meant anything in the light of eternity stands as the highest example of how earthly pursuits really are, well, vain. He was, as they say, "a *real* man" for saying so during a time when retributional justice (refer to the study of Job) was the expectation of the Hebrews.

But the miracle of the book is in Solomon's unwavering conclusion that he does actually have the answer…whereas the neighboring kings did not. They were doomed to continue searching, expecting that this tweak to the law over here or that adjustment of governmental policy over there would bring answers the people could believe.

The fact that pessimism literature ever became a distinct form of writings for the royals is proof that it never worked. If it had, there would have been one book everyone could consult for guidance on addressing the problems of life, and there wouldn't have been any need for multiple manuscripts. In other words, the existence of so many differing texts is a testimony of their failure.

Perhaps now you can understand why there is only one pessimism-literature category of books in the Bible. It *was* the answer; no other "explorations" were necessary.

Do you see? Solomon was being optimistic! He had the answers nobody else had! Ecclesiastes is *so* misunderstood...

As far as what any of this has to do with Jesus, the answer is probably obvious, but we will state it anyway, because it's just too good not to: If all of life absent God is "meaningless," "vanity," and a "chasing after the wind," then the presence of God in our lives causes the opposite. Life with God is not meaningless, he's the meaning of it all; living apart from Him is not vanity, it's exceedingly valuable; and tackling life without the Lord—which is futile, like chasing after the wind—brings abundant life, and it's worth every effort we make to chase after Him! Ecclesiastes was, of course, written before the promised Messiah arrived and completed the work of salvation on the cross, so Solomon's book bleeds with an even more powerful message of evangelism than it did then.

But don't take our word for it. As one scholar notes:

[Ecclesiastes] is thus both an evangelistic tract, calling secular people to face the implications of their secularism, and a call to realism, summoning faithful Israelites to take seriously the "futility," the "enigma" of life in this world. It forbids both secularism (living as though the existence of God has no practical usefulness for life in this world) and unrealistic optimism (expecting faith to cancel out life as it really is). Negatively, it warns us that "faith" is always a contrast to "sight" and does not provide us with a short cut fully to understand the ways of God. Positively, it calls us to a life of faith and joy.[80]

If ever there was a book that saw reality for what it is in relationship to God, Ecclesiastes is it. Jesus is the conqueror of all life's frustrations. Without the Gospel, life is pointless. All is meaningless and vain, just as the wealthiest and wisest king of Israel said. The world is insecure, chaotic, and temporary. Revisiting the outline of Ecclesiastes with fresh perspective shows us just how true that is. Again, with *just* the pessimistic bits that many question, and avoiding material that is repeated in several areas, let's look at the harsh words "the preacher" has to say about this temporal life, with contemporary rephrasing:

A generation comes and goes, and many are forgotten; the sun rises and sets, just to go back to where it rose; the wind blows in all directions, simply to return to its circuit; the streams lead to the sea, but the seas are never full; the eye never sees, and the ear never hears, enough to satisfy them; those who have gone before us have already experienced essentially all there is to experience in the world and there is nothing new under the sun; things are crooked and lacking; the very pursuit of wisdom exposes the lack thereof forever, leading to a vexed, exasperating thirst for more that no man can ever satiate; the increase of knowledge is the increase of sorrow (Ecclesiastes 1).

A quest for pleasure is superficial, leading only to emptiness; houses, vineyards, gardens, parks, pools, servants, livestock, silver, gold, women (or men)—none of it matters; hard work is just toil that never pays more than a salary, which cannot serve man other than to fill his pockets with the money he will spend on the items that titillate his hunger for fulfillment; the wise man breathes his last breath the same as the fool; life is to be hated when there is nothing to gain from it (Ecclesiastes 2).

Humanity cannot comprehend the cyclic timing of God's creation; even the most righteous have some wickedness in their hearts;

as beasts die, so, too, do people, so one is not superior to the other if this earthly life is all that counts (Ecclesiastes 3).

The oppressed are everywhere, and many will never have a friend to dry their tears; toil and hard work never lead to an end, as one must simply continue to work for life; people are lonely; even kings fail their kingdoms despite their best efforts, leaving nothing but a failed legend and a spotted record of their lives and reign (Ecclesiastes 4).

It's no surprise that there is an abortion of justice on earth; monetary investments often don't pan out; nothing we accumulate in this life can follow us into the next, so there is no point in such collection (Ecclesiastes 5).

There is much evil in this world to burden mankind; without regard to an eternity, life means as much as a passing shadow (Ecclesiastes 6).

The fullness of wisdom is always far from us; the perfect spouse or human companion cannot fix or fulfill this overwhelming search for more (Ecclesiastes 7).

No one has power over death; war will always be waged between mere humans; sickness and disease will forever affect our health while we live; the praises of mankind's achievement are only vanity; justice against evil in this life takes too long, encouraging the wicked to continue in their iniquity; malicious people can still live longer and more prosperously than the meek and righteous; good people get what bad ones deserve, and bad people get what good ones deserve, so we may as well give up and eat, drink, and be merry; we will never understand all that transpires in this life (Ecclesiastes 8).

Being righteous or evil, wise or foolish, clean or unclean, obedient or disobedient to the Law and sacrifices, keeping or breaking promises—nothing can purchase an extension of this life or guarantee we will not be forgotten by those who come after us; not even our wisdom can be carried past the grave; we cannot rely on our expectations, because the unexpected will occur as soon as we do (Ecclesiastes 9).

Foolishness has a payoff against wisdom, just as dead flies in an expensive perfume makes it stink; foolishness makes its home in high places, just like a prince who walks the road like a slave; one who digs a hole will fall into it, while one who tears down a wall will be bitten by the snake whose home was disturbed; the person who cuts stones at a quarry will be hurt by the stones, and this is true of the person who splits logs; a dull blade requires more physical strength to wield; the snake charmer who takes too long to charm a wild snake will be bitten, and the advantage of the charmer is lost; woe to the kingdom whose king is a child; the lazy person's home will spring a leak; no gossip will ever remain a secret forever (Ecclesiastes 10).

If you throw your bread into the water, it will come back to annoy you upon the waves in a few days, so instead, share your substance, because nobody knows what's about to happen; full clouds will rain; a tree that falls will lay there; those who merely sit and watch the wind will not sow, and those who merely sit and watch the rain will not reap; we can't fully understand how a baby's bones are knitted together in a mother's womb, so we can't understand the ways of God who makes them; a long life may understandably bring rejoicing, but it will also bring days of darkness and despair; everyone looks forward to inevitable judgment; so stop worrying about things like youth, because it is in vain (Ecclesiastes 11).

So remember the Creator while you're young before all these disappointments hit you and you find yourself saying you find no pleasure in your days; people go to their eternal home, and mourning is in the streets at their passing; when their spirits return to the God who gave them life in the first place, all these things will be revealed as vanity, nothing but vanity; as I taught my people knowledge, weighing and studying and compiling proverbs carefully, I set out to write happy thoughts and words of delight, but instead I wrote truth; the words of the wise inspire people to action, and the words of wisdom I have provided this world are as solidly fixed as a nail fully driven in; beware of anything beyond wisdom, because books will always abound in number, but worthless knowledge makes people weary; in the end, as a final statement, I leave you with this: Fear God, keep

His commandments, because this is the sole purpose and duty we have in this life—God sees all, and ultimately, He will expose every deed, whether good or evil, because nothing is secret on judgment day (Ecclesiastes 12).

So is Solomon cynical? Absolutely, a thousand times, *yes*. Is he negative? Not even a little bit. He's *honest* about worldly pursuits that do not take the afterlife into consideration.

Can we find any good news or positive thinking in the Ecclesiastes?

Well, apart from the most obvious message that the Father, and now the Son in our time, is the answer to everything (which should be enough by itself)...now that you mention it, yes.

One major, recurring statement in Ecclesiastes is the benefit of wisdom. As only a few examples among many: "Then I saw that there is more gain in wisdom than in folly, as there is more gain in light than in darkness" (2:13). "For the protection of wisdom is like the protection of money, and the advantage of knowledge is that wisdom preserves the life of him who has it" (7:12); "Wisdom is better than weapons of war, but one sinner destroys much good" (9:18).

Solomon also provided specific patterns for how wisdom works in practical ways, like his comment about the lazy homeowner: "Through sloth the roof sinks in, and through indolence the house leaks" (10:18).

He recognized the good things that come in life (see? he acknowledges happy moments!) are from God and should therefore be enjoyed: "There is nothing better for a person than that he should eat and drink and find enjoyment in his toil. This also, I saw, is from the hand of God" (2:24); "Go, eat your bread with joy, and drink your wine with a merry heart, for God has already approved what you do" (9:7; this verse refers to the reward of those who charitably care for the poor). And this sort of enjoyment is brought up a surprising number of times for a "pessimist" (see: 3:12; 3:22; 5:18; 8:15; 11:7–12:1).

Amazingly, the wise king endorsed random acts of enjoyment between his discourses about "vanity": "Light is sweet, and it is pleasant for the eyes to see the sun. So if a person lives many years, let him rejoice in them all" (11:7–8).

In perhaps the most powerful and oft-referenced portion of the book, Solomon acknowledged the seasons and "the time for everything under heaven," expressing that God has everything under control, He "has made everything beautiful in its time," and "whatever [He] does endures forever" (3:1–8, 11, 14).

It's also critical to note that, when Solomon is at his most negative, he speaks in the *past tense*: "So I hated life, because what is done under the sun was grievous to me, for all is vanity and a striving after wind" (2:17); "And I thought the dead who are already dead more fortunate than the living who are still alive" (4:2). "Hated," "thought": The fact that these feelings are in the past tells us that, when he reaches the finale, he will have overcome these struggles with a new message: There is hope for one who trusts in the sovereignty of Yahweh!

We've said it before, and we reserve the right to say it as many times as needed until we all can grab hold of this truth and put it into practice: We must not isolate any verses from their context, nor should we draw sensitive or offensive conclusions from our scriptural studies without knowing the material's historical and cultural background. To do otherwise results in nothing less than a violent abuse of Scripture.

Everything "the preacher" said was true. All the horrible things he said about our experience as mortals may not make us feel the warm fuzzies, but they are nonetheless words of pure, unadulterated, undiluted fact: Life without Christ is as depressing, abysmal, unfulfilling, superficial, unsatisfying, unrewarding, thankless, and fruitless as the worst volumes of the pessimism literature state. The breath in our lungs *will* cease, and all we can plead for is…an afterlife that balances it all and finally settles the score.

Thankfully, we have that in Christ. He is the answer to all our blessed hope, and His gracious role in our world simply never stops giving.

We hope this reflection has changed the way readers will view Ecclesiastes in the future. Yet, it is not the only one of Solomon's writings that is often grievously misinterpreted. In fact, the wise king created quite a humdinger with the Song of Solomon.

Song of Solomon (or Song of Songs)

This is the last of the books traditionally accredited to Solomon. Having reviewed the hill of arguments regarding his authorship, it does appear likely to these authors that Solomon did in fact write it; though, even if he didn't, the evidence shows it to be a near certainty that it was at least dedicated to him, written with him in mind, or written in the Solomonic tradition that he began. "The title associates Song of Songs with the name of Solomon and literally reads, 'The Song of Songs which is to Solomon.'"[81] For ease and brevity, we will simply refer to this book as "Songs."

Songs is a collection of love songs that tell the story of the beautiful and tender love between an unnamed man and woman. Its passages are poetic and include words of affection, reflecting the sort of romance that fits within the context of the order God created in the beginning, when He noted that everything He had established was "good" (Genesis 1:31). In this regard, we know what the book talks about and understand that we should view it as a wonderful expression of love the Creator ordained.

However, to get the elephant in the room out of the way: The book also appears to be heavily entrenched with euphemisms, many of which are sexual. This was not an accident, and it, like Ecclesiastes, was following a poetic style of literature at the time. That's why we'll here part interpretational ways from one of the most popular approaches to Songs in the Western theological world. We will discuss that interpretation now.

For those who may not be familiar with the concept of a marriage between God and His followers as a biblical symbol, it may help to read the first three chapters of Hosea. Not only was God spoken of in spousal terms by the prophets as a way of illustrating the covenantal love He had for Israel and the spiritual fidelity required of His people, but the prophet Hosea's marriage to an unfaithful wife was arranged by God to illustrate how Israel had committed infidelity against Him through the sin of idolatry. So, this symbolization is not new, making many believe it must be the spirit behind Songs.

This makes interpreting this book somewhat of a conundrum for many scholars, who still argue to this day whether Songs should be read: 1) as *only* a description of God's order of love that serves as a good pattern for couples to follow, or, 2) as many modern sources claim, as an allegory of the relationship between Christ and His Church as Bride. The overwhelming majority of academics fall into one of these two categories.

If the former interpretation is correct: The blush that rises to our cheeks is like that of a chaste, young, virgin bride: a product of God's willingness to candidly address matters of intimacy in marriage without considering such a thing to be profane, blasphemous, or irreverent. It carries a "we're all adults here" approach that handles sexual matters maturely and unashamedly. We can celebrate physical love with innocence and delight, knowing that nothing is sinful about it within the margins of marriage between a husband and wife and that this God-designed act certainly can and should apply toward more than the goal of procreation.

If the latter interpretation is correct: The blush that rises to our cheeks is a product of awkward discomfort naturally drawn from the inference that the symbol of Christ and His Bride would be described with sensual terminology. This, too, requires us to handle the subject with maturity, but to many readers, it yields the question: Why couldn't God have chosen to represent Christ and the Church in another way, one that doesn't associate the Savior with such sensitive imagery?

Either way, once some of the language is fully understood, Songs may cause a lot of readers to blush. In fact, in the Jewish world, "Because of its erotic content, some rabbis forbid the reading of Song of Songs by anyone under 30."[82] As an example of its often explicit imagery: "This thy stature is like to a palm tree, and thy breasts to clusters of grapes. I said, I will go up to the palm tree, I will take hold of the boughs thereof: now also thy breasts shall be as clusters of the vine" (Songs 7:7–8a). If this expression relates to something physical, the man in this verse is looking upon his beautiful wife and lover, appreciating her curves (and other characteristics, obviously) and comparing her to a "tree" he wants to "climb." You can then imagine the allegorical interpreter's challenge: What does a verse like this specify about Christ and the Church?

There are also Hebraic euphemisms in Songs relating certain fruits, fruit juices, spices, and other elements that were considered, according to the innuendo of the day, to be intensely erotic (you can relax, we won't go into that here). Not to be crude, but today, if we hear that two people have "knocked boots" over the weekend, we generally know the phrase doesn't refer to a couple putting on their boots and kicking each other. There are such expressions in every age and culture, and Songs is no exception, having been written with far more explicit inferences than anything having to do with "boots," even though we may not be familiar with those "colorful" references in our modern world.

Adding to lingual insinuations are scattered references to aphrodisiacs in use in that day. Songs 7:13 mentions mandrakes, which we know from the story of Leah in Genesis 30:14–16 were used for that purpose. Surprisingly few scholars who persist in interpreting Songs as the story of Christ and His Bride make these connections and address them properly, leaving the sensual overtones lingering uneasily in the air and making the interpreters look a bit negligent.

Not surprisingly, because of the sensual nature of its language and tone, Songs' inclusion in the canon was highly debated. Eventually, it was approved for inclusion, and these authors believe that decision was guided by the Designer of love, who inspired the writer of Hebrews to document: "Let marriage be held in honor among all, and let the marriage bed be undefiled" (Hebrews 13:4a; ESV). Regardless of interpretational variance, we find the value of this book not in asking whether we need it in the canon or what purpose it serves among the other sixty-five books, but in asking what we would possibly do *without* it. Songs forces us to reexamine what love and sex look like in every era as the secular world and society modifies those subjects, allowing them to become more and more defiled, in opposition to such teachings as this Hebrews verse. We can't ignore that God designed intimacy to be an act shared by man and wife in the sanctity of a thing called "marriage." (Pardon our sarcasm, but, at this rate, "marriage" is on its way to becoming an obsolete word, and it's clear from biblical teaching that sex was never supposed to be experienced outside the sanctity of a marital relationship.)

Just as importantly, we cannot ignore that the physical is inseparable from the spiritual when marital intimacy occurs. This is a sweet and lovely thing, as Songs repeatedly shows. However, when practiced outside of marriage, the spiritual element remains, but, without repentance, it can be a major stain on one's life. For instance:

> But the body is not for sexual immorality, but for the Lord, and the Lord is for the body.... Do you not know that your bodies are parts of Christ? Shall I then take away the parts of Christ and make them parts of a prostitute? Far from it! Or do you not know that the one who joins himself to a prostitute is one body *with her*? For He [God] says, "The two shall become one flesh." (1 Corinthians 6:13, 15–16; NASB)

So, whether the Songs is about a man and wife *or* is a symbol of the bond between human and Divine, the sacredness and chastity of the relationship it describes cannot be supplanted with "casual sex" or a violation of that sacred union ordained by God. To put it more simply: If Songs is "Christ and Bride," it is pure, holy, and undefiled; if Songs is "man and wife," it is pure, holy, and undefiled. Either way, the modern, Western idea that intimacy can be treated casually—or as a physical encounter that takes place outside of marriage in any way—is to soil, profane, and defile God's intent. This is at least one area where scholars unanimously agree: "The love the couple shared was exclusive and binding ([Songs] 7:10). By implication this ideal portrait excludes extramarital sex as well as all perversions and abuses of sexuality, such as promiscuity."[83]

Despite this, "as of October 2020, the latest large-scale research and statistics report [on religion] reflects that…premarital sex is agreeable to *half* of all evangelicals."[84] The Body of Christ would have no biblical grounds for handling this travesty if Songs wasn't included in the canon of Scripture. Through euphemisms and imagery, it paints the portrait of innocence and goodness that is God's plan for the order of His Creation. There's no doubt about it: Songs belongs in the Word of God.

As to how the content *should* be received, it isn't incorrect by any means to say the book is about Christ and His Bride; however, this kind of sexual language to describe the relationship isn't used anywhere else in Scripture. Faithfulness to God as represented by nuptial imagery (like that of Hosea)—imagery that's decidedly absent the sensual connotations—continues in the New Testament (in application to Christ and His Bride). This is why, awkwardness notwithstanding, we can't discount the importance of giving that interpretational method our attention. However, the glaring problem with this approach is when Songs must be compared to that image *in absolutely every single verse*, as countless scholars have persisted. In order to reach a healthy conclusion about proper interpretation that remains accountable to a reverent, worshipful attitude about Jesus, but also allows for matrimonial metaphors, we will start by looking at a few examples of how this subject has been mishandled in history. From there, we will swing back to the original thoughts of Jesus and His Church in more sensitive terms than may have been applied in the past.

Helpful theologians who have broken down the two main interpretational approaches admit that *if Songs wasn't in the canon of Holy Scripture*, there wouldn't even be a question about whether it is allegory; it would be read literally, from the perspective of man and wife, without having anything to do with God. As stated earlier, the writer was following a known style of literature at the time. Extrabiblical writings from Solomon's era have been found to be quite similar to Songs. These other works are universally accepted "as a collection of love poems that revel in a man and woman's physical passion and lovemaking," and the Greeks, after the close of the Hebrew canon, gave Songs this precise treatment.[85] The allegorical interpretation is, therefore, a late idea possibly magnified in part by Rabbi Aqiba and fellow second-century rabbis who were angered by the irreverent conduct of local Jews found singing the book's material "while wining and dining."[86]

However, another contributing development goes even further back: Around three hundred years before Christ's birth, teachers of Greek philosophy—Plato being a major contributor—taught there are two realities humans need to be concerned with: the physical and the spiritual. This was known as "dualism." Though it's not quite as easy as saying "the physical reality is evil, and the spiritual reality is sacred," that's the general idea. The Church rejected dualism in the early councils, but not until the grip of its influence was wound tightly around Greco-Roman culture, which proved to be a tough enemy to kill. St. Augustine, likely the most influential Christian theologian in Western history, also held to dualism, insisting that the only sexual act permissible for the true believer was in the interest of producing offspring. In his view, sexual desire or gratification for both males and females originated from the Fall account, because Adam and Eve were, like any members of the animal kingdom, unapologetically open about both the exhibition and function of their naked bodies in the beginning. *After* they sinned, they became ashamed of their nudity (and/or sexuality), and God's response was to make them clothes to cover themselves (Genesis 3:7, 21). Thus, God's response, in the opinion of Augustine and his contemporaries, was to limit sexual interaction to only what He saw as "good," which was to "be fruitful and multiply" (Genesis 1:28, 31). (Please note that such a theological conclusion does *not* align with the words of Paul in 1 Timothy 4:3–5 and 1 Corinthians 7:3–5. It also happens to contradict Adam's excited response to Eve—"This is now bone of my bones, and flesh of my flesh"—followed by the order God designed and approved of: "and they shall be one flesh" [Genesis 2:23a—24]. The congruency between Adam and God here is clear: "One flesh," by itself, celebrates the joining of man and wife, period. It does not require the intent of procreation to be holy or pure.) The sway of dualism, then, no doubt placed a great weight upon the shift from the natural, physical, and instructional interpretation of Songs to the allegorical/metaphorical.

Though we would never insinuate that earlier readings of Songs are more correct just because they are early, there is some merit to listening to the antique rabbinical analyses before dualism or irreverent "wining and dining" Jews entered the picture. It's more than a "whoever gets there first wins" race to a permanently indisputable finish line. As we showed in our context study of Ecclesiastes and its connection to the pessimism-literature tradition of ancient rulers, the gold mines of interpretation can be hidden from present-day culture and are very well worth digging for and paying attention to once found.

In addition to all of this is a well-known and respected principle of biblical interpretation (hermeneutics), which states: The interpreter should always assume that a biblical passage is communicating something *literal* to the reader, "unless this assumption creates an absurdity."[87] While this is true, we must still allow for euphemisms and figurative language to convey messages poetically and respectfully, even from a literal-interpretation approach. As one example: We know the woman of Songs would not really be a "tree" with "grapes" (a literal translation that "creates an absurdity"). The literal application in this moment does not cancel the figurative language ("tree" and "grapes" are her body), but it does identify the woman as a real, historical female.

If this sounds like inconsistent application—to those who would say "literal *must* stay literal, and allegorical *must* stay allegorical, therefore the woman is either a tree with grapes or she's the Bride, but she can't be merely an attractive love interest in Songs"—consider the book of Revelation. We know Satan is not bound to the physical body of a red dragon that has multiple heads and horns. His persuasion has been invisible since the beginning, yet we don't have billions of "Satan-dragon sightings" throughout history every time there has been a clear invasion of his influence. Yet, Revelation specifically self-interprets that this "dragon was...that old serpent, called the Devil, and Satan, which deceiveth the whole world" (Revelation 12:9). Therefore, the Bible *must* allow for figurative language (dragon with horns) to help describe a literal and historic place, thing, event, or person (Satan). What we have found extremely odd on our end is the number of mainstream, celebrated scholars who allow for the literal-but-figurative interpretation of Revelation, but insist upon the allegorical-only interpretation of Songs. That is inconsistent application of interpretational methods, and the scholars who maintain this don't explain how they justify tweaking the rules on this one book. The only reasons we can think of for this inconsistency is that either they've been trained to consider Songs the exception to that rule of interpretation, or they, too, feel uncomfortable allowing Songs to mean precisely what it sounds like while it upholds its position in the canon.

Certainly, again, it's an understatement to say that Songs is packed with figurative language. However, the "man and wife" interpretation *does not* "create an absurdity" like the metaphorical method (Christ having anything to do with the Bride's "grapes"), so it isn't irresponsible to maintain that the book depicts a literal couple in history. This is true even if its author chose to avoid vulgarity in his descriptions of the love scenes by using very clear, familiar (at the time) metaphors of physical romance instead of detailing intimate moments in an explicit way.

The greatest injustice of a *strictly* allegorical interpretation of Songs is that it forces one side to either accept or explain away a sensual image of Christ or His message when it doesn't need to! Those who stick to this position claim that, because the man in Songs is Jesus and the woman is the Church, when we read, "Let him kiss me with the kisses of his mouth" (Songs 1:2), we must see the "kisses" as the Word of God. Further, we must believe that the woman's dark skin in "I am black, but comely, O ye daughters of Jerusalem" (1:5), refers to sin; when "Jesus" says to the "Bride," "thy breasts to clusters of grapes" (7:7), He is referring to the Church's "nurturing doctrine"; and the "Bride's" lips, which "drop sweetness as the honeycomb" (4:11), are the Law and the Gospel.[88] These examples are quite a leap from the otherwise clear, natural, and romantic reading. What stops us from then deciding these euphemisms mean whatever we think they do in the spiritual realm? If we allow for this treatment of interpretation, in very little time, Songs could become a subjective book that bows to individual interpretation, and that could get ugly—*fast*—with a subject like this. We therefore agree with theologian Dr. Duane Garrett, in his contribution to "The Poetic and Wisdom Books" section of the *Holman Concise Bible Commentary*, when he says:

The New Testament never gives the Song an allegorical interpretation. New Testament passages that do speak of the bride of Christ do not refer to Song of Songs. [The allegorical interpretation] of Song of Songs is grossly inappropriate for worship. It is impossible to imagine a Christian praising Christ in the terms of 1:2 [kissing], 16 ["our bed is green"]; or 5:10–16 [the woman's description of her "beloved"]. It is equally bizarre to think of Jesus Christ describing His church in the terms of

7:1–9 [addressed in next paragraph];. This [strictly allegorical] interpretation has rightly been abandoned.[89]

The last passage Garrett mentions, Songs 7:1–9, involves the man's description of his lover, including feet, "thighs like jewels," belly button, "two breasts like two young roes [gazelles] that are twins," neck, eyes, nose, head, hair, posture, "breasts like grapes," breasts again "like the vine," and nose, followed by "the roof of [her] mouth like the best wine for my beloved, that goeth down sweetly, causing the lips of those that are asleep to speak." It's no wonder Garrett approves of abandoning this approach. And he's not the only one. Another source, *The Song of Songs: An Introduction and Commentary*, states that "when the woman describes her lover lying between her two breasts like a sachet of myrrh, [it is interpreted as] Jesus standing between the Old and New Testaments."[90] While this author understands the draw of the "Christ and Bride" method, as it releases teachers from having to "descend to the embarrassing matter of talking about sex from the pulpit," he acknowledges that many scholars find the method to be "a profound mistake" for the same reasons we do.[91] He goes on to discuss Songs 6:11: "I went down into the garden of nuts to see the fruits of the valley, and to see whether the vine flourished and the pomegranates budded." Humorously, he illustrates how many verses in Songs mean simply what they say:

Notice that the text of the Song doesn't say that the church is like a nut, or even that Israel is like a nut; merely that the lover went down to a garden of nuts… There seems no obvious reason why [we] should be connected with hard shells and sweet kernels, or with believers being "hidden with Christ in God." In fact, I can think of some churches that might aptly be described as "a garden of nuts," while using the image in an entirely different sense![92]

If the interpretation of Songs is improperly handled, Christ becomes sexualized. We don't need to say just how obsessed and immoral the world is right now with carnal thoughts, especially in the West, so sexualizing the Savior is the last thing any of us needs when He otherwise stands so far apart from the subject. The Word of God is a pure and holy book. Associating its Grand Hero with language intended to describe the event of a wedding bed (as opposed to the benign concept of spiritual fidelity to God represented in nuptial language elsewhere) no doubt gives a very wrong impression to believers who are young in the faith. If they have just come from the secular world into a saving trust in Christ, they won't know any better than to allow their mind to be imprinted (perhaps permanently) with some terrible, muddied portrayals of the Messiah via the allegorical interpretational method of this book. The topic of healthy, undefiled sexuality is confusing enough as it is without adding these kinds of problems to current Christian teaching. It's best to allow for the interpretation of Songs as it was originally intended.

Thus, we believe, in the interest of remaining closest to the author's intent toward his first audience (which is the very definition of trustworthy exegesis), Songs is a collection of ballads "sung" from a human male to his human wife, and the suggestive bits mean precisely what they sound like. Not only does this approach cling to the rules of proper biblical analysis, taking context and history into consideration, it also negates the awkwardness that arises from placing our relationship with the Savior in the same frame as a man appreciating his wife's "curves" (and more).

Now that we've established some groundwork, let's bring back some of the balance that can and should be present in its teaching. It's not that there is no room for appreciating the theme of Songs in any other way; the baby doesn't need to be thrown out with the bathwater on this. Accepting the "man and wife" literal approach does not discount the concept of covenantal love between God and Israel or Christ and His Bride as represented in other Scriptures and *as reflected* in Songs. And this can be done without contradicting what we've discussed: All along we've been showing that, although Christ "appears" in every *book* of the Word, He doesn't necessarily show up in every *verse*. If He did, we would have quite a bit of explaining to do in such verses as "But there was none like unto Ahab, which did sell himself to work wickedness in the sight of the Lord, whom Jezebel his wife stirred up [with her idols]." This verse is from 1 Kings (21:25)—the same book that typifies Jesus as King of all kings and Lord of all lords.

Likewise, Christ is the Kindred Redeemer or "Boaz" of Ruth, but He never approached Ruth and said, "It hath fully been shewed me, all that thou hast done unto thy mother in law" (Ruth 2:11) like Boaz did. Job was a type of Christ also, in that he: a) always trusted in the sovereignty of God; b) treasured the words of God more than food; c) faced taunting and betrayal from his closest friends; d) suffered even while he was innocent; and e) was fully lifted up and restored by the Father. When we make those connections, they are met with a corporate nod of approval by believers who see the same beautiful picture we do. Yet, we would not claim that Job typified Christ when he sat scraping his sores with broken pottery or when Yahweh appeared to him in a whirlwind to explain how Creation worked. David is a type of Christ as a great ruler and king, but nobody in their right minds would say that applied to the moments of weakness he had with Bathsheba.

The problem with taking a hard stance on one side or the other of the interpretational fence with Songs in the same way the Church has throughout history is that it places us in a restrictive box: We must either concede that *all* verses in the Songs describe man and wife or *all* verses describe Christ and Bride.

Please, for once and for all, can we agree to be free of those redundant and superfluous shackles?! We don't "see Christ" in "all" verses of any *other* book, so why does this have to be the approach with *Songs*? Balance is needed here, and balance is absolutely what is missing from traditional examinations of Songs: There is no room to see the beauty in the possibility of *both* interpretations having value when we're expected to choose a side or else be seen as indecisive and wavering like the "double-minded man, unstable in all his ways" (James 1:8). This has led to far more disputes among scholars than is necessary.

Then is Jesus reflected at all in Songs?

With the keyword "balance" in mind, yes.

In the study of Proverbs, we went against the grain by refusing to agree to the popularized ideal that Jesus is Sophia. As we stated then, that positions us in the unpopular minority. Likewise, we will again refuse to allow God's Son to be observed as the husband in Songs, because the overt sexuality simply doesn't connect with how our relationship with Christ works theologically. But with a view that distinctly separates the eroticism of Songs from the nonthreatening nuptial imagery in Israel's history from Genesis and all the way through the New Testament, we can still see that the tender love between a man and woman has always been a universal portrait of the loving relationship between God and man.

Remember, Songs is categorized as a Wisdom book. It fits in perfectly with its comrades Psalms, Proverbs, and Ecclesiastes. So, it's not surprising that, just as Jesus appears in those books *viewed as a whole work*, He shows up in the whole work of Songs in a similar way. He doesn't have to be one of the characters for that to be true. In Psalms, He is the Answer to the cries of Israel (and now Gentiles); in Proverbs, He is Wisdom personified (but not Sophia); in Ecclesiastes, He is the Reason we draw breath and the Answer to every pessimistic thought.

In Songs, He is Love—*not* to be confused with anything physical. His Kingdom is—

Not.

Of.

This.

World.

Removing His physicality in Songs "lifts Him above" the story (like the Father) as an observer from heaven—His current Kingdom until the Millennial Reign and His residence at the right hand of the Father, with whom He is "one" (John 17). Through that lens, He shares the same relationship with us as His Father has from the beginning (with the obvious difference of His humanity almost a thousand years after Songs was penned). From His heavenly seat and equality with the Father, He will always understand and acknowledge the nuptial imagery throughout Israel's history, which now (because of His First Advent) includes Gentiles.

Therefore, starting with the relationship of Yahweh over Israel, we read that sin is compared to prostitution (Isaiah 57:3; Jeremiah 3:2; 13:27; Micah 1:7); Israel's idolatry and the breaking of the Covenant is likened to a shattered, dysfunctional marriage (Hosea 1–2; Jeremiah 2–3; Isaiah 50; Ezekiel 16; 23); the coming Messianic Age is prophesied to be as a marriage and marriage feast (Isaiah 25:6; 54:1–8; 62:4–5; Hosea 2:7), as well as an "everlasting covenant" (Ezekiel 16:60; Isaiah 55:3). (By the way, the subject of the "everlasting covenant" is absent in Songs—one last argument supporting why the Messiah is not the "husband of Songs.")

Moving into the New Testament, this covenantal language continues. The Church, or the Body of Christ, is referred to as the Bride (Matthew 9:14–17; Mark 2:19–20; John 3:27–30; 2 Corinthians 11:2). Regarding fidelity and faithfulness, the meaning is kept intact throughout…along with the responsibility of righteous devotion on our part that this implies. We read in Ephesians 5:27 that the Bride of Christ should be a virtuous virgin, undefiled by spiritual adultery, "a glorious church, not having spot, or wrinkle, or any such thing; but that it should be holy and without blemish." We, the Church, "are they which are called unto the marriage supper of the Lamb" (Revelation 19:9), when we will be dressed in "fine linen, clean and white: for the fine linen is the righteousness of saints" (19:8). This magnificent feast near the end of time is an event Jesus looks forward to sharing with those who have maintained loyalty to Him, as He shared while He lived among humanity (Matthew 22:1–14; 25:1–13;

26:29; Luke 14:15–24). There is a final call for sinners to join us with Christ on this unfathomable day of celebration: "And the Spirit and the bride say, 'Come.' And let him that heareth say, 'Come.' And let him that is athirst come. And whosoever will, let him take the water of life freely" (Revelation 22:17).

This picture offers a reminder of two things: First, we have an intense duty during our time on earth to fulfill the Great Commission, telling the lost that there is Good News (Matthew 28:16–20)! Second, we don't keep the covenant with Jesus out of fear that we will lose some part of our end-times inheritance, or even out of being terrified by thoughts of hell, but because there is *joy* and only the deepest-felt fulfilment for our souls in sharing innocent, clean, wholesome intimacy in our relationship with Jesus.

Songs may not describe in every detail the relationship the Church has to its Savior, but it *does* reflect the heavenly ideal of love Yahweh always had for Israel and the Son will always have for the world. If the lines between these concepts are kept sharp, clean, and free of blurry, clumsy scribbles that contribute to the merging of eroticism and theology, we are left with a crystal-clear image—not of *sex*, but of the highest form of mutual closeness, affection, friendship, tenderness, adoration, and devotion between us and our Best Friend, precious Yeshua.

Every human knows what it's like to feel lonely. Every person who has been happily married for many years knows what it's like to have found a companion to share life with. Though there is, on this earth, a built-in expression of that companionship that remains to be physical while we live in mortal bodies—and it should be seen as good and embraced with gratitude to the One who designed it that way—it's the nonphysical and spiritual component of that marital bond that remains in view when we direct our thoughts to those members of the Trinity whose Kingdom is *also* spiritual.

The purest, most fulfilling love we will ever experience is from Jesus, who took upon Himself the worst physical suffering imaginable so that we can enjoy His love on even a more profound level when we transcend into spiritual beings and join Him for the feast of the consummation of this life as the Bride.

Tell us...is that glorious? Or is that *glorious?*

Conclusion to the Wisdom Literature

The books categorized as Wisdom literature all address ways of promoting this current life on a day-to-day basis: how to live in a way that glorifies God with wisdom, prudence, and self-control. But the purpose of shaping this human experience into something that pleases our Lord is ultimately to inherit the afterlife promised after we expire—and to take as many souls as we can along with us. There, in eternity with Christ, we will finally feel the weight of this world lifted. This world, will in fact, be replaced with a new one, where there will be no tears, "no more death, neither sorrow, nor crying, neither shall there be any more pain: for the former things are passed away" (Revelation 21:4).

Behold, He makes all things new (Revelation 21:5)!

Jesus is the Mediator of Justice Job couldn't see, the Hope and Answer the psalmists looked forward to, the Perfected Wisdom that Proverbs anticipated, the Meaning of Life that Ecclesiastes projected, and the Love of God that the Songs reflected. In all of these books put together, Jesus is the Redeemer, our Blessed *Go'el,* who far surpassed and fulfilled every expectation...

...While He also fulfilled every *prophecy.*

The Prophets

THE PROPHETIC LITERATURE of the Bible is broken into two main categories: "Major Prophets" and "Minor Prophets." The Major Prophets are Isaiah, Jeremiah, Lamentations, Ezekiel, and Daniel, called "major" only for their length (and though Lamentations is shorter, it's grouped with Jeremiah, as he is seen as the author in tradition). The shorter books are designated as "minor": Hosea, Joel, Amos, Obadiah, Jonah, Micah, Nahum, Habakkuk, Zephaniah, Haggai, Zechariah, and Malachi. Together, this represents seventeen books, all of which are equally important to the Word of God.

In a standard Bible-study book, these men would likely be handled individually, or at least grouped together by subject a few at a time, and there would be a heavy focus on Israel's mistakes as they repeatedly flourished or deteriorated based on whether or not they listened to God's words as delivered through these servants. But in a work like this one, in which the focus always leads to how Jesus is viewed in Scripture—and with the pattern of Israel's disobedience and the consequences of it having been well established already—we won't spend the additional pages needed to do that topic justice.

Just as the Law books and the Wisdom books were grouped together, the Prophets, both Major and Minor, will also be a single category as, in this work, all point to the same Person.

That raises an issue regarding the word "prophet" in the Bible. Most people, when they hear this term, think "fortune teller for God" is an accurate definition of a prophet. Therefore, it should be noted early on that, although the prophets did sometimes foretell of a future event that had precise fulfillment (both in their times and later on), there was much more than that involved with being a prophet. Like judges, prophets were directly chosen by God, and their children didn't inherit their position when the prophets passed away. Unlike kings, who were lavished in wealth and surrounded by servants, prophets were usually regular Joes, just people who were appointed to this holy position after having a radical, personal encounter with Yahweh. There were no crystal balls or tarot cards—such practices were forbidden—but the messages from God to His people came directly from Him and were reiterated through the mouths of prophets. Instead of consulting the muses or some other such pagan sorcery, the prophets sought God's voice through prayer and supplication—and many times He answered them directly. Not every message was a prediction. In fact, only one-third of the material derived from the prophets is predictive. Many times, God simply wanted to give His people a message via the prophets that would offer a new perspective on something happening in the moment.

Concerning Christ, obviously—because, of course, the Prophets are Old Testament books—everything said of Him spoke of future events, as the Messiah was a distant hope in their day. Today, the arrival, life, death, resurrection, and ascension of the Messiah is in the past. As such, the words of the Old Testament prophets about the Messiah are intrinsically linked to their New Testament fulfillments, causing us to question whether their messianic testimonies should: 1) be saved until our study on the Gospels, Acts, Epistles, and Revelation to look at the predictions and fulfillments at the same time; or 2) be covered in both our sections on the Old and the New Testaments, which naturally would lead to us address the same material twice. In the end, we opted for a third idea, in which we'll look at the words of the prophets at the end of the Old Testament study and then we'll examine their fulfillments in the New Testament study. Though this plan does mean that this part of the book will read far differently than the previous discussions and might leave readers in suspense about some of the prophecies' fulfillments, that is quite appropriate, as that's precisely how the Jews felt about their Someday Messiah. In fact, though there is much material in the academic world regarding the four hundred years of "silence" from God between the writings of the last book in the Old Testament and the first book of the New Testament (referred to as the "Intertestamental Period"), Scripture doesn't address the developments of the nation of Israel at this time. The Jews largely didn't know how their Messiah would appear (as evident in the assumptions of the Pharisees, Sadducees, and scribes), and we'd like to convey similar circumstance here. We'd like reader to "feel" instead of simply "read" this portion of our study. (This is also why the grammatical tense here will be in the present from Isaiah forward to the Gospels, as it will help transports readers to the time of the prophets.)

That said, any of the prophets can be seen as a type of Christ, in that they each sacrificed their own happiness and societal status in trade for suffering and being brought low, like servants, to obey God's directives during frightening shifts in Israel's history. Of all the studies that show how Jesus is present in the Word, the overwhelming majority focuses on the books of the prophets and Christ's fulfillment of what the prophets said. Therefore, to keep our book from parroting exhaustive information already available—and because this three-book work is already longer than those we typically release at Defender Publishing and SkyWatch Television—we'll take a truncated and condensed look at the Prophets (but we promise cliff-hangers will be resolved later in our reflections on Jesus in the books of the New Testament, which will also feature some verses not mentioned here).

This leads us to a final note before we launch: Many of the prophets' words, and some of their visions, are incredibly difficult to interpret. For instance, Ezekiel's visions involving wheels (Ezekiel 1) are highly debated and can sometimes lead to some odd theology (including some who believe the wheels were extraterrestrial flying saucers—an interpretation that we won't endorse or refute here). We believe the vast majority of readers will be relieved by our approach to stay out of these deep theological trenches to stick to what is most relevant to our study of Israel's Someday Messiah.

Let's begin with the first of the Major Prophets, Isaiah. From there, we'll examine the books in their canonical order, not in the order of chronological history.

Isaiah

Isaiah's level of education and connections to high-ranking public officials and royalty shows he is positioned for success in society, but God has other plans. When the Northern Kingdom (that retained the name "Israel") faces the Assyrian Exile, Isaiah has many reasons to fear the same fate for the Southern Kingdom (Judah) if the people don't submit to God's authority. A central theme of this lengthy book covers the concepts of God's people falling into the hands of a pagan government if they aren't obedient to His Law, even if choosing to obey drives them to give up the things they value. To avoid being exiled in the same nature as the Northern Kingdom, people of Judah have to humble themselves and show they're willing to be servants of Yahweh.

"Servants" is a key word here…and it appears that nobody is going to rise to the challenge. Giving up every grand thing in his earthly life, Isaiah stands as a righteous example of one who knows Yahweh's Kingdom is eternal, requiring a sacrifice of his temporal life in the interest of the afterlife. Someday, Isaiah prophesies, there will be an even greater example than he. That Person, as He is depicted by Isaiah, will be the Servant to outperform all servants...and He is going to experience extreme suffering.

The passage in Isaiah 52:13–53:12 speaks of how Israel's Suffering Servant will be incredibly unpopular, "despised and rejected of men" (also see 49:5–12). He will be "a man of sorrows, and acquainted with grief," "wounded for our transgressions, [and] bruised for our iniquities." Yet, He will also be "exalted and extolled, and be very high" in a way the people can't understand because He will be "numbered with the transgressors." In this bizarre picture of One who will be hated and grouped with the criminals of His day is another layer of meaning hidden behind the canvas: This One's work will flip the situation around unexpectedly when He bears "the sin of many" in His obedience, making Him worthy to make "intercession for the transgressors."

This is a concept the Israelites find hard to comprehend. (Remember, they largely hold to the Deuteronomic retributional justice pattern as a promise, not as a standard or principle.) How is such a thing possible? Who would be despised *and* exalted on high?

Isaiah explains precisely who this Man will be, and how He can be recognized: "Therefore the Lord himself shall give you a sign; Behold, a virgin shall conceive, and bear a son, and shall call his name Immanuel" (7:14). The Hebrew *Immanuel* is a name meaning "God with us," and it was to be taken literally. Someday God will be the incarnate Servant, born through a virgin, walking and talking "with us" humans upon the earth. At His birth, camels will carry important men who will "bring gold and incense; and they shall shew forth the praises of the Lord" (60:6). His arrival will thoroughly change the way government operates:

For unto us a child is born, unto us a son is given: and the government shall be upon his shoulder: and his name shall be called "Wonderful," "Counsellor," "The mighty God," "The everlasting Father," "The Prince of Peace." Of the increase of his government and peace there shall be no end, upon the throne of David, and upon his kingdom, to order it, and to establish it with judgment and with justice from henceforth even for ever. The zeal of the Lord of hosts will perform this. (Isaiah 9:6–7)

Those who follow this Man's guidance, God says through Isaiah, will be given "a place and a name better than of sons and of daughters: I will give them an everlasting name, that shall not be cut off." This will apply both to Jews and Gentiles, or "sons of the stranger, that join themselves to the Lord" (56:1–8). Every call for freedom of oppression and captivity Israel has ever cried out about to the Father will be answered and delivered in this Man (58:6–14). This Servant, a *Go'el* (59:20) who redeems Israel even without money (52:3), will come in God's timing, and the sole response of Israel is to be faithful in waiting until the Redeemer comes for the meek, broken-hearted captives (61:1).

Almost from the opening of his book, Isaiah tells of a coming Kingdom that will be established under this Redeemer, a future "concerning Judah and Jerusalem…in the last days." Isaiah says "the mountain of the Lord's house shall be established in the top of the mountains, and shall be exalted above the hills; and all nations shall flow unto it." This end-times Ruler will "judge among the nations," and there will be an end to all war (2:1–5). His ministry as King will include victory over His enemies, His reign will be one of mercy and justice (63:1–14). This "Branch" of the Father will be like a refuge amidst all other evils in that day, and "the shining of a flaming fire by night" will be upon every dwelling place of Mt. Zion (4:1–6). This Branch will also stem from Jesse (the father of King David), His Kingdom will be one of peace (11:1–9), and He will welcome the Gentiles, whose rest will be glorious and who will see a light in Him (11:10–16; 42:6). This tried-and-true Cornerstone will certainly appear as promised, God says through Isaiah, as the foretold events are a certainty (28:16). He will be a Servant in whom God's soul delights, and upon whom God has placed His Spirit (42:1).

Over and over, Isaiah acknowledges that, though many will stray before the establishment of the final Kingdom, a remnant who once and for all abandons idolatry will always be saved (6:13; 10:20–23; 17:6–8; 24:13–15; 65:8–10).

This is a lot for Israel to digest…yet Isaiah isn't quite finished. In chapter 6, the prophet has a vision:

> I saw also the Lord sitting upon a throne, high and lifted up, and his train filled the temple. Above it stood the seraphims: each one had six wings; with twain he covered his face, and with twain he covered his feet, and with twain he did fly. And one cried unto another, and said, "Holy, holy, holy, is the Lord of hosts: the whole earth is full of his glory." And the posts of the door moved at the voice of him that cried, and the house was filled with smoke.
>
> Then said I, "Woe is me! for I am undone; because I am a man of unclean lips, and I dwell in the midst of a people of unclean lips: for mine eyes have seen the King, the Lord of hosts." (Isaiah 6:1b–5)

The King, this Lord of Hosts from Isaiah's vision, appears in human form… Can it be that Isaiah has had a vision of the Immanuel?… Hmmm.

Jeremiah

Regardless of Isaiah's repeated warnings, the moral depravity of God's people rears its ugly head again, and the Jews fall into the hands of the Babylonians, who destroy the holy city of Jerusalem. As is the pattern in the Old Testament writings, God never abandons His nation. During this time, the prophet Jeremiah also stands to tell of a new relationship between God and man that will overcome all the disappointments of

Israel's history. This New Covenant, Jeremiah prophesies, will be unlike anything God's people have ever seen. The Law will no longer be a set of rules to be followed! Instead, somehow, the standards for living in obedience to God will become an inward matter. The Levitical priesthood and animal sacrifices will be replaced with something superior (Jeremiah 33:17–18). "'But this shall be the covenant that I will make with the house of Israel; After those days,' saith the Lord, 'I will put my law in their inward parts, and write it in their hearts; and will be their God, and they shall be my people'" (31:33).

Thus, in order to show Israel what they have to look forward to in their Deliverer, Jeremiah warns the people of their sin in similar, inner-person terms. Their sin is so great that it is "written with a pen of iron, and with the point of a diamond...graven upon the table of their heart, and...altars" (17:1). Through Jeremiah, the Lord speaks of the "wine cup of this fury at my hand," which is the result of such sin that "all that are in the utmost corners" of the earth are forced to drink (25:15, 23).

But in the midst of the Deliverer's coming, something terrible will come. Jeremiah looks toward this terrible moment, saying, "A voice was heard in Ramah, lamentation, and bitter weeping; Rahel [Rachel] weeping for her children refused to be comforted for her children, because they were not" (31:15).

Will a Messiah really come from the lineage of the patriarchs to stand as the Founder of this new inner work?

And what of this cup? Will He drink it, too? If so, why—and for whom?

Will He be seen as merely another leader, like a prophet, judge, or king? And will His work be carried out on earth or in the unseen dominion of the soul?

What did Jeremiah mean when he said this Man will be a "Branch," a King from the line of David, who executes perfect judgment and righteousness and sees to the restoration of Judah and of Jerusalem (23:5; 33:15–16)? What excruciating event would occur that would cause such weeping around the time of the Deliverer's birth? And who is "Rachel"?

Lamentations

Jeremiah's cries continue in the book of Lamentations, after Jerusalem and the Temple have been demolished, prophesying of the time of tribulation that will follow. The Hebrews are dismantled and fragmented, and all their ways of life, including the cultural practices of their worship, have ceased. Jeremiah, in this poetic book, until its third chapter, acknowledges that the days of glory are over, and raises the question: What hope can the Jews cling to now? Despite the Jews' willful and unremittingly reckless contributions to this dilemma, they are feeling as if God has disappeared in the wake of their land's destruction, and their penalty is now "greater than the punishment of the sin of Sodom" (Lamentations 4:6). Even the highest are being brought low as their enemies are raping "the women in Zion, and the [virgins from] the cities of Judah. Princes are hanged up by their hand: the faces of elders [are] not honoured" (5:11–12).

Lamentations captures well the anguish of a nation whose Leader is hard to see in the rising smoke of ruin. The happy laughter of men, women, and children whose burdens were once light now only echo in the wind as their land sits silent, abandoned in the aftermath of sundry seasons of iniquity: "How doth the city sit solitary, that was full of people! how is she become as a widow! she that was great among the nations, and princess among the provinces, how is she become tributary!" (1:1).

But God's mercy and capability to restore a wicked people to glory never dies. Here, in the midst of the most unbelievable crises, is a comfort…a clearly supernatural comfort that can't be explained by any source other than God in His weaving together a course of action for Israel's future. "Therefore have I hope," Jeremiah writes, "It is [because] of the Lord's mercies that we are not consumed, because his compassions fail not. They are new every morning: great is thy faithfulness!" (3:21b–23). The people will continue to survive, and their sons and daughters will not perish and bring to extinction the holy race, as God's plan is unfolding in spite of them. Though the people sit in captivity under the Babylonian government, some, like Jeremiah, know Yahweh will "have compassion according to the multitude of his mercies," draw near to those who cry out for His help, and say, "Fear not!" as they anticipate the day He will "renew [their] days as of old" (3:32, 57; 5:21).

Until then, goodness can be found for those who "hope and quietly wait for the salvation of the Lord…For the Lord will not cast off for ever" (3:26, 31).

Will laughter bubble up once again from the nation's homes? Will the Jews will see the culmination of this salvation promise in the Branch of David?

Ezekiel

Of those King Nebuchadnezzar has taken captive to Babylon, one man, Ezekiel, also sees great hope. His colorful words are unlike those of any other biblical book in many ways. As a prophet, Ezekiel knows his responsibility is to relay Yahweh's will and intent to His people, and this Ezekiel does quite graphically, often choosing to carry out public behavior as a means of shaking people up and getting their attention. In Ezekiel 4:1–8, he symbolizes the siege of Jerusalem by lying on his side, bound in rope for many days; in 5:1–4, he expresses the destruction of the holy city by cutting his hair and beard with a sharp sword; in 12:3–7, he embodies the baggage of the exiled by covering his face and digging through a wall with his bare hands, carrying the weight of his dig on bags across his shoulders in sight of all; in 12:18, he eats and drinks while trembling to represent the scarcity of food and water in this nation of violence. Such dramatizations likely stimulate a bit of gossip and the questioning of his sanity…but they no doubt communicate his intent better than words.

Ezekiel begins by noting that "in the thirtieth year, in the fourth month, in the fifth day of the month, as I was among the captives by the river of Chebar, that the heavens were opened, and I saw visions of God" (1:1). In these visions, Ezekiel watches the horrific departure of God's presence from the Temple and the holy city (8:3–4; 9:3; 10:4, 18–19; 11:22–23). As a prophet and one in touch with Yahweh, Ezekiel knows the absence of God isn't only the absence of all things good, but also of life. Spiritually, Israel is dead, lying in the graves of the forgotten.

To deepen Ezekiel's understanding and imprint upon him the magnitude of this gruesome truth, God brings Ezekiel to the massive grave, the Valley of Bones, saying, "these bones are the whole house of Israel: behold, they say, 'Our bones are dried, and our hope is lost'" (37:11). The idols the Jews set up in the very Temple of God (chapter 8) are, to Yahweh, abominations that will incur nothing but than His wrath.

But something wonderful and peculiar happens. While still experiencing his vision, Ezekiel is told by God to "prophesy and say unto [the bones], 'Thus saith the Lord God; Behold, O my people, I will open your graves, and cause you to come up out of your graves, and bring you into the land of Israel…. And shall put my spirit in you, and ye shall live'" (37:12, 14). Ezekiel foresees a day of restoration for the spiritual life of Israel. This resurrection of God creates hope in God's mercy, speaking life to the dead, imparting freedom upon Israel even while the people are sleeping in the chains of captivity. In their darkest hour, the Author of Life shows His prophet that His presence will return in a new place where a glorious river flows to bring life and healing to whatever and whoever it touches—a place where trees produce the only sustenance God's people will ever need, and the leaves of which are medicine (47:1–12).

God tells Ezekiel that these wonderful things will come on the day another, final, King David sits on the throne as a Shepherd over His people, ensuring that they live peacefully and are ever fed with good fruit (34:20–31; 37:24). The blessings of this Kingdom will be rich and plentiful, the stone hearts of God's people will be traded for ones of flesh, and God will instill His Spirit within those who follow Him (36:25–38).

Ezekiel also sees something, or *Someone*, quite extraordinary:

And above the firmament that was over their heads was the likeness of a throne, as the appearance of a sapphire stone: and upon the likeness of the throne was the likeness as the appearance of a man above upon it.... This was the appearance of the likeness of the glory of the Lord. And when I saw it, I fell upon my face. (1:26, 28)

Who might this "man" upon the throne be referring to? Is this the same being as the one in Isaiah's vision? Throughout Ezekiel's story, God frequently refers to him as the "Son of Man." Will this term someday come to mean something other than a regular man also?

Ezekiel says he will not see these prophesied events fulfilled in his day. But in the future, God's people will find a new hope, he says. Will *their* dry bones be brought back to life? And will the water that flows from God in a new Temple and a new form that offers the final salvation and restoration have something to do with the promised Deliverer?

Meanwhile, Ezekiel isn't the only prophet whose life is spent as a captive in Babylon.

Daniel

Daniel is young when he is brought in to be a servant to the king, but his wisdom as a prophet of God is evident early on, when King Nebuchadnezzar feels haunted by a disturbing dream nobody else has the ability to interpret. The dream is of a tall and mighty image or statue with a head of gold, chest of silver, abdomen and thighs of bronze, legs of iron, and feet of a mixture of iron and clay (Daniel 2:31–33). Seemingly from out of nowhere, and without the use of human hands, a giant rock is cut from a mountain and flies into the image. It breaks into pieces that fall "like the chaff of the summer threshingfloors," whereupon the wind carries the dust-like pieces away to places they will never be found, "and the stone that smote the image became a great mountain, and filled the whole earth" (2:35).

Daniel explains that the silver, bronze, iron, and the mixture of iron and clay represent kingdoms that will rise after the time of Nebuchadnezzar. The head of gold indicates the reign of Nebuchadnezzar, which, by its place at the top, will fall the farthest to its dismal, shattered fate. Daniel clarifies that the massive rock cut from the mountain is a future Kingdom that will last forever and outperform all others: "And in the days of these kings shall the God of heaven set up a kingdom, which shall never be destroyed: and the kingdom shall not be left to other people, but it shall break in pieces and consume all these kingdoms, and it shall stand for ever" (2:44).

Nebuchadnezzar is impressed by Daniel's interpretation, and says that the One whom Daniel worships is "a God of gods, and a Lord of kings" (2:47).

Sadly, this newfound exaltation from the pagan king to Yahweh doesn't last…

Daniel quickly grows in service to God, refusing a short time later to bow down in worship to the king's golden statue. Though he is not personally caught in this defiance, Shadrach, Meshach, and Abednego, Daniel's close friends, are spotted standing after they have been instructed to bow. This act of insubordination will cost them their lives, the king decrees. King Nebuchadnezzar arrogantly taunts, "Who is that God that shall deliver you out of my hands?" (3:15). Their answer is, of course, Yahweh (3:16).

This provokes the king who, in a fit of rage, orders that the furnace be heated to seven times its usual temperature and orders his men to bind the three God-fearing Hebrews and throw them into the flames. They do just that, but as they approach the furnace, the emanating heat is so intense that it immediately incinerates the king's servants. Shadrach, Meshach, and Abednego can't possibly survive, regardless of whatever "gods" they serve, the king assumes. But, as the three friends stand amidst the flames, a fourth Figure can suddenly be seen—one that the king's counselor says is "like a son of the gods" (3:25; ESV).

Shocked, King Nebuchadnezzar calls the Hebrew men out of the furnace. When they appear before him, not a single hair on their heads is singed. Having seen with his own two eyes the power of the Hebrew God for a second time, Nebuchadnezzar says, "Blessed be the God of Shadrach, Meshach, and Abednego, who hath sent his angel, and delivered his servants that trusted in him, and have changed the king's word, and yielded their bodies, that they might not serve nor worship any god, except their own God" (3:28). This proves God's authority to be more powerful than any other god of the land. Shadrach, Meshach, and Abednego are promoted in the provinces of Babylon.

Daniel's words of praise to his God for the mysteries He reveals will reverberate throughout the history of Israel: "Blessed be the name of God for ever and ever: for wisdom and might are his…he removeth kings, and setteth up kings…[and] He revealeth the deep and secret things" (2:20–22).

Yet, it is not over. After the reign of Nebuchadnezzar ceases, Daniel once again refuses to stop worshipping his God, and he is thrown by King Darius into a lions' den where he is sure to be devoured. Yet the Lord is with Daniel again; He supernaturally shuts the mouths of the ferocious beasts until the next morning, when the hungry lions are fed the conspirators who accused Daniel. King Darius' reaction to this turn of events, words about an eternal Kingdom, mirrors that of Nebuchadnezzar's, as he says that Daniel's God "is the living God, and ste[a]dfast for ever, and his kingdom [is] that which shall not be destroyed, and his dominion shall be even unto the end" (6:26).

A short time later, Daniel has a dream. In it, he sees four winds from heaven stirring up the sea and four giant creatures rising from beneath the water. Each beast is different. The first one, a lion with wings of an eagle, has its wings plucked off while Daniel watches, and it is lifted and carried to land where it stands like a man and is given a man's mind (or heart). The second, a bear with three rib bones in its mouth, is told to "arise, devour much flesh." The third, a leopard with four wings and four heads, is given "dominion." The fourth, "dreadful and terrible, and strong exceedingly," has ten horns and teeth of iron. An eleventh horn, smaller than the others and covered in eyes and a mouth, grows upward and uproots three others (7:2–8). As Daniel watches in horror, thrones are cast down from heaven, and "the Ancient of days" sit upon one. His "garment was white as snow, and the hair of his head like the pure wool: his throne was like the fiery flame, and his wheels as burning fire" (7:9). As a stream of fire issues from this Ancient One, thousands upon thousands gather in front of Him, and then, "the judgment was set, and the books were opened" (7:10). As the horn with eyes and a mouth begins to speak, it is killed, and its body is given over to the flames (7:11–12).

Then, Daniel reports something significant:

I saw in the night visions, and, behold, one like the Son of man came with the clouds of heaven, and came to the Ancient of days, and they brought him near before him. And there was given him dominion, and glory, and a kingdom, that all people, nations, and languages, should serve him: his dominion is an everlasting dominion, which shall not pass away, and his kingdom [is] that which shall not be destroyed. (7:13–14)

No other kingdom will ever triumph over the one God is preparing within His redemptive plan—even pagan kings can see that.

But will the mysterious fourth Figure in the furnace remain a mystery?

Does Daniel see a future Kingdom with an everlasting Ruler whose reign will establish a new promise of the Father following the fading away of the earthly kingdoms? This day will most certainly come, Daniel says, "and the dream is certain, and the interpretation thereof sure" (2:45). But what will it look like? How will it come about?

What do these beasts mean? And what is a "son of man"? Is it just a man? Or is it something/Someone else?

...And what does that Kingdom have to do with a big, flying rock?

Hosea

Moving into the Minor Prophets, we see Hosea, the last prophet appointed in the Northern Kingdom before the Assyrian Exile. In his lifetime, he watches as one king after another falls. Like Ezekiel, Hosea is commanded by God to not only *tell* His people what their unfaithfulness is doing, but to *show* them in a dramatic demonstration: by marrying a promiscuous woman, Gomer.

In nuptial language (see our study on the Song of Songs), Hosea refers to Israel as a wife of Yahweh, prophesying of the multiple generations of children of Israel who will suffer because of their parents' wickedness in not turning from their ways and putting away idolatry for good. There will come a day when all of God's people will see the exile, purchased with the bread, water, wool, flax, oil, wine, grain, silver, and gold that were given to them by God before they turned and offered them to Baal (Hosea 2:5–8). They will wish to come back to their first love, but it will not be with sincerity—like a wayward wife who longs merely to re-indulge in the conveniences of the Husband who cared for her—and they will therefore find that the Husband has taken back what is rightfully His (2:5, 9). The goods obtained during

Israel's idolatry will be lost, like that which is devoured by beasts of the field (2:12).

But after all is trashed, and after generations of punishment, there will come a day when Israel will be comforted, Hosea says. Like a gentle and forgiving Husband, Yahweh will establish a new marriage, a New Covenant promise, with His people. It will be like it was when Israel came up from Egypt the first time, and the idols will be remembered no more, because the Husband will wed His wife Israel to Him "for ever…in lovingkindness, and in mercies" (2:14–19). The people of God will be sown unto the Husband throughout the earth, and those who were once without mercy will have mercy, and those who were once not known as His people will be known as His people again (2:23).

The mysteries of God are many while the nation waits in captivity. Yet Hosea's words will continue to be repeated to God's people, ensuring they are never forgotten. In all of Hosea's prophecies, two verses in particular are striking: In the days beyond the Exile, Gomer and all she represents will be but a distant memory, because God will raise up His people from the dead "in the third day" (6:2)… God, through His prophet, says that "when Israel was a child, then I loved him, and called my son out of Egypt" (11:1).

Will Israel always be the Bride, and Yahweh her Husband? Or will this arrangement change in the latter days to involve other nations?

What was that about an event regarding the dead coming back to life on the third day? And what could that note about a son from Egypt mean?

Joel

Severe droughts and locusts are sweeping the land, and they've been brought on by the sin of Israel. Through His prophet, Joel, God says, "I will pour out my spirit upon all flesh; and your sons and your daughters shall prophesy, your old men shall dream dreams, your young men shall see visions: And also upon the servants and upon the handmaids in those days will I pour out my spirit" (Joel 2:28–29).

The Day of the Lord is also coming, the book of Joel repeatedly warns. This will be a judgment on the nations and kingdoms in the last days, when God's righteous Kingdom will be forever established (1:1–20; 3:1–21).

The message of Joel comes as the nation of Israel is plagued, but according to this prophet, a future event will instill the Holy Spirit of God *within* the righteous. What an amazing concept! Considering that God only rests within the Holy Temple, that is a thought worth chewing on for the Jews…though that note about a future judgment doesn't sound too good. What will *that* look like? And how can any kingdom last forever?

Does this Holy Spirit of God have something to do with that Shepherd Ezekiel sees, or the Branch or *Go'el* Isaiah speaks of?

Amos

Amos is sent by God to the Northern Kingdom, Israel, to deliver a message about the people's lackluster faith. Their relationship with God has become one of rote ritual, not love and sincerity, and as a result, they are sending the wrong signals to the rest of the surrounding world regarding who God is. His anger about this results in His rejection of their "worship":

I hate, I despise your feast days, and I will not smell in your solemn assemblies. Though ye offer me burnt offerings and your meat offerings, I will not accept them: neither will I regard the peace offerings of your fat beasts. Take thou away from me the noise of thy songs; for I will not hear the melody of thy viols. (Amos 5:21–23)

But there will be a remnant someday, Amos prophesies, that will belong to a future Davidic King who will restore David's tabernacle. The harvest in that coming era, including the Gentiles ("heathen"), will be so plentiful that the "ploughman" will even be ahead of the "reaper" (harvesters won't be able to keep up with the land's bounty). The captives of Israel will be forever freed and shall want for nothing (Amos 9:11–15).

What Amos foretells has an "inner" quality Jeremiah mentions as he speaks of a time when following God will no longer be a matter of sacrifices but of something inside each person's heart. Could this have a connection with Joel's words about the Holy Spirit of God being installed within the righteous?

Of course, the Lord's servant Isaiah also speaks of Gentiles, but who in Israel would want to include those "heathens," and how would those who have never followed the Law and sacrificial requirements ever become one with Israel? And what was that about a "remnant"?

Obadiah

Obadiah's short prophecy is against the Edomites, who are descendants of Jacob's brother Esau and, therefore, relatives of Israel. As Babylon has weakened the Jews, these relatives have seen an opportunity to exact revenge upon God's people, and judgment will therefore come upon Esau's family line.

Will they learn their lesson? Will this be the last time the Jews go against their own? Deuteronomy 28:9–10 and Amos 9:11–12 look forward to the day "the remnant of Edom" will be called by the name of God. When will this happen, and how? Will it occur through another prophet or, perhaps, through someone from the lineage of Abraham or David?

Jonah

Wicked nations and cities will always need a Savior. The prophet Jonah is sent to Nineveh, the capital city of Assyria, to show that God always extends His mercy to any people who seek redemption...even if it's those sinful Gentiles.

Though Jonah runs from God's directive to preach His message to the unrighteous inhabitants of this hated city at first, he obeys after he's swallowed by a giant fish, forced to live in the darkness and threat of death, and returns to his regular life three days later. As the prophet waits upon his hill of sunshine overlooking the city, he praises Yahweh, telling Him that He is "a gracious God, and merciful, slow to anger, and of great kindness," and one who withholds the foretold disaster if people turn from their sinful ways (Jonah 4:2). God does not favor one people over another in His extension of salvation.

But in what way does this seemingly unrelated story have to do with the future?

...And why does this bizarre reference to "three days" keep coming up?

Micah

The Jews' wickedness, as always, has purchased their troubles. Micah sees this, and warns that Israel will fall to Assyrian forces (Micah 1:6). This prophet issues a brief message that's made up of two parts: Israel's judgment (1:1–3:12) and restoration (4:1–5:15).

But when God speaks in the latter part through His prophet, Micah utters an abnormally specific detail the Hebrew nation cannot grasp. It's not that they don't understand that the Ruler who will one day reign over all Israel is eternal ("from everlasting"); nor do they have a problem realizing His lineage will trace back to Judah...

It's that part about how He will be born in Bethlehem (5:2), Micah says, existing as Peace, personified (5:5).

What's that about?

Nahum

Jonah's assistance to Nineveh does not last. Though they indeed do turn toward God for a time, they soon turn their back on Him again persecuting His people and becoming His enemies. Nahum's message is one of wrath against Israel's enemies: He tells the Assyrians they'll experience judgment like a storm from God (Nahum 1:3–6) for their idolatry (1:14), pride (2:13), murder, deceit, and wickedness against the oppressed (3:1–19).

God will always continue to bring justice, afflicting those who afflict His people, even if it isn't within their time. But Nahum alludes to a Man who, again, personifies peace; One who will bring Good News (1:15).

Will relief for God's people really come someday in the manner Nahum prophesies?

What will this message of Good News be?

Habakkuk

The Assyrians fall to the Babylonian Empire, just as Nahum has said. Habakkuk now acknowledges that there is still sin contaminating Israel. In a prayer (Habakkuk 3:1), he calls for God to "revive" His work and remember "mercy" during His wrath (3:2). The prophet praises God for "salvation with [His] anointed" and calls Him "the God of my salvation" (3:13, 18).

How long will it be until Yahweh revives His work among the

people and brings them irreversible, constant mercy? Will they have to wait another, say, six hundred years?

And who or what is this "anointed" the God of "salvation" will bring?

Zephaniah

At this same time, elsewhere, the prophet Zephaniah, a descendant of King Hezekiah (Zephaniah 1:1), is called to prophesy for the Lord. A central theme of Zephaniah's message, like Joel's, is the coming Day of the Lord (2:3)—a day when God will judge the world and "undo all that afflict" His people. Zephaniah sees that God will spare a remnant and will someday "gather her that was driven out; and I will get them praise and fame in every land where they have been put to shame.…for I will make you a name and a praise among all people of the earth, when I turn back your captivity before your eyes" (3:14–20).

Through whom will God carry out these Day-of-the-Lord judgments? Will it be someone He appoints? And how will He offer proof of this Leader's identity to all?

Haggai

Israel is freed by Cyrus, king of Persia, and thousands return to the Promised Land. The buzz of excitement about this is great. It is even said that the Lord's priest, Ezra, is among the Jews in the homeland!

However, God's people are reluctant to rebuild the Temple. The prophet Haggai watches as Jerusalem's neighboring enemies do all they can to halt the process. He understands their hesitation is born from a lack of faith in God, so he delivers a prophecy telling the people they must continue in their endeavor and, when they've finished, the glory of the Temple will be even grander than before (Haggai 2:9).

In a moment that captures the encouraging mood of Haggai's message, God gives assurance to His people through the prophet: "'I am with you,' saith the Lord" (1:13).

Haggai, as well as the rest of the Jews, knows the governor of Jerusalem, Zerubbabel—grandson of King Jehoiachin of Judah (1 Chronicles 3:17) and descendant of David—to whom the building project is given. Therefore, the people of God know the Temple, God's holy home where His presence dwells, is in the hands of a Son of David.

Will this mirror something for the Temple of the future? Will the Temple always be God's residence? Or will something about this change through the prophesied Son of David?

Zechariah

While the Temple is being rebuilt, the Lord appoints another prophet to keep His people moving: Zechariah.

Zechariah is like Haggai in his mission, but is very different from him in his words and enigmatic visions, which tend to focus more on symbolism, regarding events in the far-off future (Zechariah 1:8–6:8). In addition, Zechariah is a priest, so his prophecies about the Temple include the kind of visual details that could only be offered by one who has performed priestly duties within it. Repeatedly in his warnings, using Temple terminology, Zechariah makes it clear that those who are God's people will have abundant life and blessing, and those who are not will experience death and judgment (1:14; 12:1–5).

In a future time, God says through Zechariah, "many nations shall be joined to the Lord…and shall be my people: and I will dwell in the midst of thee, and thou shalt know that the Lord of hosts hath sent me unto thee" (2:11). God's Servant, once again called the "Branch," will "grow up out of his place, and he shall build the temple of the Lord…and he shall bear the glory, and shall sit and rule upon his throne; and he shall be a priest upon his throne" (3:8; 6:9–13). The place where the Branch-Priest dwells "shall be from sea even to sea, and from the river even to the ends of the earth" (9:10). In a forthcoming, grand day, "living waters shall go out from Jerusalem; Half of them toward the former sea, And half of them toward the hinder sea"; then, this "Lord" will be the "king over all the earth" and will be only "one Lord, and his name one" (14:8–9).

"Rejoice greatly, O daughter of Zion," God says through His prophet, "shout, O daughter of Jerusalem: behold, thy King cometh unto thee: he is just, and having salvation; lowly, and riding upon an ass, and upon a colt the foal of an ass" (9:9). We hear again that this imminent King will be linked to the "house of David," and that He will be "pierced, and they shall mourn for him, as one mourneth for his only son" (12:10).

It's clear to Zechariah that Israel will reject this King (9:1–11:17). And although they will eventually be restored and delivered (12:1–14:21), at some point the King will be paid the same price as a slave, thirty pieces of silver, which He will "cast...to the potter" (11:12–13). His hands will have wounds upon them, which He will explain by saying they are "those with which I was wounded in the house of my friends" (13:6).[93]

Due to Zechariah dutifully delivering his visions, we now see that the Branch, a High Priest of God, will be the one to build a future, worldwide Temple...but who is the Branch, and where will He build this?

This does appear to be the least of our questions!

Why does the voice behind parts of Zechariah's message sound like both the Lord and One whom the Lord has sent, while He will also "dwell" with the people? How is that even possible? What does it mean that the Lord's "name will be one"?

More puzzling: Why will such a King as the one Zechariah mentions come to Israel's people on a colt, having been "pierced," after which all will mourn as if they have lost an "only son"?

How can Israel ever reject a Leader Yahweh sends? What will cause such a tragedy? Who in their right minds would believe Him to be worth only thirty pieces of silver—the going price of a *slave*—and why does He "cast them to the potter"?

Our friend Zechariah is full of mysteries, indeed...

Malachi

As a result of the work of Ezra and Nehemiah, as well as the prophecies delivered by Haggai and Zechariah, the Temple and the wall of Jerusalem have now been rebuilt by the exiles who returned about a century ago. God's people are practicing their worship once again.

But nothing appears to be happening. God's grandiose promises have left Israel feeling empty, and His love is being called into question. As a result, the impatient Hebrews once again begin to fall away from God. Priests offer polluted food upon the altars (Malachi 1:7); young men marry wives with foreign gods, joining the Spirit of God in their covenantal marriages with the faithless (2:11, 14–15); people commit evil acts and believe themselves to be "good in the sight of the Lord" (2:17); tithes and offerings are withheld to the point that God is "robbed" (3:8); and serving God is considered "vain" (3:13–14).

In each way the people have been irreverent, they are now held accountable by Malachi, the prophet.

But Malachi is not the only messenger who will be sent to them, they learn. Malachi tells of another who will come. God speaks through the prophet, "Behold, I will send my messenger, and he shall prepare the way before me!" (3:1). As the people listen to Malachi's words and are berated for their disloyalty, they're eager to know who this messenger will be. Finally, in his last statement, God, through the prophet, says: "I will send you Elijah the prophet before the coming of the great and dreadful day of the Lord: And he shall turn the heart of the fathers to the children, and the heart of the children to their fathers, lest I come and smite the earth with a curse" (4:4–6).

Wait...*Elijah*?! Hasn't he been gone for almost five hundred years by now? What can this mean? And even if Elijah does return, what "way" is he preparing for?

Conclusion to the Prophets

As stated earlier, we'll tie up all loose ends and unanswered questions that are raised by these seventeen Old Testament books with our examination of their New Testament fulfillment contexts.

However, these seventeen aren't the only prophets of God who spoke about the Someday Messiah. Not by a long shot. They're simply considered here as they are books of the Bible, and this work is laser-focused on seeing how all the sixty-six books of the Word point to Him. As far as how many Old Testament prophecies Jesus ultimately fulfilled, the scholarly jury is still gnawing on that and will be until the Second Coming.

The list, depending on the interpreter, is usually hundreds of Scripture passages long (some lists place the number of fulfillments at around 270, and others well over 400). So, the question is not *whether* Jesus' First Coming satisfied what was spoken of Him, but how many, and what the odds are that Jesus may not have been the Messiah based on those numbers. For instance, if Jesus was merely a tragic Jewish prophet from the line of David who was born in a small town called Bethlehem, then we would have satisfied only two prophetic details: the town of His birth and His lineage. The chances are high that this same couple of facts would apply to quite a few people in Jesus' day, so the math isn't that impressive, even though it eliminates hundreds of thousands of prospects from the list of what historians say were approximately four hundred thousand Jews in the Palestinian area at the time. (Actually, it would be an even greater elimination since over

Volume One: The Old Testament

half the population was made up of owned slaves, and we know the Messiah was not prophesied to be a slave.) But each time we add the basic calculable axioms (things we know to be true) to this number and calculate probability (of whoever we think Messiah could be), the list of possible messianic candidates dramatically decreases.

So, the questions become these: What is the likelihood Christ could have accidentally fulfilled many prophecies had He not been who He said He was? What are the chances that Jesus might have been a regular guy who was in the right place and at the right time to appear to be the Messiah, but who is, in fact, not?

That's where the math gets interesting...

We mentioned *The Case for Christ: A Journalist's Personal Investigation of the Evidence of Jesus* at the beginning of this book, and it's relevant research here as well. Author Lee Strobel's book follows his journey from being an atheist skeptic and secular investigative journalist who loathed the topic of Christ and attempted to prove Him a myth, to becoming a convert when his intensive efforts failed. Strobel's account is not about a just a guy who didn't want to hear about Christ so he researched memes on Facebook one day and became a Christian after crying over a few beers with his buddies who wouldn't stop asking where his late mother was now. Far from it. Strobel *vehemently* pursued proving the historical Jesus was just a misled man whose followers stretched the truth, and his investigation led him all over the country for several years while he kept digging for the one missing element that would disprove the foundations of Christianity. Strobel's career as a researcher and writer forced him to get to the very bottom of the facts before reporting his findings. One might argue that not all journalists are honest, and that is a legitimate concern. Strobel's pursuit of the truth, however, was personal, and it was, for him, a matter of life and death to find it at all costs (the time he spent researching the subject was a season that nearly drove his wife insane) with the motive of being set free from spiritual accountability or securing his eternal soul if he was wrong. Those are high stakes, indeed.

In the midst of his search, he had multiple conversations with authorities on both sides of the argument. Renowned mathematician, Peter W. Stoner, was one he sought counsel from regarding the statistics behind Jesus and prophecy.

The coincidence of Christ accidentally fulfilling *only eight* of the Old Testament prophecies, Strobel says, is "one chance in one hundred million billion. That number is millions of times greater than the total number of people who've ever walked the planet!... [Stoner] also computed that the probability of fulfilling [only] forty-eight prophecies was one chance in a trillion, trillion, trillion, trillion, trillion, trillion, trillion, trillion, trillion, trillion, trillion, trillion, trillion!"[94]

To deny such mathematical odds would be hubris, plain and simple.

Because the meaning of some prophecies is a matter of interpretation, we won't cover each one scholars have identified. Instead, we're focusing on examples that are either: 1) commonly identified in the academic world with mountains of supportive evidence and discussion; or 2) clearly stated in Scripture and therefore easy to understand.

As one example (spoiler alert!), Psalm 34:20 says that the Someday Savior "keepeth all his bones: not one of them is broken" (see also Exodus 12:46 and Numbers 9:12—two verses regarding the treatment of the Passover lambs as sacrifice, which we discussed in the study of Exodus). This prophecy satisfies both of these requirements in that it is: 1) commonly agreed among scholars to be a messianic prophecy in the Old Testament; 2) everyone can understand what the psalmist is saying here (it's not, say, one of Ezekiel's enigmatic visions of spinning wheels or such).

When the Roman soldiers crucified victims, they usually broke the bones in the victims' legs with a club (called "crurifragium") so they could not push their body weight upward, relieving the weight from the hands and arms, improving circulation, and thus, allowing them to live longer. It's cruel, but true. If a victim was alive too long and there was a need to accelerate the process of death for any reason, preventing the victim from movement in the lower half of the body accomplished this, and the person would usually die from blood loss or asphyxiation (from poor circulation or the inability to lift one's head high enough to open the airway).

Therefore, speaking of odds, Jesus' legs *should have*, according to the common practice of the day, been broken. If they had, this one prophecy alone wouldn't have been fulfilled, and Jesus would have been just a Jewish prophet who tragically died for a measly set of principles and a reputation as a semi-popular leader of a local cult comprised of common folks. So, the fact that Jesus did not experience broken legs (John 19:33) is already a mathematical oddity, considering how He died and the fact that His method of crucifixion was an exception to the rule. A mathematician in this case would have to: 1) calculate the probability of a man dying in this exact manner when it was not the norm; 2) add the prophecy to the equation involving other potential prophetic fulfillments; and finally, 3) calculate the possibility that it happened as it did that by some fluke to an individual who *also* claimed to be the Messiah.

The results?

One serious coincidence…and all of that from only looking at one prophecy.

With that said, just who was this Jesus the Christ of Galilee who saved the world? Would all the words of Isaiah, Jeremiah, Ezekiel, Daniel, Hosea, Zechariah, and the other Old Testament prophets we've just discussed be realized in this one Man?

Luckily, we don't have to wait four hundred years during a silent Intertestamental Period to find out…

Begin volume 2.

Notes

1. Howell, Donna, Allie Anderson, and Nita Horn, *Misfits: Learning from Our Inner Outcast and How It Can Empower Us to Find Our Destiny* (Crane, MO: Defender Publishing, 2021), 57.
2. Ibid.
3. Strobel, Lee, *The Case for Christ: A Journalist's Personal Investigation of the Evidence for Jesus* (Zondervan, Kindle Edition), Kindle locations 3024–3025.
4. Ibid., locations 3030–3032.
5. Ibid.
6. Snavely, Andréa, 2017. *Christology: Jesus, Son of God in the Spirit, an Independent-Study Textbook* (Springfield, MO: Global University, 2017), 40.
7. Ibid., 42.
8. Ibid., 68.
9. Ritzema, E., "Nicene Creed," *Lexham Bible Dictionary* (Bellingham, WA: Lexham Press, 2016).

10. Feldmeth, N. P., *Pocket Dictionary of Church History: Over 300 Terms Clearly and Concisely Defined* (Downers Grove, IL: IVP Academic, 2008), 45.

11. Snavely, *Christology.* 89.

12. Ibid.

13. Feldmeth, *Pocket Dictionary.* 59.

14. Berkhof, L., *Systematic Theology* (Grand Rapids, MI: Wm. B. Eerdmans, 1938), 386.

15. Orr, J. L. Nuelsen, E. Y. Mullins, & M. O. Evans (Eds.), *International Standard Bible Encyclopaedia: Volume 1–5* (Chicago: Howard-Severance, 1915), 2,327.

16. Rusten, S. with E. Michael, *Complete Book of When & Where in the Bible and throughout History* (Wheaton, IL: Tyndale House Publishers, 2005), 152.

17. Ibid., 211.

18. Snavely, *Christology.* 148.

19. Ibid., 250.

20. Ibid., 256.

21. Ibid., 277.

22. Corduan, W., *Pocket Guide to World Religions* (Downers Grove, IL: InterVarsity Press, 2006), 38.

23. Rainbow, P. A., "Logos Christology," in R. P. Martin & P. H. Davids (Eds.), *Dictionary of the Later New Testament and Its Developments* (Downers Grove, IL: InterVarsity Press, 1997), 665.

24. Newman, Dr. Paul., *A Spirit Christology Recovering the Biblical Paradigm of Christian Faith* (Lanham, MD: University Press of America, a division of Rowman & Littlefield, 2017), 18.

25. Elwell, W. A., & Beitzel, B. J., "Theophany," *Baker Encyclopedia of the Bible: Volume 2* (Grand Rapids, MI: Baker Book, 1988), 2,052.

26. Anderson, Allie and Donna Howell, *Encounters: Extraordinary Accounts of Angelic Intervention and What the Bible* Actually *Says about God's Messengers* (Crane, MO: Defender, 2019), 188–190.

27. Ibid., 191–193.

28. Barnes, Albert, *Barnes Notes on the Whole Bible* (E4 Group, Kindle Edition), Kindle locations 2030–2035; emphasis added.

29. Ibid.

30. Kidner, Derek, *Genesis: An Introduction and Commentary: Volume 1* (Downers Grove, IL: InterVarsity, 1967), 75.

31. Meyers, C., in D. N. Freedman (Ed.), *Anchor Yale Bible Dictionary: Vol. 6* (New York: Doubleday, 1992), 544.

32. Booker, Dr. Richard, *Celebrating Jesus in the Biblical Feasts* (Shippensburg, PA: Destiny Image , expanded edition 2016), 36.

33. Trumball, Henry Clay, *The Threshold Covenant or the Beginning of Religious Rites* (New York: Charles Scribner's Sons, 1896), iii.

34. Ibid., 3.

35. Ibid., 3–4.

36. Ibid., 203–204.

37. Horn, Thomas, *The Messenger: It's Headed toward Earth! It Cannot Be Stopped! And It's Carrying the Secret of America's, the World's, and Your Tomorrow!* (Crane, MO: Defender, 2020), 37.

38. Ibid., 43–44, 54.

39. J. F. Walvoord & R. B. Zuck (Eds.), *Bible Knowledge Commentary: An Exposition of the Scriptures: Volume 1* (Wheaton, IL: Victor, 1985), 339.

40. Henry, M., & Scott, T., *Matthew Henry's Concise Commentary* (Oak Harbor, WA: Logos Research Systems, 1997), "Joshua 5:13."

41. Morris, Jastrow Jr., George A. Barton, "Chemosh," *Jewish Encyclopedia: Volume 4* (New York: Funk & Wagnalls, 1906), 9–10.

42. Ibid.

43. Cheyne, M. A., D. D., Thomas Kelly, and John Sutherland Black, "Chemosh," *Encyclopaedia Biblica: A Dictionary of the Bible: Volume 1: A–D* (London: Adam and Charles Black, 1899), column 738.

44. Morris, Jastrow Jr., George A. Barton, "Chemosh," *Jewish Encyclopedia*, 9–10.

45. Josephus, F., & Whiston, W., *Works of Josephus: Complete and Unabridged* (Peabody: Hendrickson, 1987), 247.

46. Jamieson, D. D., Robert, (n.d.). *A Commentary, Critical, Experimental, and Practical, on the Old and New Testaments: Joshua–Esther: Volume 2* (London, Glasgow: William Collins, 1872), 378.

47. Barnes, Albert, *Barnes Notes*. Kindle locations 22904–22908.

48. Barry, J. D., Mangum, D., Brown, D. R., Heiser, M. S., Custis, M., Ritzema, E., ... Bomar, D., *Faithlife Study Bible* (Bellingham, WA: Lexham, 2016), "1 Sa 8:1."

49. "1 Samuel 8:1," *Benson Commentary, Bible Hub Online*, last accessed February 7, 2022, https://biblehub.com/commentaries/benson/1_samuel/8.htm.

50. Many commentaries and theological reflections list at least these, and many more reasons. As one quick example that truncates the argument, see: "1 Samuel 8:7," *Pulpit Commentary, Bible Hub Online*, last accessed February 11, 2022, https://biblehub.com/commentaries/pulpit/1_samuel/8.htm.

51. "1 Samuel 8:13," *Pulpit Commentary, Bible Hub Online*, last accessed February 11, 2022, https://biblehub.com/commentaries/pulpit/1_samuel/8.htm.

52. "Ezra 7:6," *Cambridge Bible for Schools and Colleges, Bible Hub Online*, last accessed February 18, 2022, https://biblehub.com/commentaries/cambridge/ezra/7.htm.

53. Jamieson, R., Fausset, A. R., & Brown, D., *Commentary Critical and Explanatory on the Whole Bible: Volume 1* (Oak Harbor, WA: Logos Research Systems, 1997), 311.

54. Brueggemann, Walter, *Reverberations of Faith: A Theological Handbook of Old Testament Themes* (Louisville, KY: John Knox, 2002), 174–176.

55. Andersen, F. I., *Job: An Introduction and Commentary: Volume 14* (Downers Grove, IL: InterVarsity, 1976), 163; emphasis in original.

56. Clifford, R. J., *Wisdom Literature: Interpreting Biblical Texts Series* (Nashville: Abingdon, 2011), 80.

57. Jamieson, Fausset, & Brown, *Commentary Critical and Explanatory on the Whole Bible*, 324.

58. Henry, M., & Scott, T., *Matthew Henry's Concise Commentary* (Oak Harbor, WA: Logos Research Systems, 1997), "Job 19:23."

59. Barnes, Albert, *Barnes' Notes on the Whole Bible* (Ephesians Four Group; Howard City, MI, 2014), Kindle Edition, Kindle locations 47763–47766; bold in original.

60. Garrett, D. A., "The Poetic and Wisdom Books." In D. S. Dockery (Ed.), *Holman Concise Bible Commentary* (Nashville, TN: Broadman & Holman, 1998), 208.

61. "Job 19:25," *Benson Commentary*, Bible Hub Online, last accessed February 23, 2022, https://biblehub.com/commentaries/benson/job/19.htm.

62. Walvoord, J. F., & R. B. Zuck (Eds.), *Bible Knowledge Commentary: An Exposition of the Scriptures: Volume 2* (Wheaton, IL: Victor, 1985), 89.

63. France, R. T., *Matthew: An Introduction and Commentary: Volume 1* (Downers Grove, IL: InterVarsity, 1985), 404.

64. Exell, J. S., *Biblical Illustrator: Matthew* (Grand Rapids, MI: Baker Book, 1952), 659.

65. Footnote to Psalm 72, *NET Bible First Edition; Bible. English. NET Bible* (Biblical Studies Press; Logos Software, 2005).

66. Psalm 72, heading, *New King James Version, NKJV* (Nashville: Thomas Nelson, 1982).

67. Psalm 110, heading, *NKJV*.

68. T. D. Alexander, T. D., & B. S. Rosner (Eds.), *New Dictionary of Biblical Theology* (electronic ed.; Downers Grove, IL: InterVarsity, 2000), 183.

69. Ibid., 807.

70. Elwell, W. A., & Beitzel, B. J., "David," *Baker Encyclopedia of the Bible: Volume 1* (Grand Rapids, MI: Baker Book, 1988), 586.

71. Clifford, R. J., *Wisdom Literature*, 32.

72. Ellington, Scott, *Wisdom Literature: An Independent-Study Textbook* (Springfield, MO: Global University, 2016), 47.

73. Ibid., 174–175.

74. Ibid.

75. Ibid., 47.

76. Schwab, G. M., *Cornerstone Biblical Commentary, Vol 7: The Book of Psalms, The Book of Proverbs* (Carol Stream, IL: Tyndale House, 2009), 519.

77. Ibid.

78. Fee, Gordon D., & Hubbard, R. L., Jr. (Eds.)., *Eerdmans Companion to the Bible* (Grand Rapids, MI; Cambridge, U.K.: Eerdmans, 2011), 365.

79. Carson, D. A., R. T. France, J. A. Motyer, & G. J. Wenham (Eds.), *New Bible Commentary: 21st Century Edition* (4th ed., Leicester, England; Downers Grove, IL: Inter-Varsity, 1994), 609.

80. Ibid., 610.

81. Schwab, G., "Song of Songs 1: Book Of." In T. Longman III & P. Enns (Eds.), *Dictionary of the Old Testament: Wisdom, Poetry & Writings* (Downers Grove, IL; Nottingham, England: IVP Academic; Inter-Varsity, 2008), 739.

82. Barry, J. D., Mailhot, J., Bomar, D., Ritzema, E., & Sinclair-Wolcott, C. (Eds.). (2014). *DIY Bible Study* (Bellingham, WA: Lexham Press; 2014), under "How the Song of Songs Will Transform Your Life."

83. Garrett, D. A., "The Poetic and Wisdom Books." In D. S. Dockery (Ed.), *Holman Concise Bible Commentary* (Nashville, TN: Broadman & Holman, 1998), 255.

84. "American Worldview Inventory 2020—At a Glance…Release #11: Churches and Worldview," October 6, 2020, Cultural Research Center, Arizona Christian University, last accessed February 25, 2022, https://www.arizonachristian.edu/wp-content/uploads/2020/10/CRC_AWVI2020_Release11_Digital_04_20201006.pdf, as quoted in: Howell, Donna, and Allie Anderson, *Dark Covenant: How the Masses Are Being Groomed to Embrace the Unthinkable While the Leaders of Organized Religion Make a Deal with the Devil* (Crane, MO: Defender Publishing; 2021), 284–285.

85. Schwab, G., "Song of Songs." *Dictionary of the Old Testament*, 739–740.

86. Ibid.

87. Gibbs, Carl, *Principles of Biblical Interpretation: An Independent-Study Textbook* (4th ed. Springfield, MO: Global University, 2016), 295.

88. Garrett, D. A., "The Poetic." *Holman Concise Bible Commentary*, 253–254.

89. Ibid., 254.

90. Duguid, I. M., *The Song of Songs: An Introduction and Commentary: Volume 19* (Nottingham, England: Inter-Varsity, 2015), 25.

91. Ibid., 26.

92. Ibid., 29.

93. We are aware this verse, Zechariah 13:6, is highly debated, and some scholars believe these wounded hands to belong to the false prophet from prior verses. The evidence, however, stacks in favor of the Messiah, as we will discuss in volume 2 of this series.

94. Strobel, *Case for Christ.* Kindle locations 3024–3031.

CPSIA information can be obtained
at www.ICGtesting.com
Printed in the USA
BVHW052218301222
655376BV00014B/463